CW00541783

Jean Gurkin

with best wishes

John Patten

Father
of the House

Father
of the House

Fifty Years in Politics

John Parker

Routledge & Kegan Paul
London, Boston, Melbourne and Henley

First published in 1982
by Routledge and Kegan Paul Ltd
39 Store Street, London WC1E 7DD,
9 Park Street, Boston, Mass. 02108, USA,
296 Beaconsfield Parade, Middle Park, Melbourne, 3206, Australia and
Broadway House, Newtown Road, Henley-on-Thames, Oxon RG9 1EN
Set in 10pt IBM Journal by
Cambrian Typesetters, Farnborough, Hants
and printed in Great Britain by
Hartnoll Print, Bodmin, Cornwall
© John Parker 1982
No part of this book may be reproduced in
any form without permission from the
publisher, except for the quotation of brief
passages in criticism

Library of Congress Cataloging in Publication Data

Parker, John, 1906—

Father of the House.
Includes index.
1. Parker, John, 1906—.
2. Great Britain — Politics and government — 1936—1945.
3. Great Britain — Politics and government — 1945—.
4. Great Britain. Parliament. House of Commons — Biography.
5. Legislators — Great Britain — Biography.
I. Title.
DA585.P34A34   328.41'092'4 [B]   82—3781

ISBN 0-7100-9220-2   AACR2

To Zena and Michael

To Kate and Michael

Contents

Contents

Preface

I present an account of some of the events in which I have been interested and played an active part. I have made a special effort to give the background and period atmosphere of the events I have described in the hope that it will interest those politically active today as well as historians of the future.

I do not go into the activities of the Speakers' conferences and Procedure Committees, nor of the Historic Buildings Council, the National Trust and the Inland Waterways Amenities Advisory Council, in which I have played an active part as a member. In addition to these conservation interests I have taken an energetic part in encouraging Forestry as Chairman of Labour's Forestry group in the House.

I should say, however, that I have shown a special interest in Private Members' Bills since A.P. Herbert's Matrimonial Causes Bill (1937) and tried very hard — in view of my own experience with such bills — to remove some of the obstacles in their way. An effort to get the vote needed for the closure reduced from 100 to 50, which seems a much more attainable figure on a Friday, failed. The Procedure Committee felt it should remain the same for Private Members' Bills as for government business. However, I did secure the provision of drafting assistance in the preparation of such bills and I managed to get the 'count' abolished. Previously the House could be counted out during the lunch hour (between 1.00 pm and 1.15 pm) if 40 MPs were not present. It was easier to get supporters for a vote on a bill at the end of business, than to get them to hang about the House in the middle of the day to defeat a possible count out. This removed one of the serious obstacles in the way of Private Members' legislation.

I have also included the diary I kept on an official visit to the Soviet Union in January–February 1945, which gives an intimate picture of that country during the Second World War.

Acknowledgments

I would like to thank my wife, Zena, and my son, Michael, for painstakingly reading through my chapters as they were written and making constructive suggestions. I would also like to thank Gladys Cremer for her help in preparing the text and for the tiring job of indexing.

Each chapter as it has been written has been sent to a number of friends and companions who were present and took part in the events described. Their useful additions or corrections have been dutifully incorporated in the final draft. A list of those consulted over each chapter and other sources is attached at its end.

I would also like to thank: the *Political Quarterly* for permission to republish the articles on 'Oxford Politics in the Late 1920s' and 'The Battle for the Legitimacy Act, 1959'; *The Times* for permission to publish the obituaries of Margaret Cole and Gavin Faringdon; *The Marlburian* for the article on 'Marlborough in the Early 1920s'; and *Lincolnshire Free Press* for that in *Spalding Free Press* on 'The Merseyside Social Survey'.

Father of the House

This title is given to the Member of Parliament who has sat longest without a break; a change of constituency is not in any way relevant. In the event of more than one Member competing for the title, having been returned at the same election, the determining factor would be who had first 'signed on' as a Member. The senior Member of the House (i.e. the Father) normally takes the chair at the beginning of a new Parliament for the election or re-election of the Speaker, unless he is a Minister or a candidate for the Speakership, when the next most senior Member would do so.

The title seems first to have arisen at the end of the seventeenth century when it was given to Sir John Maynard who was first elected for the Short Parliament (1640) and continued until he died Member for Plymouth in 1690, but with a break during the Commonwealth. The all-time record is held by C.P. Villiers, who sat for no less than 63 years (1835–98) without a break, followed by William Aislabie for 60 years (1721–81) and C.N.R. Talbot for 59 years 5 months (1830–90). In the present century the longest serving Member was Lloyd George, who sat continuously for nearly 55 years (1890–1944), followed by T.P. O'Connor (1880–1929), who sat for over 49 years.

Who's Who Entry

PARKER, John CBE 1965; MP (Lab) Dagenham, since 1945; President, Fabian Society, since 1980; *b* 15 July 1906; *s* of H.A.M. Parker, schoolmaster; *m* 1943 Zena Mimardiere; one *s* Michael; *Educ*: Marlborough; St. John's College, Oxford, Chm., Oxford Univ. Labour Club, 1928; Asst to Director, Social Survey of Merseyside (Liverpool Univ.) 1929–32; Gen. Sec., New Fabian Res. Bureau, 1933–39; Fabian Society: Gen. Sec., 1939–45; Vice-Chm., 1946–50; Chm., 1950–53; Vice-President, 1972–80. Labour candidate (Holland with Boston) 1931; MP (Lab) Romford, Essex, 1935–45; PPS to Miss Ellen Wilkinson, Min. of Home Security, 1940–42; Parly Under-Sec. of State, Dominions Office, 1945–46; Member: Speaker's Conferences, 1944, 1965–67, 1973–74; Procedure Cttee, 1966–73; Parly Delegation to USSR, 1945; National Executive Labour Party, 1943–44; Executive London Labour Party, 1942–47; Select Cttee Parliamentary Disqualifications, 1956; Parly Delegations to Italy 1957 and Ethiopia 1964 and Forestry Delegation (Yugoslavia) 1971; Leader, Delegation to Windward Islands, 1965; Hon. Sec., Webb Trustees; Governor, London School of Economics 1949–81; Member: Council, Essex Univ. 1968–; Exec. Cttee Nat. Trust, 1969–81; Historic Buildings Council, 1974–; Inland Waterways Amenity Council 1968–; Chm. British Yugoslav Parly Group 1960–; Father of the House, 1979–; Chm. History of Parliament Trust, 1979–; Chm. House of Commons Pensions Fund, 1979– – Yugoslav Red Star, 1975. Trade Union: Transport and General. *Publications*: The Independent Worker and Small Family Business, 1931; Public Enterprise (Forestry Commission) 1937; Democratic Sweden (Political Parties); Modern Turkey, 1940; 42 Days in the Soviet Union, 1946; Labour Marches On, 1947; Newfoundland, 1950; (ed) Modern Yugoslav Novels (English edn), 1958–64; (comp. and ed) biographies, inc. Harold Wilson and Willy Brandt, 1964. *Recreations*: architecture and gardening. *Address*: 4 Essex Court, Temple, EC4. *T*: 01-353 8521.

I

Why Politics? Why Labour?

I was born into a political family. Both my grandfathers were enthusiastic radicals, my father was a strong Conservative, having won a scholarship to St John's College, Cambridge, in the 1890s when Kipling was all the fashion. He later spent a year at Heidelberg and returned strongly anti-German, disliking the way their young officers, as they walked down the pavements, swept all the civilians they passed into the road.

My paternal grandmother, a strong Tory and a most formidable woman, ran a successful millinery shop in Bristol following her husband's death. Sunday nights she held court surrounded in her large drawing room by her husband's friends, mostly Liberals, and my father and his friends, mostly Tories, who came to drink her whisky and argue over current political events. At Christmastime they were frequently joined by John Davies, a connection by marriage, who was Lloyd George's principal secretary (1911–22). He fascinated me as I sat in the background — all ears — with his account of L.G.'s manoeuvres at the Versailles Conference — especially the way he had sent messages to London in Welsh which he thought was a code no one could break, and the attempts of the IRA to assassinate him.

My father was a keen member of the Royal Empire Society which had a branch in Clifton, and received its literature which I duly devoured. At the age of 12 I told him I would like to become a Tory MP. He told me that was impossible as MPs had to have private means. However, he gave me for my birthday a three-volume *Life of Disraeli* which I regret to say I have never read.

My father also told me about his uncle, another John Parker. He and his two brothers, Gilbert and Herbert, had come from Wilton to Bath where they had learnt Pitman's shorthand, the latest thing. They then sailed in 1869 for India to seek their fortunes, going round the Cape as their ship was too large to go through the new Suez Canal. Gilbert fell ill and Herbert, my grandfather, brought him back to die. John stayed to become a successful journalist, editing and then owning the *Indian Daily News*. When he had made £40,000, a large sum in those days, he decided to copy Joseph Chamberlain, and returned to England to enter politics. He acquired the *Leeds Daily Mercury* and was duly adopted as a Liberal

1

candidate in that city. However, he was a very mean man, quarrelled with his local party and never became an MP. He, like my paternal grandfather, had died before I was born.

My father had fired my imagination by claiming that we were connected with the Macclesfield Parkers. An MP in Queen Anne's reign, a member of that family, had wisely anticipated the Hanoverian succession by learning German. He had greeted George I at Dover. His rise was rapid, Solicitor-General, Attorney-General, Lord Chancellor and Earl of Macclesfield. Then, in 1725, he had been impeached for bribery and corruption and heavily fined. None the less, that section of the family had remained well-off, although it had since done very little.

I have early recollections of the Suffragettes. In the summer of 1913 they burnt 'Votes for Women' with acid across the cricket table of Bristol University sports ground. The students retaliated by making a bonfire of their furniture and literature in the middle of Queens Road, Clifton, where their offices were. A student staying with us took part and got arrested; my father had to bail him out. The next Easter the Suffragettes set fire to the Hastings house of Du Cros, the local Tory MP, a strong opponent of theirs. I was staying with my mother's parents and was taken to see the damage. The fire brigade had failed to get it properly under control and it had blazed up again.

My first electoral memory is of the 1918 khaki election. Ernest Bevin was the Labour candidate in Central Bristol where my grandmother's business was. He was violently denounced in the local paper and by my father's *Daily Mail* as a dangerous Red. Thomas Inskip was successfully elected there as a Unionist to support Lloyd George's coalition government.

I followed my father's lead in becoming increasingly disillusioned with this government. I first thought that a real Tory government would be a 'good thing' – there never having been one in my lifetime, as I had been born in 1906. However, on reading some of the right-wing Tory speeches plugged by the *Daily Mail*, I was not so sure, and turned a sympathetic eye towards the Asquithian Liberals who were supported by my mother's father. Then came three General Elections in successive years 1922, 1923 and 1924. I was at school at Marlborough and argued politics with a number of school fellows. The Tory victory in 1922 and the failure of the Asquithian Liberals effectively to re-establish themselves led me to ask myself what the Labour Party stood for.

The next holiday when I was at home I decided one Sunday evening to visit Kingsley Hall in Bristol's Old Market Street, the meeting place of the Independent Labour Party. The speaker was Jimmy Maxton. He was followed by 'England Arise' and other socialist songs. The oratory, the idealism and the atmosphere 'got' me completely and so I joined the ILP at the age of 16. At later meetings I heard Ramsay Macdonald, Philip Snowden, Pat Dollan and Mrs Bruce Glasier, among others.

Then came the sudden 1923 election when Baldwin dissolved Parliament and asked for a mandate for protection. The small young Labour Parties in the rural south-west had spent all their funds on the 1922 election and were unable to put

2

up candidates. This was the case in Marlborough, part of the Devizes constituency. Together with another boy, Stopford Brooke, a keen Liberal, I managed surreptitiously to attend a Tory meeting in the town and enjoyed the spectacle of an ardent Liberal master, Dowdell, being expelled from the meeting for heckling. To begin with Labour supporters stood on one side, but, as the Election developed, the Liberals increasingly raised the 'cost of living' issue. In the last week the tide swung against the Tories and the Liberals won all the rural seats in the south-west — twenty-six — from Lands End to outside Reading including Devizes, mostly with the support of Labour votes. This helped to make possible the first Labour government. Going down town at Marlborough, I witnessed the Liberal victory celebrations as angry women stoned the windows of the local Tory office.

In the election the following year (1924) the Tories won back most of these rural seats including Devizes.

I had entered the History VI the previous autumn and was encouraged by our master, Birley[1], to read books on politics. I remember Lord Hugh Cecil's *Conservatism*, which failed to impress. Then came R.H. Tawney's *Acquisitive Society* which strongly confirmed my socialist faith. With Birley's encouragement, in due course I founded a political society, of which I was the first secretary, although few boys showed much interest.

After going to Oxford I met and heard a large number of active Labour MPs and trade unionists, together with Communists like Harry Pollitt and Saklatvala. After the General Strike and coal lockout I organized a party of students, four men and four women, to spend a week at our expense, staying with miners' families in the Rhondda, where we went down a mine and studied the dereliction left by that industrial battle. Michael Stewart, Colin Clark and Maurice Ashley were of the party.

It was not until I went to Liverpool in 1929 to work on the social survey of Merseyside that I really got to know what life was like in a northern industrial town. There, in conjunction with George Williams, the local TGW secretary, and Molly Cumella.(later a barrister and Labour councillor), I helped to organize a local Branch of SSIP (Society for Socialist Inquiry and Propaganda) which was created in 1930 by those socialists who were disillusioned by the second Labour government and wanted to complement the oratory of the ILP by constructive work. I took over a WEA (adult education) class in Barrow and learnt a great deal from the young enthusiastic engineers and draftsmen among its members. The onset of the 1931 slump confirmed me in my socialist beliefs, as I saw the suffering widespread unemployment produced on Merseyside.

2

Marlborough in the Early 1920s

I had the good fortune to be at Marlborough during the mastership of Cyril Norwood (1916–25). My father was a close friend of his, having been senior housemaster under him at Bristol Grammar School. My father and I came up and stayed at the Castle and Ball Hotel early in 1920 when I unsuccessfully attempted an open scholarship. Norwood invited us to tea and I was intrigued to hear him discuss with my father some of his difficulties. He had been a great success at Bristol where he had revived an old but flagging school. One of its governors, the Bishop of Salisbury, was also a governor of Marlborough and had backed his appointment as Master to carry out a similar job there.

Norwood had told us that on arrival he had found resentment among the staff and boys that he had come to Marlborough from being head of a grammar school. Having weak insteps he had to wear boots. The boys, who all wore shoes, save at games, at once called him 'The Boot'. He had taken nearly two years to settle in and had then carried out a number of reforms. Boys were given a great deal more freedom, school periods were cut from one hour to three-quarters, the outside School Certificate exams (the forerunners of A- and O-levels) were introduced and academic standards raised. This had entailed the superannuation of older boys who had failed to secure promotion from the lower forms. He endeavoured to conquer the 'slouch', for which the school was noted, by introducing daily PT at mid-morning under prefects trained as instructors.

Such changes, moderate as they may now seem, had aroused some opposition led by Dr James, one of the governors, who had been a master there (1872–5), Headmaster of Rossall and Rugby and was currently President of St John's College, Oxford. He produced for the governors a memo containing seven reasons why Norwood should be asked to resign. After a keen struggle, Norwood won by a majority of one, whereupon all of his opponents resigned. Their places were filled by his supporters. James then banned Norwood from entering St John's, his old college.

Some years later I secured an open history scholarship at St John's. Judge my surprise when Norwood invited me to tea and told me I would be the first old Marlburian to go up to St John's since his battle with James. He told me his side

4

of the story. On arrival at St John's, I was invited to tea, again alone, by James to be told his version. James remained President — as he could then do — until his death at 87 in 1931. The ban on Norwood had been lifted earlier and he became President (1934—46).

Norwood had also described the hectic problems which had recently arisen at Marlborough when the bursar had unwittingly accepted a double entry for the autumn term. This had only been discovered three weeks before term and he had had to buy and fit up some extra houses for juniors and place extra beds in many dormitories. This slip permanently enlarged the school by about a hundred.

As John Betjeman has said, Marlborough could be a pretty barbarous place, especially the notorious 'Upper School', for younger boys. This contained two coal fires, 'Big Fire' for four captains and a dozen good-at-games invited by them and 'Little Fire' for over 200 other juniors from in-college houses. The favoured dozen frequently paid the penalty for their privileges. They raced around till the last moment when the captains entered as the prep bell stopped. A ritual beating took place at the end of prep of all caught out of their seats. A basketing by 'Big Fire' on a Saturday night, when the victim was placed head down, clad only in an old shirt, in one of the large wastepaper baskets, covered with filth and then pulled up by ropes over one of the beams, was feared by any unpopular boy.

Houses depended, as always, very much upon the personal qualities of their housemasters. I was lucky enough to have George Turner in B1, which included boys as diverse as James Mason, the future film star, and Freddy Copleston, the future Jesuit father. The 'cult of games' was then dominant in most public schools. At Marlborough this was shown by the enormous number of blazers, ties, caps and jerseys for those who excelled at different games, which must have cost some parents a small fortune. It found its most forcible expression in one of the Field houses (C2) under a housemaster who described himself as a muscular Christian. Discipline there was truly Spartan. We bathed sensibly without costumes; the junior boys in his house were called 'hot cross bums' from the marks most of them bore across their behinds. That house was cock-house every term save one during the five years I was at Marlborough.

It was on the sixth form that Norwood had his greatest impact. Not only was the teaching of a high level, especially from the new young masters he appointed, but he encouraged discussion. I recollect a lecture he gave the sixth one morning on 'Why Shakespeare could *not* have written Shakespeare' and then asked for our replies the next week, when he also gave his own! School societies flourished, with sponsoring masters to make music, act, debate, read papers on literature, play chess and many other activities. Some housemasters disapproved. I remember the future historian, Christopher Lloyd, being forbidden to attend a paper I gave on the Restoration dramatists who again were just beginning to appear on the London stage. Marlborough definitely gave a lead in such activities. When I got to Oxford, I was at first disappointed because I had savoured most of these at school, whereas they were new to most other undergraduates.

The year I went up to Oxford (1925) Marlborough had won thirty open

5

scholarships at Oxford and Cambridge — the highest ever. Many of the young masters brought in by Norwood went on to headships elsewhere.

Marlborough was an isolated school in the country in the early 1920s. The Bath road (A4) was only tarred as far as the Aylesbury Arms one way and Savernake Forest the other. There was little lorry traffic on it. The noise of goods trains taking traffic on the old Midland and Southern Western Junction line from Southampton into the Midlands could be heard through the open windows at night.

There were three terms, two of 13½ weeks and one of 9½ with no half-terms or breaks, save an occasional extra half-holiday. Parents rarely came to see their boys during term save on Speech Day at the end of June; some mothers came up and stayed in a private house nearby during the weekend their son was confirmed. Boys were far more cut off from home contacts than now. Visits from visiting teams and to other schools provided variety for those in the first elevens or fifteen, but the school was driven in upon itself for intellectual activities.

School started with a bell at 6.30 a.m. and there was a great rush to be in Early School by 7.15 a.m. Breakfast followed at 8.00 a.m. Then after chapel came three periods broken by PT with lunch at 12.36 p.m. Boys were then allowed down to the nearer part of the town to 'brewshops'. Every afternoon from 2.30 p.m. to 3.15 p.m. boys were expected to be changed and out of their houses. Prep followed in the evening.

Those not taking part in games arranged by the house captains were sent in the winter terms on runs, with a prefect to call the roll. In summer, however, in most houses those not taking part in cricket could cycle in shorts anywhere they wished — save to a town — within a ten-mile radius. Permission could be got to go on longer rides and I well remember parties of us cycling to Stonehenge, Salisbury, Lechlade on the Thames and other places of interest after getting leave off lunch and a late pass-in. I spent many happy hours exploring Avebury, Savernake Forest, and many village churches either with a few friends or with a school society. A visit to see William Morris's house at Kelmscott remains vividly in my memory, with John Betjeman violently attacking everything Victorian!

No schoolboy ever thinks his food adequate or good. We had a very stodgy diet with plenty of suet puddings, rice and semolina and masses of potatoes. Sausages were the most popular lunch, although there was normally plenty of meat. Vegetables consisted usually of overcooked cabbage and dried peas and beans which were soaked in boiling water to expand before being served. They frequently went on expanding after being eaten. You can imagine with what results! I never remember having a salad. For breakfast and tea boys provided their own jam to kill the taste of the unpleasant First World War margarine, which was still served as late as 1924. With such a diet it was not surprising that many suffered from constipation despite the vigorous exercise most of us took.

There was little privacy. Relieving oneself was communal, with two long troughs near 'Upper School' with rows of seats separated by partitions. After breakfast queues three or four long awaited a doorless vacant place. Every ten minutes a flush cleared the whole trough beneath one. In dormitories the eldest boys took their place at one end and the youngest at the other in order of seniority. Lights were out at 9.50 p.m. Sixth-formers could go in their dressing gowns to a house classroom and do extra prep or read three or four nights a week. The others would argue for half an hour before Silence. This certainly benefited the younger boys, who listened to their elders without chiming in. It was there that I was introduced to Bernard Shaw by listening to arguments as to what he meant in some of his prefaces.

All in all, despite the barbarism from which many younger boys suffered, the sixth came into its own under Norwood. After I had gained an Oxford scholarship, my father wanted me to go to France to learn the language. I much preferred to come back to Marlborough and had two very happy terms running school societies and reading, with the helpful advice of Birley, whatever took my fancy.

Some sources

Sir John Betjeman
Father Freddy Copleston SJ (BI House)
J.R.M. Senior (BI House)
Christopher Lloyd (historian)
Professor J.Z. Young (scientist)

3

Oxford Politics in the Late 1920s

I came up to St John's from Marlborough as an Open History Scholar in October 1925 and went down in the summer of 1929.

The late 1920s at Oxford were in many ways a revival of the late nineteenth century. Apart from the General Strike (1926), there was little political interest amongst undergraduates, who were still dominated by the public-school element. Those who came up from the grammar schools tended to be penurious, and received little financial help. They took little part in university activities and concentrated on getting good enough degrees to get them into their desired teaching, business or civil service jobs on going down. Academic standards were still low, although entrance standards had been raised after the First World War. Much was made of the misfortunes of the duke of Norfolk[1] who tried for over three years to get into Christ Church but continually failed Responsions (the Entrance Exam), despite the tutoring of Father Ronald Knox, the university's Roman Catholic chaplain. Few thought that another European war was likely; many professed pacifist views and hoped that the League of Nations – despite the rise of Mussolini – would settle all future international disputes. It was not until the early 1930s, when undergraduates coming down during the slump found that those who had come down the previous year had not yet got jobs, followed by the rise of Hitler and the Spanish Civil War, that wide interest in politics suddenly developed.

The debagging cult

University life in the 1920s on the surface still appeared to be a continual struggle between 'hearties' and 'aesthetes', who debagged one another and broke up each other's rooms when a little drunk. Both were essentially public school in their support for or their revolt against the current 'cult of games' at their schools.

St John's had low academic standards apart from its scholars. Its President (Dr James)[2] known as 'The Bodger', was a former Headmaster of Rugby. As a result a large number of its commoners were wealthy Old Rugbians who would be unlikely nowadays to get into a university. They ran the Boat Club which took most of the available funds for games and, to a lesser extent, rugger and cricket. They enforced their wishes by debagging those who offended them.

The majority of undergraduates had rooms in college for their first two years — an admirable practice which enabled them to make friends on coming up — and then went into 'digs' (i.e. lodgings) when working for their finals. The JCR (Junior Common Room) had few activities but served as a meeting place for a drink and chat before dining in hall which was incumbent on all for a few evenings each week. Its officers were chosen each June by those about to go into digs from those entering their second year. One autumn the new secretary offended the third-year men and was as a consequence, debagged and had his buttocks rubbed with brown shoe polish 'to look like a couple of new rugger balls'. His attempts to remove it were watched with interest in the baths the following week; the brown polish came off with great difficulty. His critics then seized the unfortunate man and repeated the process. The secretary broke down and wept, but did not resign his post.

The Open scholars wore long gowns; they sat together in hall for dinner at separate tables for first, second and senior years. The first-year scholars took it in turn to read a Latin grace which had to be pronounced in the current modern pronunciation; failure to do this correctly led to a 'sconce' by a scholar from a higher table. This meant that a quart pot of beer had to be ordered by the man sconced. If he drank the whole of it without drawing a breath the table had to stand the cost, if not the beer was shared by the table at his expense. As I had been taught to pronounce my Latin in the old way I realized I should be in for a succession of sconces. This I avoided by telling the President that I was a Unitarian (which I was at that time) and so was barred from reading the grace.

At table the scholars were forbidden to talk shop or to mention a woman's name on pain of being sconced. This at first rather reduced conversation to discussions of what was coming on at the theatre or cinema at the beginning of the week and what one thought of what one had seen at its end. However, the mixing of scholars of different disciplines soon led to interested probings and questionings which were not considered 'shop'. Michael Stewart,[3] a classical scholar from Christ's Hospital, and I soon discovered our mutual interest in socialist politics, which we freely discussed and argued with Brian Roberts.[4] As the senior scholar of the year was a medical student, vivisection was a prominent topic. Ivor Thomas,[5] a crosscountry runner from Wales and a second-year scholar, brilliantly argued with all and sundry.

Despite occasional bullyings by its hearties, St John's possessed a strong community sense, being a moderate-sized college determined not to let its men be bested by the products of Balliol, Christ Church or New College. Hence the success of the much-criticized St John's caucus in the Union and its dramatic society, 'The Mummers'. None the less, St John's was still one of the most conservative of colleges. A large number of its dons were 'High Church and King' Tories of grammar school origin. Up to 1914 some had continued to drink to

'The King over the Water' — until they realized that the current Stuart claimant was Rupert, Crown Prince of Bavaria.

The Union as a political centre

The Oxford Union was the natural mecca of all interested in politics and enabled friendships to be made with those from other colleges. But, unlike the majority of university unions, its membership was limited to those who paid to join. It did not organize university games, clubs or dances but there was plenty of talk and a good library for non-scientists. Here leading speakers from outside could be heard; how to speak, the virtue of pertinacity and experience in intrigue could all be learnt. The leading Oxford weekly, *Isis*, edited by some of the principal aesthetes of the day such as J.B. Fernald, sometimes produced witty reports of the debates. However, most of these were written by those who were not themselves speakers; they were bored by young hopefuls trying to find something original to say late in the evening and expected them all to be of the level of a candidate in a Presidential Election (a new President and three other officers were elected each term). An exception was W.J.K. Diplock,[6] a forceful speaker, who for a time wrote reports for both the *Isis* and its rival the *Cherwell*. His anonymity breached, he thought it necessary to write in the *Isis*, vigorously defending his impartiality.

The Union was greatly over-valued; it was not what it had been in the past, the *Isis* pontificated (27 February 1929). When in the late 1920s socialists succeeded in getting debates on current issues of importance, the *Isis* attacked the Union for debating so technical and difficult a subject as unemployment. 'The debate was deplorable; speakers had read Party literature to inform themselves' (12 June 1929). The *Isis* continued to dislike solid argument and to prefer clever wisecracks of the Oscar Wilde type. The traditional amusing Eights Week debate with guest speakers such as Ronald Knox and Philip Guedalla,[7] who had been Union stars in the 1910 period, was greatly admired. It was regretted that such debates were no longer the norm (if they ever had been).

Michael Stewart and I arrived at the Union in 1925 to find it dominated by Liberals. The most outstanding of these were sons of Liberal politicians — Dingle Foot,[8] Dick Acland,[9] and Aubrey Herbert, who all became Liberal candidates in the 1929 election. They were all good speakers; they used the Union as a recruiting ground for the Liberal Club and made some appeal to the traditional Nonconformist and the ex-public-school boy who wished to break with a Tory background — but not too drastically. The General Strike set the Liberals back temporarily but, with the backing of Lloyd George and the influence of J.M. Keynes and the Liberal Yellow Book, the club doubled its not very large numbers in the late 1920s.[10] The well-known feud of the Asquith-Lloyd George families spread to Oxford; Aubrey Herbert, whose father had been a friend of Asquith, was reported to have told Lloyd George at one of his breakfasts that 'If our leaders don't behave themselves, we shall sack them.'

In contrast, socialists were almost completely absent from Union debates. We were told that the previous year A.L. Rowse,[11] then a leading Marxist, had persuaded the Labour Club to boycott the bourgeois Union after he had been laughed at for his Cornish accent. With no encouragement from senior speakers save E.F.M. Durbin,[12] young socialists had to try to make a mark late at night, usually on an unsympathetic subject.

There were a number of good Conservative speakers throughout the period. They certainly encouraged the newcomer if of the right background, but they were not so well organized as the Liberals, and many of their activities took place in bodies such as the Chatham Club. Very surprising was their continuing patronage and his repeated meddling in Oxford politics by Lord Birkenhead, then Secretary for India and a leading member of Baldwin's cabinet.

In my second term I was at home for a short time with jaundice and arrived back to call on a Tory friend who showed me a whip telling him to go to a special Union meeting that evening (9 February 1926) to vote against the motion 'That this Society respectfully, but firmly, protests against a promise recently extracted from two undergraduates because it forbids them to express their political convictions in debate and private conversation'. It transpired that in a British government raid on some Communist offices in London, a note had been found against the names of two Oxford members of the Communist Party (one an Australian) asking them to promote propaganda among Indian students. Birkenhead had then written to his old tutor, Dr Wells,[13] the Vice-Chancellor, and asked him to send the two students down at once. Dr Wells found this beyond his powers, but saw them, extracted the promise mentioned and reported them to their own colleges. The one at Queen's reported that he had been interviewed by the 87-year-old Provost, Dr McGrath,[14] who had stated that he had been a pupil of John Stuart Mill; he had told the student to say what he liked and had torn up the Vice-Chancellor's letter in front of him. When Birkenhead's intervention became known it produced a strong reaction in the Union, hence the call for a special meeting. After the above motion had been moved by Frank Lee,[15] the Labour Club chairman, Frank Pakenham (later Lord Longford) then an officer of the Conservative Association, suggested a moderate amendment which he withdrew after it had been rejected by his own supporters. An amendment was then moved to the effect that 'This House disapproves of any criticism of the disciplinary actions of the Vice-Chancellor on the part of undergraduate members of the University.' This was heavily defeated (262/147) and the original motion carried (215/92). A poll of the whole society in which many dons and country clergy voted, finally rejected the motion (403/367). The London press had a heyday; Dr Wells took no further action.

Birkenhead and Churchill

Traditionally busts of former Union Presidents who had become Prime Ministers subsequently had been placed in the Union debating hall, but no others. Anxious to create a precedent for the inclusion of his own bust (it is there now!), Birkenhead put up most of the necessary money for a bust of Lord Curzon despite his failure to become Prime Minister. This was accepted by the Standing Committee and unveiled on 28 October 1926. It was a striking ceremony. 'Where all (with two notable exceptions) were well dressed, the President [A.T. Lennox-Boyd] was best dressed (in a grey morning suit); where all were dignified, he was most dignified; where all played their parts well, he played his magnificently'.[16] Asquith unveiled the bust in a classical speech in which adjectives and nouns were largely alliterative. Birkenhead and Simon[17] followed, Birkenhead in a red tie and dark blue suit, dwelling on Curzon's faults and failures, whilst Simon sang his praises. I, however, was fascinated by watching the Mosleys. Oswald[18] who had recently won a by-election as a Labour MP, had been heavily attacked in the *Daily Mail* and boycotted by the Establishment. Lady Cynthia Mosley, his wife, was present as Curzon's daughter. As soon as the Vice-Chancellor, Dr Pember,[19] arrived, she walked over to him; she had met him when her father had been Chancellor.[20] She held him in close conversation in front of the whole audience as they collected, despite his efforts to get away. When the ceremony was over she rushed up to him and — as it was raining — asked if he could take her across the garden on his arm under his umbrella. Oswald remained silent and tagged on behind!

The Union Debating Hall was the only large meeting place in Oxford University under undergraduate control. When political societies held meetings for distinguished outside speakers, which they thought likely to be too large for their usual meeting places, they frequently hired the Union Hall. Meetings had been held there recently to listen to Baldwin and Lloyd George and one was shortly to be held for Ramsay Macdonald. Birkenhead approached the Conservative Association and asked them to get the Debating Hall banned to outside speakers in term time. He had argued, 'Suppose Nehru came to Oxford to speak. It would suggest University backing for his views if he were to address a meeting in the Union Hall.' The Tories agreed to follow his wishes and persuaded the Standing Committee to propose 'That the hire of the Debating Hall shall not be permitted during term' (26 January 1928). It was overwhelmingly defeated.

A few weeks before Birkenhead had been the main guest speaker at the Presidential debate on 23 November 1927. Dingle Foot was one of the leading contenders; greeting the guest, he humorously told the old story of Simon and F.E. Smith (Birkenhead) tossing up as to which party they would join. 'The Noble Lord lost.' Birkenhead angrily jumped to his feet saying, 'That story, which has been frequently repeated, is a stupid and foolish invention.' 'I thought better of the Noble Lord', Foot replied and brought the house down. Birkenhead was furious and when he got up to reply spent most of his time denouncing rude young men. Foot was elected President by a large majority. When I went to chat to Birkenhead after the debate I was surprised to see that he had a diamond ring on every finger and diamonds all the way down the front of his dress shirt. It suggested that there might be something in the story of his gypsy origin.

12

The next term Churchill was the guest of honour at the Presidential debate (1 March 1928). A leading contender this time was another Liberal, Aubrey Herbert. He was in the middle of his speech when Birkenhead stalked in to be greeted with catcalls and cheers. The *Isis* commented: 'There is a convention that one does not enter the Union in the middle of a speech but waits until it is finished. The foundation of this custom is unknown but it is believed to be politeness'. Birkenhead pleaded afterwards that he had forgotten the Union tradition and that the House of Commons practice was different. Herbert was elected President by a large majority.

Churchill did not loom as large a figure as Birkenhead upon the Oxford scene. Nationally, apart from his close involvement in fighting the General Strike, it was one of his more quiescent periods as a very orthodox Chancellor of the Exchequer. However, he had given hostages to fortune in the past and a number of us collected round him after the debate to ask how he reconciled his opposition to women's suffrage before 1914 with his current support of his Government's bill to give women between 21–30 the vote. Taking his two lapels in his hands with a boyish smile he replied: 'Well, these women, you know, they go to church on Sundays and they vote Conservative, what more do you want?' He continued: 'The important thing for the Conservatives is that they should keep on doing things. It doesn't matter what. If they do that they will remain in power for my lifetime. After that, the deluge can come.' I had recently heard Baldwin at a Tory meeting and found him very pedestrian and boring. His shabby suit with soup stains down his waistcoat contrasted with the well-cut dinner jackets of the club's officers.

The University Labour Club

The Oxford University Labour Club[21] had 150 members in 1925 and grew gradually to 305 in the summer of 1929 after a temporary boost during the General Strike. Its weekly meetings were well organized and lively. It had a good cross-section of student membership and gave Ruskin students one of their few close links with the university. Its visiting speakers had a wide variety of views. These included Communists such as Harry Pollitt and Saklatvala, leading Labour MPs and trade unionists, including most of the members of the 1924 government, intellectuals such as Bertrand and Dora Russell and C.E.M. Joad and dons such as G.D.H. Cole, R.H. Tawney, Harold Laski and A.D. Lindsay (the Master of Balliol). Apart from the important Ruskin contingent, the majority of its officers came from public schools; almost all of the Club members' parents were Liberals or Conservatives. Women played a much larger part in its activities than in any other university club; in fact it was lampooned as a matrimonial agency. Its intellectual level was high, most of its prominent members obtained Firsts. They largely became civil servants, journalists and dons; only a sprinkling became Parliamentary candidates and MPs.

As will be seen from the above paragraph the political interests of the Labour Club were far less focused on Union debating than those of the other political clubs. I will, therefore, describe a number of these before coming back to its Union battles.

During the period leading up to the General Strike (1926) controversy built up and the miners' leader, A.J. Cook, was violently attacked in the Tory press. He came to address the Oxford City Labour Party in the Corn Exchange on 29 January 1926 (with many undergraduates present). The *Isis* came out with the headline 'Does Mr Cook wear Purple Pants? The Question of the Hour!'[22] Whilst recommending students to stay away, it provocatively suggested that debagging was the only way to find out. Police and university authorities were terrified at a possible assault on Cook and the likely revenge outraged miners might take on Oxford undergraduates up and down the country. Hoarse from many an openair meeting, Cook quietly and movingly put the miners' case to a massively guarded meeting which hardly dared to heckle.

As a General Strike became increasingly likely, many became perturbed at the possibility of violent strife. The Union passed a resolution on 6 May 'expressing its hope that negotiations between the Government and the TUC will be continued' (carried 215/70) followed by a debate on 'The Government has diastrously mishandled the coal situation' (carried 214/141). Rumours spread that undergraduates were to be conscripted to strike-break. The Labour Club called an emergency meeting at Hannington Hall (now part of St Peter's) to protest. I arrived to find it almost full but with a large contingent of Tories determined to break up the meeting. A fight developed. Some were driven into a corner of the room; others were picked up and rolled over our heads and thrown out of the door down the steps. I got knocked to the floor and had my glasses smashed. Michael Stewart managed to bolt the door. Those outside, both supporters and opponents, knocked loudly to try to get in. Pandemonium reigned in the crowded hall. Then G.D.H. Cole and the Master of Balliol arrived hot from a meeting of Convocation to announce that the proposal for conscription had been defeated but all students 'could volunteer to keep food and other essential supplies moving'. When Lindsay got up to speak the Tories present sang 'God save the King' and then chanted 'He's a silly old bugger'. Having given their information Lindsay and Cole left the hall. A Ruskin student then asked if one of the Tories would state their case. A very tall man named Best did so; he was then asked if he was in favour of starving out the miners' wives and children. He said 'Certainly not'. 'Well then, will you contribute to a fund for their support?' A sum of £27 was then collected off the Tories as they left the hall. On coming out of the meeting the two Proctors[23] of opposing political views were seen quietly sitting at the bottom of the stairs watching the excitement. Such was the Battle of Hannington Hall.

A very large number of students, including some members of the Labour Club, went off to drive trains and move food at the docks. In the short run this seemed an exciting new experience and they fell for the propaganda to keep food and essential supplies moving. However, the Labour activists did their best to find useful work to support the strikers. It was very difficult, however, at a time of crisis to persuade young socialists just to carry on as usual. I remember attending a lecture at Exeter College one morning when all the men present were wearing red ties. The don (Atkinson) entered, took one look round and then said 'As there are no *men* present, there will be no lecture today', and walked out. Margaret Cole[24] and some students regularly motored up to London to collect the trade union paper *The British Worker* and bring copies back to Oxford which we sold whilst addressing meetings in the surrounding villages. It was then that I first met Hugh Gaitskell, one of Cole's pupils, when he motored me out to speak at Wheatley. After the Archbishop of Canterbury had been forbidden to appeal for compromise over the radio, some socialists, with the help of Cole and Lindsay, collaborated with a group of churchmen and Liberals to work for a peaceful settlement.

Two of the best-remembered Labour Club meetings were those for Ramsay Macdonald and Saklatvala. The officers took Ramsay out to the usual cheap dinner we gave our guest speakers. He was obviously piqued that he had not been invited first to dine at one of the high tables. He said he was tired and would take longer to speak by half-an-hour than he would if fresh. His handsome figure, resonant Scottish voice and socialist idealism made a deep impression on undergraduates, at least temporarily. But a number of us couldn't help noting the lack of any worked-out plans for achieving his ideals.

Saklatvala, a wealthy Indian Parsee, had first been elected as Communist MP for North Battersea in 1922; membership of the CP and of the Labour Party were not at that time incompatible. He had been invited to many recent meetings in Oxford and Cambridge but they had always been broken up. As Secretary of the Labour Club, I took great care, once he had agreed to come, to prevent trouble. We took the Oxford Town Hall for the meeting. I went the day before and placed all the keys on the exit side of the doors leading from the platform in case we had to retreat. We did not advertise the meeting and only allowed entrance to Club members. I had invited a number of friends to meet him for lunch at my digs near Ruskin. Judge my surprise when he turned up as I was about to go to a lecture. He said, 'I thought the wrong people might meet me at the station. Therefore I have come early and will write my letters here.' This he continued to do, despite partially broken glasses, as all my guests were arriving, until 1.15 p.m. Then he suddenly got up and said 'Now I can talk', and hardly stopped till we said goodbye to him just before midnight! After lunch I took him through the back streets for tea at Christ Church. We arrived in the Peckwater quad just as all the boat crews were coming up from the river. Fearing he might be recognized, I tried to shepherd him up a staircase whilst he walked up and down for five minutes admiring the architecture. Quintin Hogg,[25] who had the rooms opposite, refused to meet him as he felt unable to shake hands.

In due course we reached the Town Hall to a packed, orderly, well-stewarded meeting. He devoted a great part of his speech to defending his vote against the

15

New Prayer Book and the democratic steps he had taken to ascertain his constituents' views!

A fortnight later I received a summons to see the Proctors. 'Is it true that Mr Saklatvala is to address the Labour Club in the near future?' 'No', I replied. 'He did so two weeks ago.' Taken aback, one of them insisted that he should be told in future of all meetings likely to cause trouble so that he could be present.

A great feature of the Labour Club was the Cole Group. This met once a week in Cole's rooms in Holywell where we sat on the floor and talked. It started soon after the General Strike. The original membership was invited by Cole after consultation with Colin Clark,[26] one of the most original and striking Labour Club personalities. To begin with we all had government posts allotted to us and were then asked to prepare papers as to what we should do over three years if members of a Labour government with a majority. Cole was surprised to find that, despite a vague sympathy for guild socialism, we were all strongly parliamentary in our approach. One term Beatrice Webb came to Oxford to deliver some lectures. As she was staying with the Coles she came to these meetings. At the first one she attended a paper was read by J.E. Meade,[27] then a supporter of social credit; when he had finished, Beatrice completely demolished the paper and practically reduced him to tears. Then, before anyone could reply, she looked at her watch, said 'It is 10 o'clock, my bedtime', and stalked out of the room. We had all thought of the Webbs as a couple of old fuddy-duddies and were dumbfounded. Those reading papers at subsequent meetings when she was present were extremely cautious and rather terrified of her.

The Cole group, with his encouraging sponsorship, continued throughout his university career and had a great effect in deepening the knowledge and thought of Oxford socialists, who also benefited from help and encouragement given by A.D. Lindsay and R.H. Tawney.

Cole had written a very lively satirical revue, *The Striker Stricken*, on the General Strike, for performance at a summer school in August 1926, while the miners were still locked out. The Labour Club — with Colin Clark in one of the leading parts — decided to produce it, at the end of the following term. It was much enjoyed and established a tradition for producing similar political skits each term by Maurice Ashley and other members of the Club. The best songs in Cole's revue and these various skits became regular features of singsongs, not only amongst students, but at Fabian Summer Schools for the next thirty years.

When the 1929 General Election was called, the Club decided to play an active part and I was appointed as Election Agent. Much help was given by his friends to Colin Clark in North Dorset. Etty, the Labour candidate in Oxford City and a Ruskin don, refused all undergraduate help as likely to damage his chances. (He did badly!) We decided, therefore, to send regular parties over to help in Swindon and addressed numerous village meetings in Banbury (North Oxfordshire). One of the most successful of these was at Kelmscott where May Morris, William Morris's daughter, took the chair. On polling day we took a coach over to Swindon and canvassed all day for Dr Addison.[28] He was elected, but in Banbury and North Dorset the effect of our efforts was to build up a large enough Labour vote to prevent the Liberals winning either seat.

Despite the fact that none of us were university voters we strongly felt that a Labour candidate ought to contest one of the two Oxford University[29] seats. At a recent meeting R.H. Tawney had told us that he would like to contest a seat provided he had no chance of winning, for he felt that his war injuries would make it impossible for him to serve in the Commons. We, therefore, approached him and offered to do all the work his candidacy would require. After consulting a number of Oxford voters, he finally refused for fear that he might damage the chances of Gilbert Murray, who stood unsuccessfully as a progressive Liberal.

The fight against the Union Establishment

To return to the Union. St John's had an active Union tradition, but its speakers of all parties felt themselves cold-shouldered by the Union Establishment. A concentrated drive was, therefore, made to persuade freshmen to join and soon, with 36 per cent of its students as members, St John's had a higher membership than any other college. When the terminal elections took place to the Library and Standing Committees and for the officers, a concentrated drive by all the candidates, whatever their party, took place to get members to the poll. 'Have you voted?' echoed down the staircases. The rule against 'canvassing' for a particular candidate was thus circumvented. Such was the working of the St John's caucus. It certainly helped a number of St John's men to get on to the Union committees and so obtain the coveted chance of a paper speech (i.e. one of the opening speeches) in which to show one's ability.

Under the influence of Roger Wilson,[30] Michael Stewart and myself, the Labour Club members were led to take a more active part in Union debates. However, the Establishment steadfastly refused to hold debates on subjects of particular interest to socialists. Exasperation grew and finally came to a head when the President (Aubrey Herbert) invited two undergraduates, Osbert Lancaster[31] and Eyres Monsell, who had secured a good deal of publicity in the London press by fighting a duel in Christ Church Meadows, to speak on 'This House deplores the passing of the duel'.

Labour Club members packed the private business meeting and voted down the accounts as a protest. As a result the two officers concerned (Roger Wilson and Quintin Hogg) resigned. The duelling debate began with a motion, moved by J. Boyd Carpenter[32] deploring 'the action of certain members of the Society in rejecting the accounts ... without stating adequate reasons, affirms its complete confidence in the officers concerned and desires them to withdraw their resignations'. With many interruptions I moved an amendment to delete all criticism of the members for the action they had taken. After a keen debate on the socialists' grievance, Diplock moved the closure. The amendment was defeated and the original motion carried by a narrow majority. Michael Stewart then moved that

17

'This House do now adjourn'. After this had been debated and defeated it was moved that the galleries be cleared. Finally, the President himself moved the duelling motion. When he had finished, Colin Clark moved the substitution of 'Nationalization of the mines is the only solution of the coal problem' for the motion on duelling. After this also had been debated and rejected, Osbert Lancaster was at last called on to speak. Most Labour supporters then left the chamber and the debate was eventually counted out as there were less than 15 members present. Michael Stewart, who had just been elected Secretary, read the Minutes with great relish at the first meeting of the next term. Henceforth socialists were able to take their full share in debates on subjects they helped to choose.

The young men of ability

The Union in the late 1920s, despite the strictures of the *Isis*, proved a training ground for a considerable number of MPs, lawyers and dons.

On the Conservative side, Quintin Hogg was outstanding as a 'high-mettled orator' and debater, followed closely by Lennox Boyd, Diplock, Boyd Carpenter, Edgar Lustgarten, the journalist and broadcaster, and Malcolm Brereton, who died soon after he went down. Others to make a mark were Playfair Price and Rumbold, who entered the Diplomatic Service, Edward Hulton, the magazine proprietor, Frank Pakenham, who later joined the Labour Party, Henry D'Avigdor Goldsmid, a Tory MP, Flowerdew Lowson, who while an undergraduate stated that his main ambition was to become Lord Mayor of London (he did 1950–51), and Duff Dunbar, an original speaker, whose success at the Bar never fulfilled his earlier promise.

In addition to Dingle Foot, Acland and Herbert, the Liberals possessed a number of able speakers many of whom subsequently became Tories or socialists. Derek Walker-Smith became a Tory MP and Minister of Health (1957–60), J.P.W. Mallalieu a Labour MP and Minister; Lindley Fraser, Head of the German Service at the BBC; David Renton a National Liberal MP and Minister; Gyles Isham, an actor, country gentleman and Tory candidate; Roger Fulford an author and Liberal candidate; James Lawrie, banker and opera producer; A.D.C. Peterson, the Director of Oxford University Department of Education (1955–72); Phelps Brown, an economics professor; and Brian MacKenna a judge. Alan Tory became a Presbyterian Minister in Los Angeles and the politically ambitious Stopford Brooke settled in Tahiti to marry a French hotelier!

Michael Stewart was the outstanding Labour debater, followed closely by Roger Wilson, E.F.M. Durbin, James MacColl, who became a Labour MP and Minister, Geoffrey Wilson, a civil servant who became Chairman of the Race Relations Board (1971), Maurice Ashley a historian and journalist, Colin Clark, E.M. Reid, who joined the Canadian Foreign Service – and myself. We all made some mark.

Mocatta, who became a judge, Robert Henriques, an author and soldier,

Frank Lee, Reg Bassett, a don, and Archie Lush, who led the Monmouthshire County Council, Douglas Jay, a Labour MP and Minister, and David Ayerst, a journalist, all spoke occasionally as did Lord Ennismore (Listowel), a Labour Minister in the Lords, who was sent over to Cambridge by his father to escape Lindsay's influence at Balliol!

Prudery and anti-feminism

The Union was very much a male preserve. It had invited a number of distinguished women as guest speakers and women were allowed in the galleries. The first woman undergraduate invited to speak was Miss L.S. Sutherland,[33] the President of Somerville Debating Society, on 18 November 1926. She opposed the motion that 'The Women's colleges of this University should be levelled to the ground' which the House ungallantly carried (223/198). There was a very prudish approach to what could be mentioned in debate. Alan Tory, a respectable Nonconformist, was soundly ticked off by the *Isis* for telling, in the presence of women in the gallery, the story of Churchill tapping the rotund Haldane[34] and asking him what he proposed to call his expected child. 'If it is a boy I shall call it George, after our gracious King. If it is a girl Mary, after our gracious Queen. But if, as I strongly suspect, it is only wind, I shall call it Winston.' Quintin Hogg was rebuked for saying 'The first Queen Elizabeth was known as the Virgin Queen. As a queen she was a great success.' After a great battle on the Standing Committee, I was allowed to introduce the motion (14 February 1929) 'That Birth Control should be made a National Policy', but only on condition that the galleries were banned to all women! It was carried (290/120).

Three other Union debates made a particularly deep impression on my mind. The first was on capital punishment, where an admirable case for its abolition was made by Lawrence Housman[35] (carried 204/118). His guest opponent, Gilbert Frankau[36] horrified his audience by his account of the slick guillotining he had watched in French market squares in the middle of the night. The best debating speech in favour of socialism I heard there was by Sir Oswald Mosley, in which he wiped the floor with Sir Mitchell Banks, a Tory MP. Yet he left an unpleasant flavour in one's mouth! Following some of Mussolini's earlier escapades, a debate took place on 'Recent Events have shown the Impracticability of the League of Nations' (defeated 47/105). Diplock had pointed out that 'Law to be enforced must have a police force. The League has none'. The *Isis*[37] commented: 'a gentleman of neat intelligence this'.

In contrast I remember there was an amused and cynical attitude over a debate in which the President (Stopford Brooke), a keen 'lion hunter', invited the Greek King,[38] an exile but no orator, to propose that 'The House would prefer an athletic to an aesthetic education'. It subsequently transpired that Brooke, already a Liberal candidate, had invited the snobbish wife of his Tory opponent to meet the King in the hope that she would persuade her husband to drop a pending libel action against him. (She succeeded!)

Political tradition at Oxford

How can the subsequent success of so many of the Oxford Union contenders of this period be accounted for? Despite the general lack of interest in politics among undergraduates, the strength of the Oxford political tradition was outstanding. All Souls and Balliol in particular had long had enormous influence in the political field which they continued to exercise. Public affairs were widely and keenly discussed by an able minority of undergraduates and dons. Many tutors encouraged their bright students to go into public life either in Parliament or the various branches of the civil service in preference to business. This tradition had no doubt arisen when Oxford students were mainly drawn from the ruling classes, but it continued after the widening of Oxford's intake. Alongside this direct contribution from the university, Ruskin had already begun important work in educating the political as well as the industrial Labour Movement. There was nothing like so wide an interest in politics at Cambridge or in other universities save at the London School of Economics.

Since the Second World War the vast growth in the total number of university students and of grants to enable the bright children of the less wealthy to go to universities, combined with the creation of many politics departments at other universities, has lessened the earlier advantages of Oxford graduates in this whole field.

The Labour Club represented a very important stream of new thought. This particular generation established a continuing socialist tradition on a more solid basis than that of the immediate post First World War period. It was the largest and most influential of the university socialist clubs. Only that of the LSE approached it in size. In addition to its support of the Cole group, it organized a good deal of serious study by other groups, particularly into long-term problems, and made useful contributions to the discussions and organization of the University Labour Federation.

Some sources

Oxford Union Minute Books
Isis files
Roger Wilson
Michael Stewart
Colin Clark
J.P.W. Mallalieu

4

Holland with Boston, 1930-31

I had taken an active part in organizing the 1929 Election activities of the Oxford Labour Club, during which I had met Christopher Addison (his daughter was a Club member). The Club had helped to get him elected at Swindon. He became Under-Minister of Agriculture and recommended me to the Holland with Boston Labour Party when they wanted a candidate.

The seat had had an unusual history. Traditionally Liberal, it had been surprisingly won by Labour in 1918. W.S. Royce had been Tory candidate there in 1910. He was said to be the first local man to put up for 200 years, having been born in the local workhouse and emigrated to South Africa where he made a fortune building railways. He had returned and farmed in the area. He had been too sympathetic to the agricultural workers' claims, and so was dropped as Tory candidate in 1918. He at once joined the Labour Party and was elected in a three-cornered fight. Once elected, he had steadily increased his majority until his sudden death in 1924. Hugh Dalton just failed to hold the seat in the subsequent by-election. The Labour vote continued high until another by-election in March 1929. Lloyd George had then poured his funds and speakers into the area. Blindell, the Liberal, won with Labour second, and two rival Tories at the bottom. In the ensuing General Election (May 1929) Blindell forged ahead with the Tory a good second and Labour a poor third.

No one therefore wanted the seat, which was why I was selected in May 1930 as Labour candidate at the age of 23. There was a continual shortage of cash; Royce, a wealthy man, had paid almost all expenses. The agent had to collect his 'salary' by selling tea around the villages.

I agreed to come over from Liverpool at my own expense whenever required and stayed with local supporters. I took a week of my holiday in September 1930 going around the large constituency, and came over for May Day and other special rallies. The chief Labour support was among the agricultural workers in the villages, who were numerous in that most fertile arable part of England. Our weakest areas were towns like Boston and Spalding. Most of our village meetings were held in pubs between elections.

I was scandalized to find that local schoolchildren had to spend all their school holidays, save for bank holidays, in the autumn working at potato picking. An approach to Charles Trevelyan, the Education Minister, led him to insist on at least a week's school holiday at Christmas and another at Easter; this was locally unpopular, as parents thus lost some of their children's earnings. Basic agricultural wages, fixed on a county basis, were 33 shillings a week; these were the best in the whole country. I well remember calling on a skilled agricultural worker to find him giving bread and dripping to his three growing boys for their main meal.

Some housewives earned money by 'pea-picking'. This was a home industry. Dried peas were supplied by canners, spread out on the kitchen table and the black peas picked out. The sound peas were then collected, expanded in boiling water and mixed with a green-pea soup to market as Garden Peas, a product replaced later by frozen peas.

Many farmers did well in this prosperous area in the slump. In the Spalding area 96 paid supertax according to one of our members who was employed in the local tax office. One large farmer had already started to spray his potato fields by plane.

The General Election of October 1931 created difficulties, owing to lack of funds locally. A number of friends generously helped with what they could spare and we organized a month's campaign. My invalid Tory father sent me a generous donation he could ill afford. My sister and I drove around in an old Fiat with a 'dicky' seat in the boot, and an effort was made to reach each of the sixty villages at least twice during the campaign. To start with, audiences were small. Opponents tried to hold me up so I would miss the later meetings that evening. At one meeting I remember the parson and school-teacher sitting in the front row, and then an outraged farmer led in his workers and sat at the back, each with his shotgun across his knees. As he loudly heckled, the parson and teacher thought at any moment they would be in the line of fire. However, my chairman ordered me to go on to the next meeting in good time. The farmer and his men let off their guns with loud bangs as we left, but fortunately did not hit the car's tyres — or my sister or myself! It was a fine autumn, but each evening a fog came up from the canals and ditches and we had great difficulty in getting back to our hostess, an aunt of Lionel Robbins, the economist. My sister succeeded on one occasion in backing our Fiat, covered with Labour posters, through the fence of an outraged neighbour whose house was decked with Tory posters!

The campaign appeared to be going well, with workers in the fields waving as we passed, until the last few days, after Snowden's speech saying a Labour victory would endanger Post Office Savings. The Tory candidate had been withdrawn by the casting vote of his chairman and Blindell was elected as a National Liberal, but dropped 5,000 votes on the joint Liberal-Tory votes of the 1929 General Election. I was lucky to keep just under 9,000 votes which Labour had had before, but was defeated by over 20,000.

Our main colour was yellow, and when the result was announced at the Boston Town Hall, a large hostile crowd had collected and shouted 'Dirty Chinese' at us as we slowly and in as dignified a manner as possible walked through it to the Labour headquarters, whilst an indignant woman rolled up a newspaper and hit me on the head as I passed.

I had repeated Disraeli at the declaration, saying 'You will not hear me now but a time will come when you will'. I went back and spoke to a friendly meeting in 1945 when Labour did much better.

A source

Beryl Hughes (my sister)

5
Merseyside Social Survey, 1929-33

The following article was written for the *Spalding Free Press* on 7 October 1930.

WHAT IS A SOCIAL SURVEY?
Things it Reveals
by John Parker, BA(Oxon)

In this article Mr Parker, prospective Parliamentary Labour candidate for the Holland with Boston division, explains the scope and nature of the investigation work on which he is engaged.

On my visits to different parts of this constituency I have been widely asked what work exactly I was engaged upon on the Merseyside Social Survey, and what value such a survey had. In this article I will attempt to show some of the very wide subjects in which our survey is interested.

As our work is nowhere near completion, this can best be done by explaining first of all the original survey carried out in London 30 or 40 years ago. All of the surveys being carried out today owe it an immense debt as blazing the path we are humbly attempting to follow. And we can only hope that the nation will gain a few benefits from our work to place beside the great number which resulted from this first survey.

It is extraordinary that the nation should have so little idea of what it really owes to the late Charles Booth. The credit for the work he made possible was taken by politicians who would have been unable to carry out their reforms if he had not provided them with the necessary information about social conditions. But Charles Booth was quite prepared to let others take the credit if the people benefited.

Took seventeen years

A shortage of funds and public indifference to begin with made his task long and

24

difficult. He did not shirk hard work, and was always thorough in his methods. It took seventeen years to complete his gigantic work on *London and Labour*, and he published it in as many volumes. Much of this work would be considered superfluous today; a great deal of it was not of interest to the general reader. But it was the first scientific attempt to find out the conditions of life in which the great mass of the people of London were born, lived, worked and died.

It showed the circumstances in which the London mother brought her child into the world and the assistance (or rather lack of assistance) that was available to advise her both before and after her delivery. It showed the stark reality of the fight of the unemployed father and mother to keep a roof above their heads, and to find food for their children, and clothing and boots for them to go to school. Education could only be a farce when the children were ill-nourished and in bad health. Teachers had to devote a large part of their time to keeping their class awake and to repeating again and again the same dull lesson. They were obliged to hammer in by constant repetition things which fit and properly fed children would easily have grasped.

Alongside the difficulties of the unemployed in finding work and in keeping his family was shown the position of the family dependent upon the casual worker and the difficulty of housekeeping when work and wages are irregular. For the first time it became generally known what happened when the head of the family fell ill or suffered an accident at his work. The tragedy of the family too poor to pay the doctor's fees for care of a suffering child was realized in all its poignancy. Overcrowding was displayed with that miserable inadequacy of proper sanitary conditions that brought ill-health.

Social conditions

Many of these evils were guessed at before Charles Booth's work. What was not known was the condition of the people — their normal life in all their activities, at home and in work, or when out of work. Such information had not been collected and studied as a whole to see what could be done to remedy the principal social ills. Individual hard cases might receive assistance from Lady Bountiful, but a whole nation could not. Social questions became for the first time the direct concern of Parliament. For when Keir Hardie had astounded the House of Commons by telling MPs that they must consider the condition of the unemployed, Gladstone had retorted that unemployment was not a question that should be discussed in Parliament.

This attitude rapidly changed when so much information on social questions became available. Charles Booth showed where the shoe pinched and so enabled social reform to become a live issue. The pressure of public opinion that his work had aroused compelled Parliament to take action.

Multitude of improvements

It is not too much to say that Charles Booth made possible a multitude of improvements. The development of maternity hospitals and children's clinics has been an attempt to solve one of the difficulties he found. Permission for Local Authorities to feed necessitous children in the schools is another. The medical inspection and physical training of school children have been attempts to give children healthy bodies so that they can take full advantage of the teaching they receive in school. Workmen's Compensation on a large scale, Health Insurance and Unemployment Insurance for the town worker all became possible when Booth showed the need for them. The widespread housing programmes carried out by our big towns in recent years are another result, although they have not as a rule brought good houses within reach of the less well-paid workers. One of the greatest boons of all has been the pensions for old people and for widows. The old can now live with their children without thinking themselves a burden, and widows are not forced to send their children to orphanages in order that they may go out to work themselves.

Surveys today

Today surveys are being carried out in London, Liverpool, Sheffield and elsewhere to find out how far our national life has been affected by changes since Booth's day. These surveys are being carried out directly by the universities and have many advantages which Booth had not. They will also be able to see how the improvements which Booth made possible are working, and if they can be bettered. Housing is an obvious example. Only those who are fairly well-off have been able to move to the new houses built since the war. If those with large families and low wages are to get better houses, it would seem that some way of reducing rents to meet their means must be found.

On questions such as this the surveys were able to offer the government valuable assistance in drawing up their recent Housing Bill.

Again, has the old age pension completely solved the difficulties it was designed to meet? From my own investigation of this question at Liverpool I should say that the pension is just sufficient to enable an old couple to live with their children but that, if the pensioner does not wish to live with his children — or has none, and is alone in the world — the position is very different. An old woman living by herself in a room or cottage can hardly end her days happily on 10 shillings per week. After paying for rent, light and heating she will be able to afford little beyond tea and bread unless she is healthy and fortunate enough to add to her income by charing or hawking. This example — and I could quote plenty of similar ones — suggests that it will be necessary to do something to meet such cases. But without adequate investigations the extent of such difficulties would not be known and no satisfactory attempts could be made to meet them.

Family income and expenditure

A subject of great interest today is that of the incomes of different working-class families, and how they spend them. An interesting discovery we have made is that the better-off families spend a very high proportion of their incomes on fruit and vegetables, but that on a reduction of wages these are the first things they economize in to the disadvantage of their health. The opposite is also true, for when families improve their incomes they buy far more fruit and vegetables. This discovery shows that an improvement in the standard of life in the big towns would be a direct advantage to the countryside, and that the proposed reduction of their standard of life will be a grave disadvantage to the countryside.

It is a great pity that some university cannot provide the funds and staff to carry out a similar study of an English countryside area such as this county of Holland. The problems of the countryside are in many ways of a distinctive character and require distinctive solutions. The omission of the agricultural worker from the unemployment insurance system for so long a time is an obvious oversight due to neglect of a study of this kind. The unfair competition of Irish labour is another problem that has never been faced.

'Knowledge is power' runs the old saying. Nowhere is it more true than in politics. A nation which desires a healthy social life must know itself in order to lay firmly the foundations of future progress.

6

Contacts with the Oxford Group
Movement, 1931–33

In the course of the 1920s Buchmanism,[1] a form of religious revivalism, insinuated itself into certain Oxford circles. It had an informal ceremony of 'sharing' in which the penitent ran over his sins and perplexities with other members of his group. It made an elitist approach to the well-to-do student. This led it to welcome the name 'Oxford Group Movement' when it was given to students on a visit to South Africa. The name aroused much hostility at the university, but had considerable snob value outside. In the late 1930s it gradually took the name 'Moral Rearmament'. I did not attend any of its meetings at Oxford.

Sometime in 1931, while I was working in Liverpool on the Merseyside Survey, I received a letter from Murray Senior, an old school friend then at Oxford, telling me he would be in St Helen's and inviting me to join him for a meal one evening. Accordingly I motored over. Asking a boy in the street where the address was, I was surprised by the reply 'You mean where the Oxford Group Movement is staying?' Senior welcomed me and we went out for a meal and a talk. He had apparently been jilted by his girlfriend, and had been comforted by some Buchmanite student friends, who had invited him to join in an attempt to 'convert' industrial England. St Helen's was the third town they had visited on the way north from Oxford. Doubts were already troubling him and he was delighted to have a talk. He had found the attitude of some of those leading this group rather distasteful.

The previous evening, after a meeting, he had passed a crowded pub when he felt an urge to go inside and ask those there to come to the next group meeting. At the door his courage had deserted him and he turned away. However, after he had walked a few yards the urge to go into the pub returned. As a result, he went in and asked the woman behind the bar if he could make an appeal to all present to come to that night's meeting. She swore at him and told him 'Get the hell out of here'. He couldn't help wondering why he had received 'a call' to go into the pub if this was to be the result!

We went to the crowded meeting with many inquisitive as to what would happen there. An Anglican parson and Congregational minister graced the platform, but the proceedings were run by self-possessed Oxford students. One of them rose from the floor and described the lazy life he had lived before conversion; the local young men were open-mouthed at the quantity of whisky he said he had then consumed. Another 'laid bare his soul' and asked what he should do. 'Take a good dose of Epsom Salts' a local lad prescribed amid laughter. A little later a tramp arose at the back of the hall who was recognized and welcomed by the chairman as having followed the group from previous meetings on their tour. To the enjoyment of much of the audience he soon went into the fruity details of his past life and sexual experiences. The Congregational minister rose from his seat and said 'I have never listened to such filth at a public meeting' and forthwith left the platform. The tramp was encouraged to continue his story. The parson then left too.

After an evening of self-revelation enjoyed by most present, the meeting ended. The chairman descended on me and was introduced, 'What do you do?' I told him I worked on a social survey to find the facts on which to build better social services. 'All completely unnecessary, England will be converted within the next two years and then all will be well.'

After leaving Liverpool I was out of work for some months and put in for a number of jobs. One was that of tutor to a boy of 17 whose parents hoped to get him into an Oxford college. I was invited up to Lancashire to be interviewed. After a tiring train journey I arrived at Crank Hall, Crank, a small country house in one of the few rural areas in the centre of the county. The boy's mother welcomed me with a boiled egg for tea and then asked the boy to take me for a walk to get acquainted. He told me his father was a director of Pilkington's Glassworks, but did not make clear why he himself had left Marlborough. Suddenly we came to a stile and, looking over, there was St Helen's and the Pilkington Glassworks below. I recalled in amusing vein my previous visit to St Helen's. To my surprise the boy drew himself up to his full height and said 'My mother and I are keen supporters of the Oxford Group Movement.' Over dinner the father made me welcome. After telling me what was wanted and asking a number of questions, he said 'I expect you are tired and would like an early night.' I went up to overhear a keen debate in the bedroom next door between father who favoured my appointment and son and mother who were strongly against. I did not get that job!

Some years later I entertained Murray Senior and his wife to dinner. As I launched into an account of my unsuccessful visit to Crank, Murray kicked me under the table to dry up. After the meal he said that he had never told his wife of his time in the Oxford Group Movement!

7
Getting Elected, 1935

On coming to London to take over the Secretaryship of the New Fabian Research Bureau in September 1933 I was recommended by Teddy Radice, my predecessor, as a possible candidate to Brixton Labour Party, where he had been the candidate in the 1931 election. I was shortlisted and went to a Selection Conference where I was defeated by Marcus Lipton, who subsequently became Brixton's MP (1945–78).

I was not, however, keen at that time to become a candidate, as I was anxious to build up the NFRB into an effective socialist research body. However, I was asked to take an adult education (WEA) class in Becontree, the newly built LCC estate to the east of London. This was breaking new ground and I found myself with an enthusiastic class on current affairs at the Woodward Hall. The first free Sunday I came down with some friends and explored the still incomplete estate, with rail lines still operating down the principal avenues to deliver bricks, doors, windows and other building materials.

Early in the summer of 1934 I was nominated by Liverpool friends and short-listed for the Kirkdale division, but had to stand down, as the NFRB Executive considered a Liverpool seat was too far from London and would interfere with my work for NFRB.

Becontree was part of the Romford division which consisted of Romford, Barking, Dagenham, Hornchurch, including Upminster and part of Brentwood. A normal-size constituency at the Redistribution in 1918, its electorate had grown to 167,000 by 1935, due to the building of the Becontree estate and a large number of private estates further out. The seat had been won for Labour in 1929 by Harry Muggeridge, the father of Malcolm Muggeridge, by an 8,000 majority over the Tory, but with a large Liberal vote of over 15,000. In 1931 he had slightly increased his vote but the Liberal withdrew and W.G.D. Hutchinson, the National Conservative, had been elected with a majority of over 18,000.

Early in 1935 Harry Muggeridge announced that, with failing eyesight, he would not be standing again. Members of my WEA class were active members of the local Labour Party and asked me if I would agree to be nominated. This I gladly did. An important industry in the old town of Barking was the gas works

30

and Arthur Whiting, an official of the Municipal and General Workers' Union, which covered its employees, was also nominated. Barking Council had recently decided to open a birth control clinic which he had strongly opposed. A Stepney councillor was also nominated and I was finally selected as Barking's nominee for the wider Romford division by 33 to 27, getting most of my support from Becontree.

The Romford division was organized on almost federal lines with each of its four parties operating separately. Communications were difficult as few members of the Labour Party possessed cars. At the Selection Conference held in May, the number of delegates from each party was determined by its individual membership. Barking, with its large membership in Becontree, had the biggest number of delegates.

Five candidates were shortlisted. They included D.N. Pritt, a well-known KC and the favourite; H.J. Nathan, a former Liberal solicitor; G. Holock, a Post Office worker; and Ernest Davies, whose father, Emil Davies, had fought the seat in 1922, 1923 and 1924. Pritt and Nathan each offered £150 a year and £150 towards election expenses. I offered nothing financially.

Each candidate in alphabetical order spoke for ten minutes, and answered questions for ten minutes. I was told afterwards by my supporters that Pritt, despite his Left views, had opposed birth control (he had a Catholic wife) and Nathan had given such a long list of his activities that he had been asked what time he could give the division. On the first vote I led with 50, Pritt had 27, Nathan 23, and the other two 11 and 9. On the final vote I had 70 to Pritt's 50. My initial support came mainly from Barking, but I picked up most of the Dagenham vote in the final count.

To get known, even to active Party members, was a difficult task and when the election came in October was far from completed. I remember spending one Sunday that summer with a Dagenham party on an excursion to Clacton by train. My open-necked red shirt was a great success! On the return journey many of us gathered in the guard's van for a singsong which ended with 'Lily of Laguna' and 'Knees up Mother Brown'.

An agent was sent in by Transport House who had not been warned of the immensity of the task before him. 'This is not a constituency', he said 'it is a continent.' A press rumour started that the ILP was likely to field a candidate as I had declared myself in favour of rearmament against Hitler, but he didn't turn up. The Liberals at the last moment decided not to fight. There was, therefore, much speculation as to where the large vote they had received in 1929 would go.

We organized four or five meetings a night for a three-week campaign. I stayed with George E. Button, the chairman of the division, who lived in Hornchurch, and was driven to meetings each night by E.H. Mitchell, the party's secretary, who came from Upminster. I bought an old car to run around the division during the day. Transport House supplied only two Labour peers (Listowel and Faringdon) as speakers. Few councillors were keen to talk on national issues, so we had to depend on getting friends, frequently students from Oxford and London, to fill gaps. Harold Laski was a great help. Transport having failed to turn up, he arrived at one meeting himself driving a baker's horse and van!

The division included the Warley ward of Brentwood. My agent booked meetings by mistake at schools some miles outside at the villages of Great and Little Warley. Looking for my meeting on a pouring wet night, I saw one being held and walked on to the platform of a Tory meeting to the loud cheers of those present.

My opponent, W.G.D. Hutchinson, was a former actor. He invited me to lunch soon after my adoption. During the meal a call came through from a constituent. He replied in a Cockney accent saying he was the butler and would pass on the message. During the campaign I wrote and then phoned him to challenge him to a debate. Back came his Cockney accent! He refused a few minutes later when he rang me back in his normal voice.

He was a great help to me during the campaign! For he lost his temper when heckled. A strong woman supporter of mine was cross-eyed. She followed him around asking awkward questions. 'Thank the Lord I am not your husband and don't have to look at your face every morning at breakfast' was a reply which circulated all round the neighbouring pubs. He upset the local Liberals when their chairman, a Methodist minister, raised his hand to ask a question to be greeted with 'You may leave the room if you want to'. Without knowing who he was I, fortunately, had answered his questions fully!

Owing to the size of the electorate, the count at Barking Town Hall was postponed till the next morning. After seeing the disappointing results all over the country the previous evening we were not optimistic. It took until 12 noon to check the votes. Counting them started with those on top which had come in last from Romford and Hornchurch. The trend at first was obvious and at one stage there was a 10,000 Tory lead. At that point Hutchinson arrived with his mother and a bottle of champagne. The tide then began to turn as the Dagenham and Barking votes came up. We drew equal and then the Labour votes drew ahead to give an 8,000 majority (55,723 − 47,416). Being the early afternoon, few Labour supporters were present to cheer the victory. Hutchinson wisely withdrew to drink his champagne behind a screen. Over 250 supporters of the ILP and Socialist Party of Great Britain spoilt their voting papers by writing 'Socialism for Ever' across them.

On election day a strong supporter of mine gave birth to a son at a polling station. He was named John Parker Knowles. At a victory celebration his proud mother handed him to me to nurse. I hurriedly handed him over to his father when I saw the photographer of the local paper about to snap me standing beside his mother and nursing the child! Some years later the father told me this son had become an architect.

With such a large electorate the legal maximum expenses allowed to each candidate was £4,198. The Tories spent £1,433, of which Hutchinson told me he put up £1,200. The total Labour expenses were £631, much of which came from local trade union branches or was raised by the 9,000 individual members of the Party.

So I became the second youngest Labour MP and one of the youngest in the whole House.

Some sources
(with posts held in 1935)

Ted Hennem (Leader, Dagenham Council)
Arthur G. Pearce (Secretary, Dagenham Labour Party and Trades Council)
A.F.J. Chorley (Dagenham Charter Mayor 1937)
Glyn Richards (Editor *Romford Recorder*)
W.J. Russell (Clerk to D.N. Pritt; Romford Councillor)

8

The New Fabian Research
Bureau, 1931-39

Easton Lodge conferences

As Margaret Cole has related in *The Story of Fabian Socialism*, a good deal of uneasiness developed among many socialists in the summer of 1930 due to the apparent lack of purpose and drive shown by the minority Labour government; this led to the holding of three exploratory weekend conferences in the second half of 1930 at Lady Warwick's Easton Lodge,[1] a country house near Dunmow, in Essex, out of which developed first SSIP (Society for Socialist Inquiry and Propaganda) and then the NFRB (New Fabian Research Bureau). Lady Warwick, an aristocratic socialist convert of Blatchford and one-time mistress of Edward VII, gladly provided hospitality. The Coles and friends, such as H.L. Beales,[2] G.R. Mitchison[3] and C.M. Lloyd,[4] took the initiative in getting these conferences together, and invited those likely to be interested, but they received a great deal of help from the former members of the Cole group which had come together under Cole's sponsorship in the Oxford Labour Club in the late 1920s. These included Evan Durbin, E.A. Radice[5] and James Meade in addition to other Oxford socialists such as Hugh Gaitskell and Elizabeth Harmer[6] who had not been members of the Cole group. Colin Clark, C.T. Saunders[7] and myself, who had been members of this group, founded a northern outpost of the new movement.

After leaving Oxford in 1929, I had obtained a post as an assistant to the Director of the Social Survey of Merseyside run by Liverpool University. Caradog Jones was the Director, being a lecturer in the Department of Social Sciences, of which Carr Saunders was the head. They had recently recruited Colin Clark as Deputy Director in view of the experience he had gained as an assistant on the London Social Survey in the previous year. We had been close friends in the Oxford Labour Club and I owed my job in large part to the strong recommendation he gave me. After about nine months Colin moved to London to work in the Cabinet Office and I was joined on the Merseyside Survey by Saunders.

Those who attended the Easton Lodge gatherings came from a wide cross-section of the Labour Movement, excluding the Communists. Lansbury, Cripps

34

and Attlee were all MPs and members of Macdonald's government; there were many former guild socialists like William Mellor, Ellen Wilkinson and Frank Horrabin; tutors and organizers active in the WEA, such as R.H. Tawney and Hugh Gaitskell; W.R. Blair of the CWS; lawyers like D.N. Pritt,[8] and G.R. Mitchison, and important trade unionists such as Ernest Bevin, Arthur Pugh[9] and Harold Clay.[10] By the new year (1931) a new society (SSIP) had come into being to try to rejuvenate the Labour Movement.

A strong underlying feeling at all these gatherings was that no effective work had been done to try and translate the vague but strong socialist enthusiasm that had produced the Labour government in 1929 into practical programmes for creating a socialist society. The Fabian Society had become almost comatose in the 1920s. So it was felt that a new research body also was required to carry out creative thinking. After securing the goodwill of the Webbs and Arthur Henderson, and the far-from-enthusiastic support of Macdonald, the Coles therefore organized further conferences at Easton Lodge in the early months of 1931 which led to the creation of the New Fabian Research Bureau.

Organization of NFRB

A Provisional Committee of thirty-seven to establish such a body was set up on 1 February and it was officially founded at a conference on 14 March. This elected a Selection Committee which reported proposals for its officers and executive, which were accepted on 22 March. At the meeting on 14 March it was decided that NFRB should have an individual membership with no trade union block vote. This was intended to prevent any similar sequel to that which had taken place in the Fabian Research Department (later Labour Research Department) which had been converted into an organization mainly to assist trade unions in wage negotiations. The NFRB was to do long-term research and leave the Labour Party's Research Department to carry out day-to-day research. The meeting on 22 March was chaired by W.A. Robson.[11] The following five officers were appointed: Clem Attlee (Chairman), C.M. Lloyd (Vice-Chairman), Dick Mitchison (Treasurer), G.D.H. Cole (Honorary Secretary) and Hugh Gaitskell (Assistant Honorary Secretary). An Executive Committee of ten was also set up from among those who had attended these conferences. It consisted of Philip Noel Baker,[12] H.L. Beales, Dr Stella Churchill (a practising doctor), Colin Clark, Harold Clay, Barbara Drake,[13] Mary Agnes Hamilton (a biographer), Miss Symons,[14] Professor Levy (economist) and W.A. Robson. They were given powers to co-opt and decided to organize three main committees (Economic Policy, Political Policy and International Affairs).

The first Executive Committee meeting at which all save two of the officers were present was held on 30 March 1931. Margaret Cole was co-opted and it was agreed that membership of NFRB should be confined to 'individual members of the Labour Party'. Others could become associate members. The purposes of the

NFRB were defined as 'research, holding of conferences and publication of results'. It was firmly laid down that NFRB as such should have no policy and that only the author or committee carrying out research was to be held responsible for the views expressed; readers, however, were to be appointed by the Executive Committee to vet publications for facts and readability. Rules were to be drafted. Subscriptions were to be 10s.6d. a year; 21s. for associates. Cole reported that £400 income a year had been guaranteed, but £1,000 was to be aimed at by an Appeals Committee. Work was to go ahead on economic policy; Cole was to draw up a draft and send it to Clark, Levy, Beales and Gaitskell for criticism. Work on political policy was to be postponed, but an early conference was to be organized on international policy to get research started in that field.

Clark reported that I had organized with Molly Cumella a group in Liverpool to do research on local housing policy. Other groups were set up in Oxford under Meade and in Cambridge under Clark and Shove (an economics don). It was decided that such groups outside London should be asked to work with both NFRB and SSIP; most took the character of SSIP 'branches'.

At a conference held at Easton Lodge on 8–10 May, the International Affairs Committee was officially set up. Leonard Woolf[15] agreed to act as Chairman with S.D. Bailey[16] as Secretary. The committee members, drawn from a panel of forty-two, included Arnold Foster (a League of Nations enthusiast), Noel Baker and Lauterpacht, (a distinguished international lawyer); H.R.G. Greaves[16] and Gaitskell were subsequently co-opted. Greaves later became its Secretary. There was widespread feeling among the founding members of NFRB that the Labour Movement had neglected its study of international questions, was deficient in knowledge of what was happening abroad and lacking in contacts with foreign socialists. However, it still proved difficult to get an active working committee despite Leonard Woolf's devotion. Attlee had taken the Chair at the May conference at discussions on USSR economic policy and on arbitration in international affairs. Other sessions dealt with the League of Nations, the ILO and cartels and tariffs.

The Political Section, under the chairmanship of W.A. Robson, got off the ground more slowly, carefully drawing up a comprehensive plan of research. It included R.S.T. Chorley,[17] Ivor Jennings,[18] and Harold Laski, all LSE dons; H.R.G. Greaves, James MacColl[19] and W.T. Wells[19] subsequently became active members. An Education Committee under Tawney and Mrs Drake (Secretary) replaced one dropped by Transport House, and a Housing Committee under J.H. Martin[20] and F.J. Osborn[21] also started work. These came at first under the Economics Section, but always acted very independently. The Haldane Society of Labour Lawyers, which had been founded in 1928, willingly agreed to act as the Legal Research Committee of NFRB. Meanwhile the Economic Section under Cole's leadership, after some discussion, had assumed the nationalization of all major industries and set up a number of sub-committees to study (1) the form and scope of socialization, (2) economic planning, supply of capital and flight from the pound, (3) finance and industrial fluctuations, (4) foreign trade,

(5) industrial research, (6) appointment of staff, wages and conditions and workers' control, (7) wages, social services and taxation, (8) socialist economic theory and price policy. Special committees were set up to study the railways and the conclusions of the Macmillan Report on banking.

Later Easton Lodge conferences

The later Easton Lodge conferences combined work on the setting up of NFRB with informed discussions, attended by invited specialists on issues as diverse as unemployment insurance, reform of Parliament, control of basic industries, empire questions and agricultural policy. Nine such conferences were held in the early part of 1931 and two on 'Banking Policy' and 'The Causes of Defeat' after the general election of 1931 in January and April 1932.

Margaret Cole has described the attractive, informal and casual atmosphere which pervaded these conferences, which numbered fourteen in all between the summer of 1930 and April 1932. A wide variety of invited specialists and interested enthusiasts attended. I got a lift from Liverpool to attend two, one concerned mainly with the organization of NFRB and the other on agricultural policy (4/6 July 1931). With other young men, I slept in a ramshackle outhouse, was fascinated to meet H.G. Wells with his high falsetto voice, who lived with the Baroness Budberg, in a nearby cottage, and watched with amazement Lady Warwick consuming a whole dish of new potatoes as she murmured 'No slimming for me. I like my Edwardian curves. I have no intention of attempting the boy-like figures young women affect today.' I heard Ernest Bevin speak at the Agricultural Policy conference and was greatly impressed.

At a Business Meeting on 16 May 1931, it was reported that SSIP and NFRB were now working and had obtained adjoining offices at 23 Abingdon Street[22] — opposite Parliament. The two organizations had £305 in hand and three years' guarantee for £975 with an estimated expenditure of £990. The chief contributors were Stafford Cripps, Pritt and Mitchison, all successful barristers. E.A. Radice, another of the 'Cole group', was appointed Director of Research from 1 August 1931, at £400 a year (salary joint with SSIP). He was to be assisted by Honor Scott[23] (£3 10s. a week to be paid by SSIP) and Enid Jeeves (typist for £3 10s a week shared with SSIP).

Radice was given leave of absence to contest Brixton in the 1931 General Election and announced that he was resigning on 21 March 1932 to obtain an Oxford job he expected to take up on 1 October. He was not offered this job, was re-appointed, to resign finally in July 1933 to accept a Commonwealth Scholarship in the USA. In the meantime, SSIP had been dissolved when the Socialist League was established (6 November 1932). Radice had given much of his time to SSIP but decided to stay with NFRB which moved its offices to John Street, Bedford Row. Honor Scott had been dropped (July 1932); E.W. Darling, originally a general clerical factotum, had been appointed Assistant Secretary early in 1933.

My appointment

I was approached by Radice after his first resignation in March 1932, on behalf of an NFRB Appointments Committee, to know whether I would accept his post. I said 'Yes', was told that his Oxford job was 'in the bag' and gave in my resignation to the Merseyside Survey to date from the end of July. A fortnight before I was due to leave Liverpool I was told Teddy Radice would be continuing with the NFRB. I was therefore 'out on a limb' and had to return home to Bristol unemployed to look for a job in the middle of the slump.

When Radice announced his second resignation on 15 May 1933, a staffing committee was set up (Attlee, Cole, Gaitskell, Mitchison and Radice) by the Executive Committee. It was decided to appoint a full-time General Secretary at not more than £300 a year 'whose qualifications should be among others: 1. a knowledge of the Labour Movement and, 2. a sound knowledge of economics.'

Six applicants were to be considered and two were interviewed. It was finally decided to offer me the post, after I had seen Mitchison, on the following conditions: (1) The appointment to be from 1 September 1933 subject to three months' notice on either side, provided that no such notice was to be given before 1 June 1934. (2) The appointment to be a full-time one starting at £250 a year. The salary could be raised to £300, but not above that figure. No objection was to be taken to the General Secretary taking one tutorial class. (3) The post to be vacated should the General Secretary be accepted as a Parliamentary Labour candidate without consent of the EC or be elected to Parliament; the attitude of the EC would be that consent would not be given if for a distant constituency likely to interfere with Bureau work.

I accepted with a feeling that I owed the job in large part to the fact that both Radice and Cole felt an obligation to me after what had happened the previous year.

I did not personally know Mitchison, the Treasurer and one of the appointing Committee. Radice therefore arranged for me to come up to London to see him at his Hammersmith home for coffee after dinner. I arrived to find the Coles being entertained by the Mitchisons at what had obviously been a good dinner. Dick asked me to take a walk 'round the houses' to talk about the job and form an opinion of me. As we set out, I overheard Margaret say to Douglas 'I thought we had intended this job for my young brother, Richmond.'

I arrived in September at the John Street office to find that decisions had recently been taken to establish a quarterly journal which I was to edit, and to hold a series of weekend conferences. I arranged for the first of the latter to be held at the Royal Star Hotel, Maidstone, on 'Some Aspects of Socialist Planning', which proved a popular venue, especially when a fair was being held nearby. I attended the Labour Party conference at Hastings, the first of many I went to, to publicize the NFRB.

I found the membership of the NFRB was small and practically stationary. The first annual report (31 March 1932) had shown a membership of 143. It had dropped to 132 (1 April 1933) and had only reached 158 (1 April 1934). The number of members attending early AGMs varied between 12 and 30, and all officers and the Executive Committee were re-elected unopposed.

Much of the research originally initiated had either been completed or had collapsed. A full report on the progress of research had been completed (30 June 1933). It was decided to abolish the Economic Section and set up a Research Committee (29 September 1933) consisting of the officers and chairmen of the main committees to supervise all of the Bureau's research and initiate new work. A report was received on discussions held with Hugh Dalton, a member of the Labour NEC. The Labour Party had recently decided to draw up a new pro-gramme and gladly accepted NFRB's offer of help; it had invited research studies on the Stock Exchange, National Investment Board, Industrial Compensation, Parliamentary Procedure, the Second Chamber, Housing Policy and Armaments Socialization. The Research Committee decided to ask the Haldane Society to do work on priorities in land nationalization and wartime control of industry.

I threw myself not only into getting work started, but — more difficult — completed. The result was that the numbers of MSS received in the office rose appreciably over the next few months, as did the number of pamphlets we published.

My candidacy

I had worked very well with Douglas Cole (the Honorary Secretary) who had been one of my tutors at Oxford and for whom I had a high regard; but he had a strong anti-Parliamentary bias which dated from his guild socialist days. I had been active politically whilst in Liverpool, where I had run the local SSIP branch. Friends there suggested in the early summer of 1934 that I should let my name go forward for the Kirkdale constituency. This I did, and when I was put on a shortlist of two, I sounded out Margaret Cole and Dick Mitchison, who were sympathetic to my going ahead. I did not approach Cole, as he was away as usual in Oxford. I put forward the plea to the EC that, although Liverpool was some way from London, it had far better train communications than many places nearer. However, Cole strongly opposed and the EC 'declined to grant the General Secretary permission to run for a constituency in Liverpool on the grounds that it was too far from London and likely to interfere with his duties with NFRB' (9 July 1934). I had, therefore, to withdraw from the Kirkdale selection confer-ence at the last moment.

Cole then told me that he would propose at the next EC that 'the General Secretary should never be allowed to be a Parliamentary candidate'. I fought back and circulated a paper to the EC giving my reasons for wishing to stand. I was strongly backed by Pritt and at the EC (8 October 1934) Cole had only one supporter. He thereupon resigned as Honorary Secretary. Fortunately, Margaret agreed to take over and so began our long and close collaboration as General

Secretary and Honorary Secretary of NFRB, and later of the Fabian Society, which continued until the end of the war in 1945. However, Douglas Cole agreed to remain on the EC and became Vice-Chairman at the next AGM (25 May 1935).

A financial crisis

Not having been in on all the early discussions at the foundation of NFRB, I had not fully realized how limited our financial resources were, and how dependent we were upon one or two wealthy benefactors. The increased output of the Bureau, without a corresponding increase in income, led to a financial crisis early in 1935 and a sub-committee was set up to report (1 April 1935). The Coles had a reputation for creating organizations and then walking out. E.F.M. Durbin, who had become Assistant Honorary Secretary when Gaitskell went to Austria in 1933, and I became apprehensive when we talked of possible economies to tide the Bureau over whilst membership and income were built up and were told that perhaps dissolution would be better than 'May Committee cuts'.[24] We went to Cripps and Pritt, our chief benefactors, and obtained their strong backing. They felt that all the money they had put up so far for NFRB would have been a complete waste if the Bureau did not try to weather the storm. The sub-committee recommended to the EC on 29 April 1935 that: (1) there was no case for closing the NFRB; (2) the *Quarterly* costs were to be cut by £50 a year (its creation had been costly and unremunerative); (3) it would not help the position of the Bureau to ask the General Secretary to resign; (4) Darling, the Assistant Secretary, was to be given six months' notice (he resigned soon after); (5) the General Secretary's offer of a 10 per cent cut in salary (it had recently risen to £300 a year) was accepted; (6) Enid Jeeves (typist) was asked to take a 5 per cent cut in salary.

The recommendations were agreed. At the next EC the offer of John Cripps,[25] Stafford's son, to come for a year's work as Assistant Secretary from June 1935 was accepted, his salary to be paid by Beatrice Webb. Meanwhile, membership had about doubled from 158 (1 April 1934) to 292 (1 April 1935) as a result of a membership drive.

Changes in staff and organization

As permitted by the NFRB Executive, I had taken a WEA class in Barking after coming to London. Early in 1935 Harry Muggeridge, who had been Labour MP for Romford (1929—31), which included Barking, announced that he would not be standing again. I was asked by members of my class to let my name go forward for selection as candidate, and was so nominated. Pritt had been the favourite for this nomination; he kindly motored me down to and back from the Selection Conference where I defeated him by 70 votes to 50. I felt very embarrassed on the return journey, as he had largely made it possible for me to stand. The NFRB Executive raised no obstacles and in the 1935 General Election gave John Cripps, who stood at Exeter, and myself leave of absence. Following my election in October the Executive agreed that I should continue as General Secretary for 6 months on a half-time basis (£150 a year) and then review the position. I usually attended the NFRB office in the morning and Parliament the rest of the day. I paid half the salary of Irene Roussin, my secretary, who dealt with both my NFRB and Parliamentary correspondence. On 10 March 1936, Durbin moved that I should continue as General Secretary on a half-time basis (with three months' notice on either side) and that an Assistant Secretary should be appointed from September 1936 (at £200 − £250 a year); it was hoped 'to recruit a University man who wished to do research or become a barrister'.

The reputation of NFRB had steadily mounted as a recognized training ground for service in the Labour Movement. From the galaxy of talent which sought the job, Bill Nield[26] was selected. He energetically built up membership before leaving to work at Transport House for the Labour Party. He was succeeded by another Oxford Socialist, H.D. Hughes.[27] A number of useful voluntary workers, including Lewis Clive,[28] Evan James [29] and Joan Bulmer[30] now joined the staff.

Meanwhile, at the 1937 AGM (4 June) it was decided to recast the NFRB's organization. Addison became President, Cole became Chairman, Mitchison Vice-Chairman, Margaret Cole Honorary Secretary, George Wansborough[31] Treasurer, with Durbin and Gaitskell as joint Honorary Research Secretaries. The Executive in future was to consist, in addition to the officers, of seven elected and up to seven co-opted members. The elected members comprised Franklin and Martin, housing experts; Haldane, an electrical engineer; Mrs Drake, W.A. Robson, Woolf and Pritt (Colin Clark had left to go to Australia). The co-opted members included R.W.B. (Otto) Clarke,[32] a journalist on the *Financial News*, H.R.G. Greaves, H.V. Berry, who worked in the City, and Geoffrey Wilson,[33] a social worker and barrister.

Meanwhile, NFRB had been forced to migrate to 37 Great James' Street; our landlords at 17 John Street had strongly objected to a display of Labour posters during the 1935 General Election.

Publications

In the summer of 1935 Cole had negotiated with Victor Gollancz for a joint publication of NFRB pamphlets and some of its books which were to be distributed by the firm's agents. It was agreed that Gollancz should buy NFRB pamphlets at 2.8d for each sixpence. This help was of great benefit to pamphlet sales. These rose, but the majority of bookshops disliked finding the space to display pamphlets which were mainly sold to those keenly interested or actively engaged in the field covered. They sold reasonably well and frequently made a small profit; reprints, however, were rarely needed. Books offered a bigger return to the bookseller and usually had a wider appeal; some sold well. Gollancz also agreed that his reader, Rubinstein, should read all NFRB publications for libel before publication. A number of important works, such as a *Study of the Flour Milling Industry*, had finally to be dropped for fear of libel. It was apparently libellous to attack the owners of an industry when there were only a few, like the millers, but quite in order if there were a large number, like the coal owners. I remember an interesting lunch with Gollancz at the Ivy Restaurant when discussing NFRB publications. He noticed an American at the next table drinking a glass of milk whilst eating a steak. He said suddenly 'John, please change seats with me. It makes me feel sick to see milk and meat taken together; despite the fact that I am a Christian convert, I had a strict Jewish upbringing.'

In all forty-two research pamphlets were published by NFRB between 1932 and 1939. They covered a wide variety of subjects. No less than five dealt with taxation and public finances, mostly by Colin Clark and Durbin, including one by Wansborough on banking and financial policy and one edited by Barbara Wootton;[34] another five were on socialization, including one on workers' control, four with the reform of local government and three with education. The International Section was the most prolific, producing no fewer than ten. These included H.R.G. Greaves's *The Prevention of War* (1934). *Why the USSR joined the League* (1935), with an introduction by Hugh Dalton, had been anonymously written by Konni Zilliacus,[35] a League of Nations official, who had been Secretary to Arthur Henderson at the Disarmament Conference (1932—3). After discussions with the International Section he also wrote *The Road to War* with an introduction by Clem Attlee; it was later published as a Penguin.

The *Quarterly* was used for articles considered too short for pamphlets, of immediate importance or needing further discussion. It proved very difficult to edit, being such 'a mixed bag' and had few outside sales. A consultative library of research documents by members of NFRB was available for consultation at its offices.

Starting with *Twelve Studies in Soviet Russia*, NFRB sponsored a large number of books, most of which were published by Gollancz. A visit to the Soviet Union in 1932 by writers as diverse as Hugh Dalton, Raymond Postgate,[36] D.N. Pritt, Naomi Mitchison[37] and Margaret Cole (the editor) produced a volume which tried to be impartial and objective, but was certainly coloured by the powerful attraction which a planned economy had for many western socialists at a time of world slump. The most critical study was that of John Morgan, an agricultural journalist, who saw the unhappy results forced collectivization was having for the countryside in the period leading up to Stalin's purges.

This book was followed by *Studies in Capital and Investment*, edited by G.D.H. Cole, and by Ivor Jennings's *Parliamentary Reform*, the outcome of much discussion at the Political Committee. Many of its proposals were accepted by the Labour Party and the greater part carried through in 1945. Had that not been done, the legislative programme of 1945—51 could not have become law. The history of this project was typical of many of those carried out first by

NFRB and later by the Fabian Society (1939–45). First a research project by an individual member, then full discussion by a committee and publication as a pamphlet or book for discussion within the wider Labour Movement, then a policy document put to Party Conference by the National Executive, accepting these ideas wholly or in part which was usually endorsed and so became part of the Party's policy, and thus of the legislative programme carried out in 1945/51.

Other books of this kind were *The Socialization of Iron and Steel* written by R.W.B. Clarke under the name of Ingot. This played an important part in the battles on iron and steel nationalization. Another of importance was *The Electricity Supply Industry*, by Graeme Haldane, an electrical engineer. A similar study of the gas industry was made available, although unpublished because of its length. Meantime, W.A. Robson edited in 1937 *Public Enterprise*, a full-length study of existing industries and services under public control. This included chapters on the post office, the BBC, London Transport and the Co-operative Movement; I contributed one on the Forestry Commission. Although not uncritical, these studies accepted the idea of the independent corporation and undoubtedly influenced the forms the Labour government adopted in its nationalization schemes after 1945. A study was also made on *The Government Regulation of Industry*.

In the same year (1937) the Bureau decided to send a team of inquirers to Sweden where the apparent success of the Social Democratic government in dealing with the depression had excited wide interest. This party included the Coles, Gaitskell, Mitchison, Hughes and myself officially from NFRB, in addition to James MacColl, Geoffrey Wilson, Raymond Postgate, R.W.B. Clarke, Christopher Mayhew,[38] and Charles Smith.[39] The resultant book *Democratic Sweden* was edited by Margaret Cole and Smith. Surprisingly, little interest was shown in the American New Deal, save in the development of the Tennessee Valley Authority. E.A. Radice, on a Commonwealth Scholarship in the USA in 1934, thought that Roosevelt's policy[40] was 'more akin to Fascism than to the economic order desired by Socialists. It provided warnings of what to avoid rather than examples of how to act.' Leonard Woolf and the International Section commissioned a series of studies of Eastern Europe which were published as *Hitler's Route to Bagdad* just as the war started. This drew attention to the Nazi economic penetration of the Balkans which had already taken place. Barbara Ward's[41] study of Yugoslavia after Hitler's seizure of Austria and Czechoslovakia was particularly illuminating.

Further research

Periodic reviews of its research programme were carried out by NFRB's Research Committee which had been set up in 1933. The amount of work planned, which was in fact completed to a reasonable standard, was remarkable, but there always remained gaps difficult to fill in an organization where research work was unpaid.

Retail distribution long remained undealt with and a special research grant for a year (September 1937 — September 1938) was obtained to enable Peter Vinter[42] to make a study of this subject. It proved too difficult to find the necessary sources and the project had to remain incomplete. Frank Pakenham donated £1,000 in 1938 to enable the three following research workers to be employed for a year on particular projects: Charles Smith (food policy), Christopher Mayhew (planned investment), Polly Hill[43] (unemployment services). These were just completed before the war started.

Meanwhile, as a result of NFRB discussion groups and weekend conferences, new policies for discussion within the Labour Movement were produced on housing, rent rebates, education, health services, Greater London government, world population problems and 'The Need for Social Control of Industrial Location'. At controversial conferences on constitutional questions Harold Laski spoke on 'The Relation of the Cabinet (or Front Bench) to the Parliamentary Labour Party, the TUC and Party Conference', whilst Michael Stewart advocated 'Total Abolition of a Second Chamber'. 'The need for a Labour Foreign Policy' was debated with equal vigour at a number of similar conferences. In conjunction with the Haldane Society, reports were prepared on 'The Law of Libel' and 'The Right of Assembly'. A draft bill to prohibit the wearing of political uniforms was passed, via Herbert Morrison, to the Home Office when it was preparing the legislation successfully passed on this subject.

A number of the younger members of NFRB began to play an active part in local Labour parties, where some became councillors, whilst others were active in their relevant trade unions, where some became members of their staff, particularly in their research departments.

The NFRB continued to grow. Its membership reached 403 (1936), 615 (1937) and 792 (1938), 71 per cent of the latter from addresses in London, Oxford and Cambridge. This growth made NFRB less dependent upon wealthy benefactors. Cripps and Pritt first halved their annual donations and then stopped them altogether when they were each in turn expelled from the Labour Party.

NFRB takes over Fabian Society

The NFRB had no contact in its work with the older society, although a few students, such as Colin Clark and I, when at Oxford, had joined it as a way of joining the Labour Party to which it was affiliated. Those NFRB members, however, who were also members of the older Fabian Society came to feel that the two organizations were duplicating much of their work, and supported Emil Davies,[44] its Treasurer, in desiring an amalgamation. F.W. Galton,[45] who had been Secretary of the Fabian Society since 1920, and E.J. Howell,[46] its bookshop manager, were both ready to retire, which became possible when Davies had raised a fund to enable them to receive modest pensions. Negotiations were opened in the summer of 1938. The two Coles, Wansborough and I were appointed as NFRB negotiators and it was agreed that we should take over and run one week of the Fabian summer school to be held at Dartington, near Totnes in South Devon.

The older Society appointed E.R. Pease,[47] the Honorary Secretary, who had been General Secretary 1891—1913, Galton, Davies and E.G.M. Fletcher[48] as their negotiators. Progress was slow at first, but a key meeting took place at the height of the Munich crisis which certainly hastened full agreement. This was ratified by both executives in November and December and became effective in July 1939 when the NFRB staff migrated to the Dartmouth Street office just before the war. Beatrice Webb blessed the Union by lunching Sidney, Shaw, Pease and Galton from the older society, and the Coles, Durbin, Gaitskell and myself from the NFRB at the London School of Economics where her slightest wish was law. Shaw asked me why a young man like myself should waste his time in Parliament when local government provided more effective opportunities for useful work. Galton drily remarked that Shaw's achievements on the St Pancras Vestry — his one public office — had not been an outstanding success.

The Fabian Society had been one of the founding bodies of the Labour Party in 1900 to which it was affiliated. But the NFRB had never been affiliated to the Labour Party. Apart from G.D.H. Cole, there was no strong opposition to the Fabian Society remaining affiliated. A self-denying ordinance, however, was incorporated in the rules of the amalgamated society to the effect that

> No resolution of a political character, expressing an opinion or calling for action, other than that in relation to the running of the Society itself, shall be put forward in the name of the Society. Delegates to conferences of the Labour Party, or any other conference shall be appointed by the Executive Committee without any mandatory instructions.

This safeguard satisfied Cole and other NFRB members who felt that the Society would thus be able to continue on similar lines the work done by NFRB. More controversial was the insistence by NFRB that there should be a rule in the new constitution for the election by postal ballot of fifteen members (in addition to the Treasurer) and the co-option of not more than nine others. It was felt that many of those most helpful in the organization and carrying out of research might not be known to the mass of members, and so would fail to secure election in a contested fight. This has certainly been borne out by the facts, but has not prevented many attempts by 'purists' to insist that all members of the EC should be democratically elected.

At the date of the amalgamation with the older society, NFRB had just over 800 members. On paper the older society had over 1,600; about 200 were members of both bodies. A vigorous purge of all members of the older society who were more than three months in arrears with their subscriptions brought its number down to about 800. So after amalgamation had been completed the society drew its membership about equally from both organizations. On 1 January

1940 it totalled 1,715. The officers of the joint society were drawn mainly from NFRB. G.D.H. Cole became Chairman, Emil Davies Treasurer, Margaret Cole Honorary Secretary, and Durbin Honorary Research Secretary. Beatrice Webb accepted the post of President to signify her support of the rejuvenated society. Of the elected members of the Executive, seven were drawn from NFRB, five from the older society and two had been members of both.

In the whole course of Labour history there can be no similar case in which a research organization so small in membership and so limited in financial resources as NFRB has had so great an influence in a short period on party policy and subsequent legislation. For the NFRB provided the Labour Party at a critical period in its history with a rallying point for the conduct of research that was independent, socialist in content and within the party. It was essentially a small intimate personal body closely bound together by a keen devotion to its work and aims.

The distinctive features of both the NFRB and the Fabian Society were carried forward into the revived society with its independent socialist research within the Labour Party, its discussion groups and conferences and, above all, its self-denying ordinance which has prevented its being identified with any particular point of view in policy controversies. As Sidney Webb long ago remarked, the work of the Fabian Society is the *work of individual Fabians*. The active part played subsequently by members of NFRB and the Fabian Society in Parliament, in the civil service and local government, has continued this all-important tradition to the present day.

The revived Fabian Society, after its merger with NFRB, was able to take the great opportunities for expansion which the Second World War provided, not only in the field of research but also in that of socialist education left vacant by the electoral truce during the wartime National government. Local societies grew up all over the country and national membership swelled to close on 8,000 by the end of the war.

It thus became a very different body indeed from what the NFRB had been.

Some sources

NFRB and Fabian records
Cole Papers
Margaret Cole
H.D. Hughes
E.A. Radice
Colin Clark
W.A. Robson
H.R.G. Greaves
Enid Jeeves
Lady Longford
Elizabeth Durbin

9
The Late 1930s

The election of Attlee as Leader

The question of Labour leadership was the first issue to arise after my election. I had known Hugh Dalton for some years, through his participation in NFRB conferences. He lobbied strongly on the need to replace Attlee by Morrison as Leader. I was invited to dine at his home to find F. Watkins, Fred Bellenger and Commander Fletcher, a Liberal convert, also being canvassed. A number of other MPs came in later, nominally to meet Zilliacus and discuss foreign policy. They included Ellen Wilkinson, at whom Dalton made 'a dead set' when the talk turned to the question of leadership. Others present included Creech Jones, Chuter Ede and John Wilmot.

Attlee, Dalton said, had become Leader by accident. Had Morrison or Dalton survived the defeat of 1931, one of them, he thought, would have become Leader.

After the Labour débâcle in 1931, which left only 45 Labour MPs, Lansbury alone of the Cabinet had kept his seat; of the Junior Ministers only Attlee and Cripps. Lansbury had, therefore, been elected Leader, with Attlee who had been in the House since 1922, as his Deputy. Cripps had only been brought into the house to be Solicitor-General in 1930 and so was inexperienced.

Cripps greatly impressed the Parliamentary Labour Party by his vigorous and lively attacks on the National government. His brilliant nineteen days' cross-examination of the colliery officials at the inquiry into the Gresford colliery disaster, at which 235 miners had lost their lives in September 1934, had won the respect of large sections of the Labour Movement. However, he found himself increasingly in opposition to majority opinion in the party. So when Lansbury fell and broke his leg (December 1934) the Parliamentary Labour Party asked Attlee, his deputy, to take over the Leadership in his absence, which lasted until July 1935.

After Lansbury's return it was felt that an avowed pacifist was hardly the right Leader, in view of the rise of Hitler and Labour's support for League sanctions against Mussolini over his invasion of Ethiopia. Cripps in the meantime had further alienated the trade unions by his support of 'working-class sanctions', which entailed a refusal to handle goods for Italy. Attlee backed the official policy of support for League sanctions and had secured the confidence of Ernest Bevin and the leading trade unionists. The PLP therefore confirmed him as Leader when Lansbury finally resigned in October. So he had led the party into the General Election of 1935.

At the first meeting of the new PLP, Attlee was in the chair; Attlee, Morrison and Greenwood were all nominated as Leader. David Kirkwood, a Clydesider, indicated his strong support for Morrison. All three were asked if they would give their full time to the work of the PLP. Attlee indicated that he would carry on as before; Greenwood said 'yes'. Morrison, however, made a long speech saying that Labour had only won control of the London County Council a year before, that it provided great opportunities for Labour to prove it could rule for which there had been no time to show so far, and that therefore he was certain arrangements could be made to enable him to carry out both jobs. Had he given a straight 'yes' he would certainly have led on the first vote although I doubt he would have done so on the second. Instead on the first vote Attlee got 58, Morrison 44 and Greenwood 33. Most of Greenwood's vote came from northern trade union MPs who belonged to a masons' lodge organized by Scott Lindsay, the Secretary of the PLP. Attlee got most of the votes of those who had served with him in the 1931–5 Parliament. On the second vote Attlee got 88 and Morrison 48, so nearly all of Greenwood's vote went to Attlee.

The Abdication

Soon after the Election George V died and Edward VIII became King. It was not long before people began to ask when he was going to get married. Then rumours began to circulate about his affair with Mrs Simpson. I remember overhearing some Tory backbencher saying to colleagues: 'Why even the Labour MPs know now about Mrs Simpson.'

The King handled the matter with remarkable stupidity. Whilst a non-church-goer, he yet attached great importance to having a church wedding with Mrs Simpson before his coronation. Had he been prepared first to be crowned he could almost certainly have got away with a morganatic marriage at a later date. Stories that circulated at the time were very damaging to him. Firstly, it was said he had paid Mr Simpson a large sum down for his wife. Secondly, that he had sent a note to the judge officiating at Mrs Simpson's divorce case saying it would be to his advantage if the case went through smoothly. Thirdly, that he had invited a number of debutantes for the weekend to Fort Belverdere to meet him and Mrs Simpson. After a day in the open Mrs Simpson had said to the King: 'Don't let us trouble to dress for dinner', and he had agreed. However, his secretary had then told him that the girls had all brought their best evening frocks and would welcome a chance to wear them. Edward had therefore changed his mind. When all had arrived dressed for dinner Mrs Simpson had gone up to him and 'ticked him off' in front of the assembled company for so doing. His secretary had told her later that what she and the King said to one another in private was their affair but he was King and should be treated with respect in public. She had made an outraged protest to Edward as a result, demanding the man's dismissal.

Baldwin handled the affair with great delicacy as it developed, never moving ahead of public opinion which had only become aware of the position when the British press broke its silence. He had had a reconciliation with his Labour son, Oliver, who came up to the House every evening to keep backbench Labour MPs informed and win their support for his father's actions. As Prince of Wales Edward had been a very popular figure. The popular reaction against his proposal to marry a twice-divorced American surprised MPs. I remember attending a cinema show on the Sunday night, after the affair became public, at the London Pavilion. At that time it was customary to end a show with the National Anthem. Everyone got up to walk out as 'God Save The King' began instead of standing to attention. On the previous Thursday, Churchill had put a plea to Baldwin in the House for no precipitate action. When he repeated the plea on Monday, he was howled down by MPs fresh from reactions in their constituencies.

There was much division among MPs as to the next step. Some suggested that, in view of her father's stammer, Princess Elizabeth should be made Queen with Queen Mary as Regent. At a PLP meeting, Ellen Wilkinson and half a dozen MPs suggested the creation of a republic. Attlee easily carried support for the succession of George VI and it was left to Jimmy Maxton and the ILP to put the case for a republic in the House.

My own view was that Britain was very well rid of Edward VIII in view of his pro-German sympathy. Had he been King at the time of Dunkirk he might well have copied Leopold of the Belgians in suggesting surrender to Hitler, which would have been very damaging to morale.

Rise of Hitler

When I first came to London (1933) I shared a flat in Lamb's Conduit Street with a half-French cousin who was taking a law degree at LSE. When he returned to France (1935) I obtained a flat on the top floor of 12 Great Ormond Street, which I shared with Otto Clarke, a journalist on the *Financial News*. We got this flat at a cheap rent as a month before two German women refugees had committed suicide there. The elder had been a Social Democratic MP. Some young German, claiming to be a member of the socialist 'New Beginning', had made up to the younger woman. They suddenly found their contacts in Germany disappearing and committed suicide when they realized they had given them away.

The start of the Spanish Civil War roused strong passions throughout the Labour Movement, not only in Parliament, but in the constituencies. In Romford we raised the funds to buy and fit out an ambulance to send to Republican

Spain. Particular frustration was felt at the refusal of the British and French governments to allow arms to be sent to Spain while Fascist Italy and Germany poured in arms for Franco.

Whilst raising funds for Spanish medical aid, I got to know Sylvia Pankhurst who believed strongly that the 'bomber would always get through' and London would be destroyed if a world war started. She thus also collected funds for a memorial to 'The Dead to Come', which took the form of a bomb. She asked me to unveil it in 1937 at Woodford on the edge of Epping Forest which I agreed to do. She was accompanied by Richard, her boy of 11. She took me on one side and said 'As a good Suffragette I do not believe in being dominated by a man but I also believe I should not be denied the pleasures of Motherhood. So I looked around and found a suitable male with both brains and good physique. This boy is our offspring.'

The reaction to Hitler's continuing success in Germany was striking. A large number of Tory MPs had fought as wartime officers in the First World War. They were resolved, if at all possible, to avoid another German war in which their sons would be combatants. When I was a student at Oxford (1925—9) many Germans of liberal views visited the university preaching the iniquity of the Versailles Treaty and particularly the absurdity of the Polish Corridor. French visitors were few and far between and it was widely assumed that Austria, a non-viable remnant of the Habsburg monarchy, would soon unite with Germany as its socialists then desired.

So long as Hitler was able to claim he was only taking German ethnic territories which wanted to join the Reich, the majority of MPs felt he should not be forcibly opposed however much the more far sighted saw he was aiming at world domination. Hence the acceptance of Chamberlain's appeasement at Munich (1938). It was not until Hitler took over the Czech rump of Czechoslovakia in March 1939 that the majority of Tory MPs realized that war was inevitable and the government gave guarantees to Poland and Romania which it could do little to back up.

Reactions in my constituency became reluctantly pro-war as events developed. If unavoidable, it was felt a stand must be made *against* Nazism. At this stage there were few hopes for a better world at the end of the struggle, especially after the Soviet-German Pact (1939).

European visits

I travelled extensively on the Continent in these years. Hugh Dalton, in conjunction with Zilliacus, a member of the League of Nations Secretariat who had been Arthur Henderson's Secretary at the Disarmament Conference, organized a fortnight's school at Geneva in the summer of 1935. Dalton drew up a list of younger socialists and trade unionists who were invited to rally the school in support of collective security. I attended, and among the twenty-eight invited members were Hugh Gaitskell, Michael Stewart, George Brown, Ellis Smith, Ted Willis, then an officer of the Labour League of Youth, and Bill Nield, an officer of the Oxford University Labour Club. Russia had recently joined the League and her representative there spoke appealingly to us for joint action against Fascism.

After leaving Geneva I met Richard Greaves, a young don at LSE. Together with Hamilton Fyfe, editor of the *Daily Herald*, and another friend, we motored through Germany to Denmark, being particularly appalled by the crude anti-Jewish billboards displayed in Thuringia and noting the building of shelters in Berlin.

In August 1938, in company with Christopher Mayhew and Charles Smith, who worked for me at NFRB, I motored in an old Austin Seven across Germany to Czechoslovakia. There we first visited Sudetenland and talked with the leaders of the Henlein Movement (for union with Germany). Although their activities were perfectly legal, they deliberately created an air of conspiracy about them. In Prague we met some leading Czech MPs. Benes was certain Britain, France and the USSR would all support Czechoslovakia if Hitler attacked. We were shown airfields being built or enlarged to enable Russian planes to come in to land.

We then crossed into Poland on the Assumption (15 August), a national holiday. Great demonstrations were being held jointly by the Socialists and Peasant Party demanding free elections and strong opposition to Hitler. At the same time they celebrated the victory over the Russian invaders in 1920! When we got to Warsaw we visited the British Embassy where we met a number of young diplomats from the Polish Foreign Office. Their main concern was the wickedness of the Czechs in taking Teschen from them in 1920! They pooh-poohed any danger from Hitler! So strong, however, were the campaigns against the government that it agreed to free elections being held that autumn. These were duly cancelled after Munich.

In the autumn of 1938 war suddenly seemed likely. Hospitals were cleared of all save acute cases and anti-aircraft guns were brought into central London whilst barrage balloons floated overhead. Chamberlain's appeasement of Hitler at Munich brought immediate relief that war had not started followed by a feeling both in Parliament and the country of national disgrace. We at once organized a series of public meetings throughout the Romford division. These were crowded to the doors, particularly in the Tory areas, by people who wanted to know what was likely to happen. After three weeks the meetings suddenly fell away.

Popular Front

The Spanish Civil War, followed by the continuing aggression of Mussolini and Hitler, led many to consider what could be done to force the Chamberlain government to make a stand. Among intellectuals, especially at Oxford, Cambridge and the LSE, the Communists made many converts from those who did not know the extent of Stalin's purges. They pressed at first for a United Front with Labour. Then they turned to a Popular Front which was to include Liberals and anti-Chamberlain Tories. Despite being banned by Labour's National Executive, the Popular Front made considerable progress, especially after Munich.

At a by-election in Oxford in October 1938, the Labour and Liberal candidates stood down in favour of Lindsay, the Master of Balliol, who put up as an Independent Progressive against Quintin Hogg, the official Tory. The university appeared largely to back Lindsay, and the town Hogg. Despite a lively campaign, Hogg won easily. I spoke for Lindsay on the same platform as Ted Heath, then an undergraduate opposed to Chamberlain.

This was followed by a by-election at Bridgwater, normally a Tory stronghold. Again the local Labour and Liberal candidates agreed to stand down. Vernon Bartlett, a broadcaster and *News Chronicle* journalist, stood as an Independent anti-Chamberlain candidate. I went down to speak for him with the backing of forty-four Labour MPs. I was greeted at the station by two young ladies who asked if I was the visiting MP and waved me towards a car with Tory colours. They were very chagrined when I said: 'I fear the wrong colours, ladies.'

The meeting in the Town Hall was packed to the doors. The speakers included Wickham Steed,[1] who gave a long discourse on foreign policy far above the heads of the audience; then came John Foot, Miss Josephy and other Liberals, who all attacked the wicked Tories. I tried to put a balanced Labour case combining domestic and foreign issues. At 9.30 Bartlett arrived with Dick Acland (Liberal MP for North Devon), who had taken him round the villages on the Acland estate[2] near Porlock. Bartlett was tired and said he would just answer questions. These were mainly on domestic issues such as old age pensions.

Then at 10.00 p.m. sharp the Chairman called the meeting to an end. Suddenly, to my great surprise, the whole meeting, which had been very quiet till then, rose to its feet, picked Bartlett up and carried him shoulder-high, waving his colours (purple and gold) through cheering crowds to the town centre. I had never seen such enthusiasm and said to a fellow speaker: 'He must be in.' He was. He had 19,540 to the Tory's 17,208.

This success gave a big boost to the Popular Front campaign. Cripps had backed such a campaign before Munich. Early in 1939 he demanded that the National Executive should change its policy. His uncompromising and arrogant approach, however, alienated many and ultimately led to the temporary expulsion from the party of himself and his principal supporters.

Despite official disapproval, many local Popular Fronts were planned, and undoubtedly would have come about if the expected General Election had come in the autumn of 1939. Banbury was one of those seats where one of the Early family (blanket makers at Witney) agreed to stand. Hugh Dalton, although a member of the National Executive, hoped for a serious break in the Tory Party. He encouraged any arrangements likely to lead to a defeat of a Chamberlain candidate. I went down to Oxford on his behalf to see Professor Lindemann,[3] one of Churchill's cronies, to find out if any collaboration was possible with his supporters, as the local Tories had only defeated a proposal in the spring of 1939 to field an official Conservative to fight Churchill at Epping by three to two. I made no progress, as Lindemann had flu and could not talk to me.

Modern Turkey

I had long been an admirer of Kemal Ataturk, and early in 1939 Christopher Mayhew, Charles Smith and myself contracted to write a book on *Modern Turkey* for George Routledge & Sons. We read all we could on the subject in English and French and had that in German translated. We then arranged, through the Turkish Embassy in London, to visit Turkey and interview and question Ministers there.

We set out on our visit early in August, booking passages on an Italian boat from Venice to Istanbul. After spending a few days viewing Venice and bathing on the Lido, we arrived at the quay to see our boat away on the horizon, as we had been given the wrong departure time by our travel agent. By a two to one majority we decided to pursue the boat by train and try to pick it up at Brindisi where we just got aboard as it was about to depart.

There was a crowd of young Germans on board with an English-speaking Nazi leader. Christopher Mayhew got into violent dispute with him as night fell. Charles and I left him with some apprehension, fearing they might throw him overboard after we had gone to bed. The Germans got off at different points of call in Greece, no doubt spying out the land.

On arriving at Piraeus the Greek dockers made very obvious their dislike of the Italian crew. We spent a day visiting the Parthenon where our English-speaking guide declaimed the whole of Pericles' speech in favour of democracy, ending up by saying 'under the present dictatorship of Metaxas it is illegal to make this speech'.

We arrived at Istanbul with the sun setting on its domes and minarets. After Italy and Germany, with their uncritical worship of Duce and Führer, the Turkish attitude to Ataturk, who had died recently, was refreshing. Whilst greatly admiring his military successes and re-creation of Turkey after the débâcle in 1918, many amusing stories were told of him, sometimes at his expense, and some of his decisions criticized, such as the creation of a new capital in the interior of Anatolia at Ankara instead of a better-watered site further west, such as Eskishiher.

At Ankara we not only interviewed Ministers, as arranged, but also met Knatchbull Hugeson, who had just come out as British Ambassador. His first appointment as a young diplomat had been on the staff of the British Embassy at Istanbul in the days of Sultan Abdul the Damned. He said he found it difficult to get his staff to go around and see the country; they all so much preferred the surroundings of Istanbul, the old capital, in summer. We travelled to Konya, Kayseri, where we saw a large Russian-built cotton mill, and then through the Cilician gates in the Taurus mountains to Adana, and, as guest of the local governor, spent a pleasant Sunday bathing on a sandy beach. The contrast between the educated middle-class trained up under Ataturk and the primitive Anatolian villages was striking. Everywhere we saw signs of new factories, railways and schools, largely financed by loans obtained from the British, French, Germans and Russians, who all sought influence in Turkey.

Suddenly we were warned of the likely outbreak of war with Germany and we hurriedly returned by plane to arrive just before hostilities commenced.

Mayhew, who was a territorial, was at once called up. Charles Smith and I completed the book (*Modern Turkey*) which sold well, especially among British officers in Egypt, as it was widely believed Hitler would attack Russia and try to reach the Baku oilfields through Turkey and that British troops would attempt to fight him on the Anatolian steppes. However, he was held up early in 1941 by the need first to conquer Yugoslavia and Greece and decided to attack the USSR without first invading Turkey.

Some sources

Ben Pimlott, *Dalton's Diaries*
Ted Hennem
Michael Stewart
Richard Greaves
Christopher Mayhew

10

My Visit to Austria, 1935

Britain had come out in the autumn of 1935 in support of sanctions against Mussolini over his Ethiopian aggression. The Austrian Fascist government of Schuschnigg seemed very unstable. In view of the international situation, the National Council of Labour decided to send a small delegation to Austria to see what help could be given to the Austrian socialists, particularly those who had been imprisoned following the Fascist seizure of power in 1934. This was led by David Grenfell, a respected Welsh Labour MP, who had been a miner as a young man and had organized miners of many nationalities into a union in Nova Scotia where he had emigrated for some years. He had a natural gift for languages and spoke a smattering of many. Grenfell asked me to accompany him as the General Secretary of the New Fabian Research Bureau and as a young MP interested in that part of Europe. We were accompanied by Elwyn Jones (later the Lord Chancellor), a young Labour lawyer not long down from Cambridge. He had been out in Austria for six months in 1934 helping to organize the legal defence of socialists with funds supplied by the National Council of Labour. Before going we talked to Hugh Gaitskell and Naomi Mitchison who had been out in Austria since the Fascist coup and gave us much useful information. We also saw the Austrian Ambassador in London and asked him to arrange for us to see the Austrian Chancellor, which he succeeded in doing.

We travelled out by plane, stopping down at Nuremberg. We arrived in Vienna not long before Christmas in the depths of a snowy winter. Poverty seemed very widespread and we were struck by the way 'cabbies' fought for our custom instead of queuing up. We went to the British Embassy in the evening soon after our arrival and saw Walter Selby, our Ambassador. He received us very formally and told us very firmly over drinks that we had wasted our time coming out to Vienna, as the Chancellor would certainly not see us. David Grenfell neatly floored him by telling him we had an appointment next morning at 11.00 a.m.

It was a cold sunny day when we went to the Chancellor's headquarters which was massively guarded. As we walked up the stairs machine-guns were trained on us. We were then placed in a little ante-room where Dolfuss had been murdered by the Nazis. A new piece had been let into the carpet where he had bled to death and a light burned on the wall above.

We then entered Schuschnigg's room, where I was struck by the white marble death mask of Dolfuss on his desk. After receiving us, Schuschnigg asked David Grenfell to present our case. He listened nervously, tossing his leg up and down in its shiny black boot whilst Schmidt (later I believe one of Hitler's interpreters) translated. When Schmidt cut out anything Grenfell interrupted in German to insist on its inclusion. Each of us pressed on Schuschnigg the need to conciliate British opinion in view of his position between Hitler and Mussolini, who were not then in alliance, and the possibility that Mussolini might fail in his Ethiopian adventure if the League of Nations sanctions were made to work — as we hoped. We asked for an amnesty for all the socialists in jail since the fighting, not only to impress western democratic opinion, but to strengthen his own regime against the danger from Hitler. After asking a number of questions, he promised that there would be a general amnesty for all socialists 'save those who had committed murder'. After some questioning, he defined this as meaning all those who had had arms in their hands when arrested during the fighting. He insisted that we should say nothing about our talks publicly, but that he would announce the amnesty as a Christmas goodwill gesture on the part of his government. If he did not carry out his promise, we would be free to criticize him on our return home. From what we were subsequently told, he carried out this promise and there was a substantial 'jail-delivery' of socialists, a number of whom subsequently told me that if they had remained in jail they would certainly have been executed when Hitler invaded Austria.

We stayed a number of days in Austria before returning. Socialists made contact with us and walked about with us quite openly — the government appearing to have little popular backing in Vienna. Plain-clothes police followed us very obviously. Whenever we sat down for a talk in a cafe, socialists filled all the surrounding tables so that the police could not overhear our conversation.

We visited a number of jails where socialists and Nazis were imprisoned together in the same room — usually very crowded and with little privacy. There was noticeably considerable friction between them. In one prison yard we saw where the murderers of Dolfuss had been hanged. The older prisons appeared from the prisoners to have a much pleasanter regime than the newer ones — one of which was run by an undoubted martinet.

I was taken ill with sinus trouble — the only time I have ever had it — and spent a day in bed in our hotel whilst Grenfell and Elwyn Jones visited a prison in Graz. The socialists brought a Dr W. Griffel to see me; he was a member of the Socialist Medical Association in Vienna and had manned a medical aid post for the members of the socialist 'Schutzbund' engaged in fighting during the uprising in 1934.

After the 'Anschluss' in 1938 both David Grenfell and myself were instrumental in helping Dr Griffel to come to England. He was one of the fifty Austrian doctors selected by the BMA for admission to practise in this country and, after qualifying in Edinburgh, joined the staff of the Medical Officer of Health in St Helens, Lancashire. He established the first Mass Radiography Unit for civilians at the Pilkington glass factory in St Helens. He subsequently became consultant chest physician in Preston and retired to Bloxham in Oxfordshire where he was active in the National Trust.

I made a quick recovery and we travelled back by train across a snowbound Europe wondering how far Schuschnigg would carry out his promises. Elwyn and I were fascinated by the way Dai Grenfell managed to find enough Dutch to flirt with a Dutch nurse in our carriage. The National Council of Labour seemed very impressed by the account of our visits.

Some sources

Lord Elwyn Jones
Dr. W. Griffel
Dr F. Scheu (Austrian correspondent, *Daily Herald* 1935)
Several other Austrian socialists

II

A Peace Mission that Failed, 1937

In the autumn of 1937 Reg Sorenson, the Labour MP for Leyton, was asked to go on a mission to Germany by a group of German émigrés to try and find out the whereabouts of political prisoners, particularly Thaelmann, the Communist leader. George Lansbury, the former Labour Leader, had had some correspondence with Hess, who was then Hitler's No. 2, and was anxious to follow up various statements that Hitler had made in favour of world peace now that the Nazis had seized the power they had sought in Germany. At Lansbury's request Sorenson decided to pursue Hitler's professions of peace whilst carrying out his other mission. Sorenson asked me to accompany him as one of the younger Labour MPs. I gladly agreed. For, although completely sceptical about the Nazi regime, I saw no harm in trying to find out what was happening in Germany.

We were accompanied by a young American who was a good German linguist and acted as our interpreter. We first flew to Paris to meet our German émigrés for a discussion. Our young American mistook 13.00 hours for 3.00 p.m. and so we missed our train to Brussels. However, we took a plane and arrived there in time to board a night-stopping train from Brussels to Hanover which appeared to be continually picking up or dropping sacks of potatoes. Our British passports did not indicate that we were MPs (mine gave my occupation as 'Secretary') and we easily crossed the German frontier and arrived in the early hours in Hanover where we slept the remainder of the night at a small hotel immediately opposite a statute of George II who was also Elector of Hanover.

We had been asked to find out whether Thaelmann was imprisoned in Hanover. Early in the morning we visited the jail and, producing our cards as British MPs, asked to see the Governor. We were immediately shown in and asked him if we could see Thaelmann. The Governor gave us the information we sought by his embarrassment and by his statement that he must first contact Berlin for instructions before granting our wish. After a hectic telephone call this was refused. We left, soon realizing that we were being followed by plain-clothes police.

Reg Sorenson had taken an active part in distributing food and other necessities in that area in the disturbed period following the First World War. We called on a number of his contacts and talked to them about conditions in Germany. One of these was a young man, married to an English wife, whose father had been a keen Social Democrat and trade unionist. Both father and son made it clear they now took no part in politics. Another was a very vigorous general's daughter who was an Anthroposophist — a follower of Dr Steiner, whose religious philosophy embodied an original educational theory. Hitler had suppressed the sect. Her brother, a former German officer, had worked in the Foreign Service until it was discovered that he had a Jewish grandparent. After he had been dismissed from his job, he had committed suicide to avoid his wife being harassed because of his 'taint'. We had some qualms as to whether these contacts might suffer as a result of meeting us, but they assured us they would not as they were now known to be non-political.

Arriving in Berlin we called next day at Hess's headquarters with Lansbury's letter of introduction. This was in a Baroque mansion. We were told Hess had left that morning for Munich, but that his ADC would see us. Three double doors were successively opened by two airmen, who stood to attention, one pair after another, with a raised arm and a 'Heil Hitler'. At the end on a raised dais stood the ADC who advanced to greet us in English. He read Lansbury's letter and apologized for Hess's absence. A young man of about 30, he was surrounded by veterans of the First World War wearing their iron crosses and obviously enjoyed 'wiping his boots' on them and humiliating them in our presence. He would arrange for us to meet the head of the British Section of their Foreign Office and in the meantime told one of the young airmen who spoke English to take us to lunch in the canteen of the newly built Air Ministry (it survived the war) where we might meet Hermann Goering. However Goering was not there. On one wall was a vast wall map in different-coloured woods showing very plainly how much of the world was then part of the British Empire. We were struck by the apparent 'equality' with which officers, typists and men lunched together. I asked our airman if he had been abroad. O yes, he said, he had been to Austria and Czechoslovakia to train pro-Nazi pilots! Had he been to England? No, but he might come any time dropping bombs!

As can be imagined, these remarks left us rather nonplussed for our visit to the Foreign Office. There we were greeted by von Hassell, later Ambassador in Italy and one of those who died a fearsome death for his part in the 1944 attempt on Hitler's life. At this time he alternated with Ribbentrop who was Ambassador in London, going there when Ribbentrop was absent. Hassell spoke perfect English and gave the impression of being an Old Etonian with his somewhat aristocratic manner. He was widely believed to be closely connected with Lady Astor's Cliveden set, but on this occasion was obviously anxious to prove before his subordinates how good a Nazi he was.

Hassell opened politely by saying 'O, Mr Sorenson, I read your article in the *New Stateman* recently . . .' Reg had written no article in that paper. He replied by developing Lansbury's thesis. If Germany really believed in peace could she not cut her expenditure on arms and thus prove to the world how genuine her intentions were? Could she not release and pardon all political prisoners as a gesture of goodwill? Hassell indignantly attacked such suggestions. The Nazis had made great mistakes when they came to power. They should have killed seven times as many opponents as they did and wiped out those decadent elements who had destroyed Germany's good name. He particularly regretted the damage done by the publicity given to Dimitrov's trial which ought not to have been allowed.

We left Berlin the next day amid the dropping leaves and pouring rain of a late October day. Sorenson first went to Paris to report to the group of émigrés. He was shadowed continuously by a man in a certain kind of brown boots who he spotted at a railway station and again at a post office and elsewhere. He found it impossible to get a plane to Paris and took a sleeper. On mounting to an upper sleeping berth he spotted the 'brown boots' underneath, which disappeared after the frontier had been crossed.

I returned directly to London feeling that the coming war was now inevitable. Reg Sorenson sadly told Lansbury of the failure of our mission. When I reported to Clem Attlee he grimly remarked 'When war breaks out we shall have no choice'.

A source

Reg Sorensen

12

Evacuation, 1939

Evacuation was part of the general scheme of Civil Defence. In the Civil Defence Act of 1939 the country was divided into evacuation, neutral and reception areas. Dagenham was at first registered as a neutral area. Strong local feeling that it ought to be an evacuation area led to the sending of a deputation to the Minister on 31 January 1939. Evacuation from Dagenham was finally agreed only eight weeks before it came into operation.

When the Second World War appeared imminent, late in August, the various schemes for evacuating school children and mothers with children were hurriedly carried out. There had been 23,047 children on the roll of maintained schools in Dagenham in July 1939. 7,797 school children were involved in the first voluntary evacuation between 1 and 4 September. A trickle followed them in the next few weeks. From Dagenham and other riverside boroughs it was decided to take most of these evacuees by boat to receiving areas in Norfolk and Suffolk. From Lowestoft, Yarmouth and Felixstowe they were conveyed into the rural areas behind the coast.

Great discomfort was experienced by many of the mothers with children who were difficult to accommodate, and the majority soon returned to look after their husbands and enjoy their own homes. The school children evacuees remained an important feature of wartime society whenever the bombing of industrial areas created serious and continuing problems.

Within two or three days of leaving home a large contingent of the Dagenham school children had arrived in south-west Norfolk in the area around the towns of East Dereham and Swaffham. Local women from the Women's Institutes found homes for them. Teachers from Dagenham arranged with their Norfolk colleagues how best to share the limited and often primitive school buildings and to dovetail their various activities. A wide range of welfare activities fell upon their shoulders which were far outside their normal experience and to which most of them responded with initiative and devotion.

The absence of bombing in the early months of the first year of 'phony war' led to a drift back home of many evacuees as the autumn advanced. However, a large number remained — especially among those who had 'settled in'. When serious bombing started, a further large evacuation took place, this time mainly to Somerset to be followed by further drifting home and new evacuations, as the bombing of London eased up or worsened in intensity. How teachers and pupils managed any real schooling under such conditions was indeed a mystery.

The initial evacuation to Norfolk highlighted many of the problems which continued to arise for Dagenham children throughout the war. Differing home conditions in other exporting areas no doubt produced other problems elsewhere. The child population from Dagenham came largely from new council house estates – the LCC in particular had built very extensively at Becontree between 1926 and 1933. At home the children were used to running water, a bathroom with inside WC, electric light and gas cooking. Many of the houses they came to in rural Norfolk obtained their water from well or spring, cooked on a kitchen range, were lit by oil lamps and had to use a tin bath in the kitchen filled with water heated by the range, and a draughty outside ash closet away from the house at the end of the garden. No wonder adjustment to these conditions was not easy.

About three weeks after their arrival, I went down to Norfolk to see how the evacuees were getting on. An enthusiastic schoolmaster, who was in charge of one of the evacuated schools, met me and told me something of his problems and difficulties and what he thought might be done by the authorities to help. The main problems affecting his charges – bed-wetting and constipation – he thought, however, were largely outside their field. He took me to meet local officials and particularly the women in charge of billeting. They at once raised the problem of bed-wetting; evacuation they felt had shown that it was much more widespread among children than social workers had believed. How far this was due to a physical disability and how far to inadequate training by their mothers they hotly disputed, although it was generally agreed that the feeling of neglect felt by many children as a result of the evacuation had greatly aggravated the problem. Local foster parents faced by persistent bed-wetters had reacted strongly. Some laboured on manfully with mackintosh sheets, but the majority had sent them back to the billeting officers and they were being slept on the floors of village halls and similar buildings. It was a seemingly intractable problem for which they could suggest no solution. It was natural that there was large early return from their number.

Harvest was just starting as the evacuees arrived. Fields in arable Norfolk, although larger than in many parts of the country, were still bound by hedges which harboured a large population of rabbits and other wildlife. As the reaping machines trundled round the fields rabbits took refuge in the middle of the ever-smaller areas of standing corn. From time to time one made a bolt for the safety of the surrounding headland. Village boys joined by evacuees awaited with sticks to knock them on the head and take them home for the pot. At harvest the rabbit had always formed an important part of the local diet. The distribution of meat supplies took some time to catch up on evacuation and the rabbit was therefore widely fed to the new arrivals. A rumour quickly grew up that it was responsible for the constipation which affected so many of them, though this was more likely due to their desire to postpone using the outside ash closets as long as possible.

The schoolmaster suggested that we should call on some of his problem cases, talk to the foster parents and see how the children were settling in. He was struck by the fact that all of his difficult cases were boys. Girls seemed able to adjust themselves more easily.

The first family we visited was of a successful farmer and his wife, who I will call Clark — both in their middle thirties — who had been greatly disappointed at their inability to have children. When billeting was being arranged the wife had put in a strong request for two boys and had been give two strong and healthy brothers of 12 and 10 from a not-very-adequate Dagenham home. The boys had arrived tired and dirty after their journey and were at once bathed — to their intense indignation — in front of the kitchen range and then put to sleep, in a large double bed in the spare bedroom which was the housewife's pride. One of the boys messed in the bed during the night and they both put their fingers in it and spread it all over the wallpaper. Mrs Clark was naturally indignant, gave them each a good smacked bottom and made them clean up the mess as far as possible. The schoolmaster had listened to the stories of both foster parents and the boys and done his best to calm them down. When we arrived Mrs Clark had prepared a good spread for tea. The boys arrived whistling cheerfully, called Mrs Clark 'Mum' and quickly got down to a good meal. We decided that they had 'settled in'. As we went out, we met Mr Clark who said they were good lads and very helpful to him about the farm.

After visiting a number of farmworkers and other families with smaller houses we called on another farmer — this time a small one. Here they had a young family of their own and had happily fitted in Johnny, a big boy of 13, who had been billeted on them. The housewife, who I will call Mrs Smith, however, had come to the schoolmaster for help as Johnny had refused to take a bath. She had twice heated the water and prepared the bath for him in the kitchen but each time he had deliberately stayed out until the water was cold. Now he 'stank to high heaven'. 'Get the bath ready at 4 o'clock this afternoon', the master had replied, 'and I will bring Johnny home after school'. He did so, told him firmly to take off his clothes, and get into the bath and threatened to scrub him personally if Mrs Smith was not satisfied as to his cleanliness. Johnny had scrubbed himself vigorously, got out of the bath and danced around with his towel, holding out his feet and hands for Mrs Smith's approval. 'Now then,' said the schoolmaster, 'You are to come straight home from school every Tuesday and Mrs Smith will have the bath ready for you. If you don't bath I am asking Mr Smith to tan the hide off you.' 'Right, Sir,' Johnny had replied. 'None the less, I think', said the master, 'we had better call and see if Johnny is there, as today is his bath day.'

It was one of those houses frequent in the countryside where the front door is only used on 'state occasions' and everyone normally uses the back door. It was open and as we walked into the kitchen the schoolmaster called out 'I have

63

brought someone to see you, Mrs Smith'. 'Excuse me not getting up but you will see I am busy,' she replied. A tin bath steamed with hot water before the range with a chamber pot beside it. Mrs Smith sat in a comfortable farmhouse chair whilst Johnny lay across her knees with his trousers down. A basin of warm soapy water stood on a stool beside her which she was purposefully syringing up his behind. 'Johnny has just told me that he has been bunged up for over a week so I am giving him a bath inside before he has one outside', she said. Johnny winked at me and said 'I have so many rabbits inside me she is having to put a ferret up me to flush 'em out.' When she had finished her ministrations Mrs Smith gave us a cup of tea whilst Johnny had a good turnout. Mrs Smith produced a large piece of cardboard to cover the jerry when he had finished. Johnny went ahead with bathing his outside and then joined us for tea. Her son of 12, who had been an interested spectator throughout the proceedings, was then told to empty the jerry! Privacy, at least for the young, did not appear to exist in the Smith household.

Johnny returned home some weeks afterwards. He made himself known to me at an election meeting in Dagenham in the 1950s chortling at the memory of that afternoon. He had kept in touch with the Smiths and visited them on a number of occasions. He said he had been happy with them.

The subsequent history of the Clarks and the two boys was interesting. At the end of the war when the boys were 18 and 16 they all came to see me to ask my help. The two boys had last heard from their parents at Christmas 1941. All subsequent letters to them had remained unanswered. The Clarks, with the enthusiastic support of the boys, wished to adopt them. This had proved impossible as it was legally necessary to get their parents' consent. All efforts to trace them had been unsuccessful. Both boys had become enthusiastic 'Young Farmers'. Mr Clark proposed in due course to buy a farm for the eldest and take the other into partnership at his own farm. At my suggestion the two boys took the Clarks' name by deed poll and Mr Clark made a will dividing all he had after his wife's death between the two boys. They accepted this as a happy solution to their problems.

Nearly 2000 evacuees from Dagenham remained in the reception areas after the war. These were mainly old people, but there were 270 children who did not return. In some cases they remained at their own wish and with their parents' consent at their foster homes. In some cases the parents may have been killed in raids but undoubtedly a number of their parents had taken the opportunity to disappear and thus wash their hands of any further responsibility for their children. It is to be hoped that in most of these cases they found greater happiness with foster parents than they would have done in their parents' homes.

Some sources

Danger over Dagenham 1939—45, edited John O'Leary
Evacuation Survey (1940) by Margaret Cole and Robin Padley

13

Some Wartime Activities

Constituency problems

Having the largest electorate in the country, I received an enormous correspondence during the war years, varying from problems arising from bombing to rationing, evacuation — which grew and dropped in line with German raiding — allowances and pensions. At an early stage a battle developed with the service departments as they tried to forbid servicemen to approach MPs. Finally MPs insisted that, if any serviceman had first used the normal channels for dealing with his grievances and was still dissatisfied with the outcome, he must have the right to raise them through his MP.

The Romford Divisional Labour Party and the various local parties continued to function well during the war. Activities were adjusted after the blitz started. Saturday afternoon meetings with a tea — and sometimes a social to follow — became the order of the day. I fitted in my surgeries to try and cover the area without clashing with other events.

Bombing and shelters

Ellen Wilkinson, as a former Communist, soon rumbled the attempts of the Communist Party to plant party members as secretaries on MPs such as herself and the Liberal, Wilfrid Roberts, who were active supporters of the Republican cause in the Spanish Civil War. Wanting a reliable secretary, she approached me to know if my sister Beryl Hughes would consider the post. She agreed to do so and followed Ellen into the Home Office to deal with her constituency cases when Ellen joined the Churchill government.

Ellen was given the task of dealing with the effects of the German bombing, particularly in the provision of shelters. I felt flattered when she asked me to serve as her PPS and to travel across the country and report to her on any problems I came across. A weekly committee was set up under her chairmanship which included the two London Regional Commissioners for Civil Defence,

Admiral Evans[1] and Charlie Key,[2] and representatives of all departments concerned, in addition to the Home Office, such as Health (to provide Elsan closets and prevent the spread of disease), Food (for canteens), and of course the Treasury.

From time to time Father Grosser, the 'Red' priest from Stepney, and Mrs Henriques, who represented the Jewish community, also attended, as did the leaders of the various institutions which provided an educational programme in some of the shelters.

The great problem at first was that people automatically went to shelter in cellars and any holes in the ground which they thought would provide some greater security than their home and/or Anderson shelter. We soon found from experience that, if the building was of brick or stone alone and unreinforced by steel girders, it was likely to collapse like a pack of cards if a bomb dropped in its vicinity, but otherwise would usually remain standing unless it got a direct hit. We had, therefore, to locate alternative shelters near danger spots and then go around and persuade people to use them.

In London the tube stations were at once occupied by families who brought their bedding down nightly when the siren sounded and 'booked' their places. At an early meeting, Ellen's committee decided to order large numbers of tiered wooden bunks to accommodate as many as possible. The weekly minutes went to the Prime Minister. Back came a note 'Why not use the large number of spare hammocks at the Admiralty?'

Fortunately, Admiral Evans (of 'The Broke') was a useful and very active member of the committee. He insisted we reject the PM's advice on the ground that boys of fourteen or fifteen would pitch out and break their heads on the floor. We therefore persisted in seeking, and finally got, our bunks, despite continuing pressure from Churchill to use hammocks.

The cost of getting the necessary number of Elsan closets was large. Ellen made a point of going through the minutes of the previous week and asking each department what had been done to implement them. On one occasion the Treasury representative stated he had referred the matter back to his superiors in view of the cost of this proposal. Ellen's eyes flashed and her red hair quivered with rage 'There is a war on and decisions of this committee must be immediately acted upon. If I have any further sabotage I shall go straight to the Prime Minister and report the matter.' The unfortunate Treasury official shivered. Henceforth all decisions were promptly carried out. From time to time, especially when bombing was bad, Ellen and members of the committee went around the shelters to hear the complaints and collect suggestions. The Admiral always put on his full 'canonicals', as Ellen called them, i.e. his full uniform and decorations, to help reinforce morale.

The problems varied in different parts of the country. I spent a whole week one late December in Glasgow when daylight never appeared. The Germans were sending raids from Norway across Britain to Brittany and vice versa, dropping bombs mainly on Glasgow and Liverpool. They had bombed along a main road in the moonlight through the riverside area in Glasgow thinking it was the Clyde and they were hitting the shipyards. As a result, all smoke possible was being discharged to deny future bombers any landmarks below. Pat Dollan, the Lord Provost, was dealing with local problems. This did not prevent him from giving me an official lunch when the leading councillors, and their ladies joined in a discussion of what could best be done. All were formally introduced 'Councillor and Mistress Buchanan' and so on. I asked Pat whether he favoured a Scottish Parliament. 'Not if it were to meet in Edinburgh', he replied. 'I get all I want now', he added.

I was in Bristol for the first of its bad raids, which fortunately ended at midnight having started at 7 p.m. The next morning I walked down from my parents' house near the Downs over St Michael's Hill to catch the London train from Temple Meads. The centre of the city was a magnificent if fearsome sight, with flames everywhere. The tower of St Nicholas crashed as I crossed Bristol Bridge. I made my way to the station along Victoria Street through blazing buildings on either side. The city was filled with fire engines which had come in from all round, but the equipment was not standardized and many could not use the local hydrants. Morrison had already set to work to standardize all fire-fighting equipment but this took time. Having breakfast on the train, I sat opposite Benno Moisewitch, the pianist. He was proud to have completed his recital during the blitz. This was being broadcast from the Colston Hall. His audience had speedily disappeared!

Early the previous evening I had visited a crowded church crypt near the Floating Harbour, which provided no effective shelter, and then went into the equally crowded Hotwells old railway tunnel where water was pouring through the roof on to tarpaulins stretched above bedding which could not possibly be kept dry. Bristol was finding it particularly difficult to provide reasonable shelters.

Fabian Society

A few weeks after the outbreak of war the telephone operator at the Fabian Society told me she had had a leg-pull. Someone who gave his name as Bernard Shaw wanted to talk to me. It was indeed the great man, aged 83, who was anxious to receive a report of the discussions to take place on war aims at a forthcoming conference.

After the advent of the Churchill government the Fabian Society began to grow nationally with increasing rapidity as public opinion turned to what was to happen after the war. The evidence the Society gave to the Beveridge Committee largely determined its recommendations, which were widely welcomed. Margaret Cole, as the Honorary Secretary, and I gave a great deal of time to building up the Society, particularly its research, which continued despite bombing. Leonard Woolf, for example, came up from Rodmell to attend committees when necessary. He took an active part at one held in March 1941. The next day the press reported that his wife, Virginia, had committed suicide the previous day. The Society's role as a forum for discussions particularly at conferences, summer schools and meetings, was outstanding.

Increasing unrest in the Labour Party at the electoral truce encouraged the growth of local Fabian Societies for the discussion of immediate and postwar problems. Among other places I visited Llandudno to help the Callaghans form a society, mainly for members of the Inland Revenue Staff Association who had been evacuated there. Jim, who was then its Assistant Secretary, was anxious to 'settle them in' before he joined the navy.

After working for two years for Ellen Wilkinson as her PPS, I was advised by Jim Griffiths to resign and adopt a more critical attitude to the government. This I did. None the less, I was asked by Attlee in 1944 to second the Address in reply to the King's Speech. The Fabian Society had recently published a pamphlet (*The Dutch State Coal Mines* by Llewellyn Morgan) which appealed to mines' managers to support coal nationalization. It had been written anonymously by civil servants, of whom Harold Wilson was one. Some Tory backbenchers strongly disapproved of Attlee's invitation and I had to stand down. He then invited Tom Fraser, an able, recently elected young miner, to take my place.

Electoral truce fades

Under the electoral truce it had been agreed that when a by-election took place, an MP from the same party as the former MP should replace him. Owing to the overwhelming Tory majority, most vacancies appeared in Tory seats. Early in 1942 a wave of disillusion set in with Churchill's National government, which came to a head with John Wardlaw Milne's unsuccessful vote of 'No Confidence in the central direction of the war' on 1–2 July, when he aroused the scornful laughter of MPs by suggesting the Duke of Gloucester as Commander-in-Chief. Already in February 1942 six sitting MPs (two elected as National Labour and four as National Liberal) had announced that they would henceforth sit as Independents. A 'Popular Front' began to develop where it was thought an 'Independent Progressive' might get in. In March 1942 Grantham was thus won followed by Rugby and Wallasey (April) and Maldon (June). In all these cases a large part of the local Labour Party had supported the victors unofficially. In September 1942 Sir Richard Acland (Liberal MP for Barnstaple) and friends founded the Commonwealth Party to 'contest all by-elections where a reactionary candidate was in the field and not opposed by a Labour or Progressive candidate'.

Commonwealth

Foremost among Acland's supporters was J.B. Priestley, who had acquired a large following with his brilliant wartime broadcasts. I attended an early meeting of its founders to find out their views. This took place at Edward Hulton's Mayfair house where we sat — as bombs dropped outside — in the blackout at mahogany tables lit by silver candlesticks. Hulton's *Picture Post* had been a big success in rallying opinion against Hitler before the war, and suggesting the kind of world which ought to follow. Among those present were A.L. Rowse, the historian, Tom Driberg, the journalist, who had won Maldon as an Independent Progressive, and H.G. Wells. Acland launched into an account of his activities. He said he hoped to get the support of Canon Collins and a number of distinguished churchmen. Wells interrupted in his high falsetto voice with 'If we have clergy in the organization I will have nothing to do with it.' He walked out forthwith. Priestley made it clear he wanted the organization also to arrange public meetings — if need be at lunchtime — so he could be in closer contact with live audiences than he could then be on the BBC.

There was a steady build-up of the anti-government vote as the war continued, although only thirteen seats changed hands. Surprise results were wins by Commonwealth at Eddisbury (April 1943) and Skipton (January 1944) by young RAF men in Tory strongholds. The most spectacular change was at West Derbyshire (February 1944).

This was traditionally a pocket borough of the Duke of Devonshire, whose seat at Chatsworth was within its boundaries. Frequently the Duke's heir, the Marquess of Hartington, had been its MP. An exception had been in 1918 and 1922 when C.F. White (senior), a former agent of the Duke who had quarrelled with him, stood and was elected as a Liberal. Lord Hartington had been elected unopposed in 1923, 1924, 1929, 1931 and 1935. When he succeeded to the title in 1938 he was replaced by H.P. Hunloke, a naturalized American who had married one of the Duke's daughters. C.F. White (junior), a Labour member of Derbyshire County Council, had then stood unsuccessfully.

In January 1944 Hunloke decided to divorce his wife in a case which attracted a good deal of publicity. Whereupon the Duke asked him to resign 'the family seat', which he did forthwith. The Duke's action was strongly criticized. A riproaring by-election followed in which Lord Hartington was the government candidate. He was opposed by C.F. White (junior), who resigned from the Labour Party to fight as an Independent candidate. Only two[3] Labour MPs were prepared to go down and support the government candidate. White was elected by a large majority (16,636 to 11,775) over Lord Hartington, who was unfortunately killed soon after in the Normandy landing. In 1945 White rejoined the Labour Party but only just retained the seat.

More significant for the country as a whole was the capture of Chelmsford, an outer London constituency, by Commonwealth in April 1945 by a 6,431 majority. Here again the successful MP subsequently joined the Labour Party after being elected at the General Election with a reduced majority.

On the National Executive

To my surprise, I was elected to Labour's National Executive at Whitsun 1943 and sat until December 1944, owing to a change of conference date. This was due, in part, to a series of accidents. Herbert Morrison decided to stand for Treasurer, but was defeated, leaving a vacancy in the constituency section; Nye Bevan refused to stand, as he thought it would compromise his independence. Mounting opinion was rising against the electoral truce. The leadership carefully contrived that pacifists, such as Rhys Davies, should continue as their main critics at conference, and so sought to prevent a clash on this issue. However, I had attacked the electoral truce at meetings which won me a good deal of support. Local Fabian Societies got their parties, in many areas, to back me. My Romford CLP had a block vote of 9,000 with its large membership, which was a useful base. The next year both Morrison and Nye Bevan stood for the constituency section and so I lost my seat.

1944 Education Bill

As the war took a more favourable turn, interest in reconstruction plans after the war mounted. Three areas came to the fore where widely discussed reforms needed legislation; housing and urban planning, the implementation of the Beveridge report on the social services and education. The latter subject seemed less likely to endanger the coalition and was accepted by Churchill under pressure from Bevin and the Labour members of the Cabinet. Butler, anxious to live down his Munich reputation, with the assistance of Chuter Ede, drafted a comprehensive bill, after discussions with the Roman and Anglican churches over their denominational schools. To occupy the time of a restive House, Churchill decided to take all stages of the bill on the floor of the House.

The Labour shadow front bench gave little thought as to how best to handle the bill beyond asking Alfred Barnes to take charge. He asked me to help him, which I agreed to do, and then only showed up for one or two amendments to clauses. Educational administration was not one of my interests and I had to depend on Cove, Messer and, for later amendments, Nye Bevan, to deal with much of the detailed criticism. On behalf of the party, I welcomed the bill on Second Reading on 19 January 1944, particularly for its intention to provide secondary education for all children over 11. Points pressed unsuccessfully in committee were the abolition of all fees for secondary schools supported by the Ministry, definite dates for raising the school-leaving age to 15 and 16, the refusal to transfer children from approved schools and remand homes to the care of the Ministry, an extended number of days for day release training and a promise that school milk would be free.

A Tory reform group of about 40 was anxious to remove the prewar reactionary Tory image and backed a number of amendments. It was admirably led by

Thelma Cazalet Keir and had the support of Hogg, Thorneycroft, Eccles and most of the women MPs. The committee stage lasted from 8 February to 5 April. A Labour amendment to abolish all fees in secondary education was defeated 183/97, with only two Labour MPs, not in the government, voting with the majority. A Tory reform amendment setting a firm date for raising the school-leaving age to 16 failed by 172/137. A week later another amendment, to include a clause requiring equal pay for men and women teachers, was proposed. This was moved by Mrs Cazalet Keir and supported by Hogg and Thorneycroft. I had persuaded Labour MPs not to put down their own amendment but to vote for the Tory one. Butler replied turning down this amendment. I then followed and stated 'I would like to say that our Party have definitely taken the line that equal pay for equal work is Party policy. We shall vote for this amendment if pressed to a division.' When the vote took place the government was defeated 117/116.

Churchill was furious as the Second Front was about to open and demanded both a vote of confidence, recalling his backwoodsmen for this purpose, and a reversal of the vote which had been carried. I supported the government on the vote of confidence but abstained on the equal pay vote. The Education Bill finally became law on 3 August 1944.

The Labour party had at that time no clear education programme of its own but found the main proposals of the bill acceptable. No pressure was put on Labour MPs in favour of comprehensive education which was only beginning to be discussed in educational circles.

A visit to Ireland, 1944

Interest in the Beveridge Report spread to Ireland and I was invited through the Fabian Society to do a speaking tour there on the subject. I applied to the Home Office for permission to go but got no reply. I then consulted Ellen Wilkinson, a junior Minister at the Home Office, who told me not to ask again but to go. I accordingly crossed from Stranraer to Larne early in May 1944. I addressed a large interested meeting at Belfast University and then one under Nationalist auspices in Newry. I was told there that I might have difficulties about crossing the border. If so, I was to return to Newry and they would row me across Carlingford Lough to the South. However, I showed my passport on the train at the border and was allowed to proceed. So I arrived in Dublin, lit up with no blackout, and with plenty of food and masses of Spanish oranges in the shops. My host was Owen Sheehy Skeffington,[4] a socialist don at Trinity College with a charming French wife. His father, a pacifist, had been shot by the British for a breach of curfew regulations during the 1916 rising. A meeting held in Trinity was well attended not only by members of the Irish Labour Party and other progressives but by members of all the socialist factions in the country.

A large number of prominent Irishmen met me during my stay, making clear their antipathy to the Nazis and their sympathy with the Allied cause. There was general support for De Valera's declaration of neutrality at the start of the war but apprehension had arisen about a possible German invasion from Brittany to cross Ireland to attack the harbours in northern Ireland where convoys from the USA sheltered after crossing the Atlantic. I was told De Valera had stationed the small Irish army in the south to meet a possible invasion. However, he would not allow British or American troops to cross the border to help them unless a German attack actually materialized. Satisfaction was felt that many American troops — including Irish Americans — might then be involved.

I was also told that many German and British airmen had come down in Ireland during the raids on Liverpool and had been interned. However, recently the guards around the British internment camp had been removed, but those around the German camp had remained in place. Christopher Mayhew's younger brother, Paul, was one of the British airmen who was thus able to escape to Britain. (He was killed on a subsequent sortie.)

I do not think that pro-British feeling can ever have been as strong in Ireland as it was at this time. On my return from Dun Laoghaire (I asked how it was pronounced and was told Kingstown!) I cross to Holyhead. There had been a late snowstorm which had broken down some of the branches of the red may in full blossom in Trinity Gardens. Snowdon and the surrounding heights glittered white in the sunshine. The boat was filled with Irishmen in mufti, serving in the British forces, returning from leave in Ireland. On arrival the Captain announced that a German submarine had been located on the seabed under the lightship off Dublin, but it had not surfaced in pursuit during the passage!

Candidacies

Hugh Gaitskell had first been put in touch with his South Leeds constituency when they were seeking a candidate in 1937, thanks to my contact through the University Labour Federation with Marjorie Brett, the daughter of the local agent. He did not, however, enter Parliament until 1945.

The Fabian schools during the war, particularly those at Dartington and Frensham, were attended by a large number who were subsequently elected as MPs in 1945 or soon after. These included such diverse characters as Austen Albu, H.L. Austin, Hubert Beaumont, Arthur Blenkinsop, Tom Braddock, Barbara Castle, F.A. Cobb, Terence Donovan, Maurice Edelman, John Lewis, Ian Mikardo, G.R. Mitchison, Maurice Orbach, R.W.G. Mackay, Arthur Palmer, Dr Segal, Arthur Skeffington, H.C. Usborne, Eirene White and Konni Zilliacus. Among MPs who attended were Fred Bellenger, Arthur Creech Jones, Alfred Edwards, Jim Griffiths and Ellis Smith. Many visited schools when on leave from the services.

The Coles spent much of their holidays at these wartime schools which were also enlivened by Victor Gollancz, the Left Book Club publisher, Kingsley

Martin, the editor of the *New Statesman* and contributors such as Harold Laski, Leonard Woolf, Barbara Wootton, C.E.M. Joad and Frank Horrabin.

My wife, on seeing Labour's 1945 Parliamentary intake, said 'Why, it looks like an enormous Fabian school'.

Early in the war, whilst awaiting call-up, the Dartington School had been visited by Tony Crosland, David Ginsberg and Roy Jenkins, who later entered the House; H.D. Hughes, Christopher Mayhew and Charles Smith, who had worked for the Society in 1939, all won seats in 1945. E.G.M. Fletcher, Geoffrey de Freitas, Commander Pursey, Michael Stewart and W.T. Wells, who had all worked voluntarily for it before the war, were also successful, as was James MacColl in 1950; Scholefield Allen, Dryden Brook and Colonel Hamilton, who had worked actively with local societies, were also elected in 1945.

As the war drew to its conclusion a flood of would-be Labour candidates descended on 11 Dartmouth Street to seek a recommendation from me. I remember a Rear Admiral arriving in full uniform. I asked him what were his qualifications. He said a Tory MP had recently spoken to officers at Portsmouth and he had been asked to propose a vote of thanks. He had been congratulated on his speech and told by the MP he ought to stand for Parliament as a Tory. 'What do they stand for?' he had asked. The MP had sent him some Tory literature. 'I did not agree with a word of it, so I must be Labour!' I did *not* forward his name to Labour headquarters. Earlier, after the Watford by-election in 1943, the unsuccessful Commonwealth candidate (Raymond Blackburn) had arrived the next day to join the Labour Party (he was elected for Northfield in 1945).

Many local Fabian Societies wrote and asked me for suggestions as to possible candidates they might nominate at their constituency parties. Amongst those I suggested, who were successful, were Harold Wilson (Ormskirk), Jim Callaghan (Cardiff South), Hilary Marquand (Cardiff East) and Julian Snow (Portsmouth Central).

I had known Geoffrey Bing before the war when he was working for Spanish Medical Aid. He came to see me to secure my support for Hornchurch when my seat was divided. I told him he had no chance, but the local chairman, the favourite, had recently opposed the opening of Sunday cinemas, and Bing won by one vote. I did not recognize him owing to a face lift he had had following a war accident when parachuting.

A frequent visitor to the Fabian bookshop at this time was Tony Benn, then a Westminster schoolboy, who frequently called in to seek advice as to what to read.

Despite the growing signs of a swing to Labour, many Labour MPs feared that Churchill's name and war record would produce a Tory majority when the Election came. In my desire to make this less likely I joined with Jim Griffiths on the Speaker's Conference in 1944, to support the 'Alternative Vote'. We were the only two Labour Members to do so. It was a view I was soon to reject.

The reputation of the Fabian Society in the Labour Movement and the country as a whole was outstanding. It even penetrated Germany where my name, as its

General Secretary, was placed on the blacklist of those to be shot at once when the Nazis had carried out their occupation.

Some sources

Ted Hennem
Beryl Hughes
A Place for Everyone by Nigel Middleton and Sophia Weitzman
(Chapter 1 — The Bill the Whips Liked (July 1943 — August 1944))
Hansard
Charles de Peyer
Christopher Mayhew

14

Attlee (1883-1967)
and Churchill (1874-1965)

Attlee, it is now generally agreed, was for long underestimated as a political leader. When elected, he certainly held the majority views of the party on collective security unlike the more ebullient Cripps. It was also widely felt that Labour needed a good team man in contrast to MacDonald's personal showmanship. This explains, in part, the preference shown by Bevin and other trade union leaders for Attlee as against Morrison. Yet there was a good deal of criticism in the Parliamentary Party over the rather dull speeches he made, especially on foreign policy during the lead-up to the war. John Dugdale and Peter Thurtle, who acted voluntarily as his research assistants, 'tore their hair' at the unexciting use he made of their briefs and a serious attempt was made during his illness at the beginning of the war to replace him as leader.

Attlee a good chairman

Attlee came into his own in the negotiations leading up to the formation of the Churchill government in 1940; it was generally agreed that he had secured for Labour the necessary key positions in the government if the National government was to work and he became respected as Deputy Leader in the House. This was followed by the creation for him of the post of Deputy Prime Minister in February 1942.

Attlee had shown his ability as Chairman of the PLP in the years leading up to the war. He invariably let the discussion develop and then at a suitable time came in with his own suggestions which usually presented a consensus of opinion. It was widely reported that he was a far better Chairman of the War Cabinet when Churchill was away, for Churchill tended to make speeches at the Cabinet whereas Attlee sought agreement and got through far more business.

I once attended a Cabinet meeting in place of my boss, Addison, early in the Labour government of 1945. The issue before the meeting was what could be done to honour the pledge of 'First In, First Out' for servicemen after the sudden surrender of Japan following Hiroshima. Lt-Gen. Sir Ian Jacob of the Imperial

General Staff gave all the facts. The wounded and prisoners of war could be flown home. Most of the troops in the Far East would have to travel back by the two *Queens* which were too big to go through the Suez Canal. All of this would take considerable time. Were troops to be left in the forces unnecessarily in Europe in order to honour the pledge? Attlee opened the discussion and made his suggestions. He then went round the table. The views expressed were not entirely the same, but all differed considerably from his. He then made a second speech admirably pulling the arguments together into a consensus which was very different from his own first statement. He finished by saying 'I think we are all agreed. Good. Next business.'

Another attempt was made to replace him during the bad winter of 1947. It was reported that Stafford Cripps had called on him and suggested that he make way for Bevin as PM. Thereupon Attlee phoned Bevin and said 'I have Cripps with me. He says you want to be PM'. On receiving Bevin's answer he turned to Cripps and said 'He doesn't want the job, good morning'.

Attlee definitely grew in the job and developed the short staccato statement that proved very effective in pricking some of Churchill's more extravagant attacks in the 1945 election. His review of Churchill's *History of the English-speaking Peoples*, was a classic: 'Very good for schoolboys, Clem Attlee'.

I remember an occasion at the PLP when Harold Davies delivered a scintillating speech against the H-bomb and asked Clem 'to destroy it'. Clem carried on doodling until the applause had died down. Then he looked up over his glasses and said 'Yes, Harold, that is something we'll have to watch. Next business.'

As Chairman of a very divergent team, which included Bevan, Bevin, Cripps, Dalton and Morrison, he got them to reach decisions which were carried out. One of his biggest successes was the grant of Indian Independence. Despite the troubles resulting from partition, it was indeed fortunate that Churchill was not PM at that juncture, as his intransigence about India would undoubtedly have involved Britain in a 'Vietnam' type War of Independence.

He was a shy man with no small talk save about his beloved cricket. He made a point of coming into the tea room with his PPS regularly so as to be available to any MP who wished to raise a matter with him. Attlee's success in holding his team together failed with his illness in 1951 after eleven years in office (since 1940) when the Labour government broke up.

Some early impressions of Churchill

My first feeling about Churchill when I entered the House in 1935 was that he was a spent force. He took very definite lines on Nazi rearmament, India and the Abdication and thus won support and opposition from different and often conflicting groups of MPs.

His vigorous attacks on the government alienated many Tory backbenchers. He also did himself no good with his personal attack on Hore Belisha over the

Sandys case. His resolute and continuing campaign on the German danger and the need to rearm to meet it, gradually, however, impressed the House. It was considered natural that he should enter the government when war broke out, but there was much criticism of the Narvik expedition which was compared with his Dardanelles campaign in 1915.

With the fall of the Chamberlain government, which Churchill did his best to defend in the House, the question of who should become PM at once arose. Despite the distrust in the Labour Party, dating back to the General Strike (1926) and the Tonypandy episode (1911), there was a feeling that he alone of the Tories could inspire the country at this juncture. Many Tories would have preferred Halifax, but he was not acceptable to the Labour Party. Despite Labour's small number of seats in the Commons, a National government could not command the necessary support in the country without Labour — and trade union backing. In the early days of the Churchill government at least forty Tories showed their obvious sympathy for Chamberlain by cheering him when he entered and receiving Churchill with silent disapproval which sometimes produced Labour cheers for him. A vendetta against him was carried on by a few. His son Randolph had entered Parliament under the electoral truce for Preston and, on joining the army, had received a military rank. 'What are the qualifications of the Hon Gentleman for this post?' queried Sir Archibald Southby.[1] When Churchill answered him he murmured 'What has Vic Oliver (Churchill's comedian son-in-law) done to be left out?' Churchill later went up to him in the Lobby and said 'Did I hear you aright, when you asked what has Vic Oliver done to be left out?' Sir Archibald replied 'Yes.' With great self control Churchill restrained himself, turned on his heel and walked away.

Churchill becomes Tory Leader

Remembering the fate of Lloyd George after the First World War, Churchill very carefully prepared the way to be appointed Conservative Leader to follow Chamberlain in October 1940, to secure himself against future attacks from that quarter. By so doing, he definitely injured his National appeal and strengthened the growing demand in the Labour Party for ending the electoral truce.

Churchill sometimes resented the criticisms made of him in the House, especially by Stokes and Bevan often in secret sessions. When he came back from a very successful visit to USA he proposed to broadcast his report to Parliament to the country. At once the House was up in arms and insisted that he first report to it where he could be criticized before broadcasting. Had he not wisely given way an unfavourable vote would undoubtedly have taken place.

When the war ended the long-standing resentment against Chamberlain and the men of Munich welled up accompanied by a revival of the past distrust of Churchill. The Labour Party had decided, in view of his services as wartime PM, not to oppose him in the General Election. His Woodford constituency was close to mine. At every meeting I was asked why Labour was not fighting him. An unknown Independent secured 10,488 votes to Churchill's 27,688 in a safe Tory suburban seat.

One of the rumours that circulated in the later days of the Italian campaign was that Churchill had sent some agents to go through Italian state records and destroy all the favourable remarks he had made about Mussolini's regime in its early days of power. He found it difficult after he ceased to be PM to accept the new situation. It was reported that he embarrassed an Air Marshall by ordering a personal plane from the RAF, as though still PM, to take him to the Far East. This was refused. He also fell out with the Speaker by expecting privileges in the House in excess of those normally given to the Leader of the Opposition. As a result, he refused to attend any of the Speaker's receptions. I witnessed a most surprising happening. At the first reception Attlee gave to junior ministers and their wives at 10 Downing Street, after the Election, he also invited the Churchills as a courtesy to their wartime collaboration. Churchill and his wife acted as though they were the hosts, both in receiving guests and in saying farewell. Mrs Attlee was most embarrassed and did not know what to do. They were not invited again.

With increasing age he got somewhat forgetful. Megan Lloyd George told me he had embarrassed her some years after her father's death by saying 'I have not seen David about for some time. What has happened to him?'

After his second stroke in 1955, he came regularly to the House and sat on the government bench below the gangway to listen to the PM's questions. When getting up one day with his two sticks to walk out, I overheard one young Tory say to another 'The old man's getting very ga ga nowadays.' He turned to them and said 'He is also very hard of hearing.'

In view of his wartime services, his constituency continued to return him until 1964, until just before his death, despite his infirmity. He had served as an MP for sixty years, being first elected in 1900. After two breaks he sat for forty years from 1924 without one, and so became Father of the House.

Some sources

Dalton's Diaries
Hansard

15
Bevin (1883-1951)
and Morrison (1888-1965)

Early contacts with Bevin

Ernest Bevin was respected in Bristol, my native town, by political and industrial opponents and had become a legend before my time. I had joined his Transport and General Workers' Union in Liverpool where I worked with George Williams, the local Secretary, to found a branch of the Society for Socialist Inquiry and Propaganda (SSIP), which Bevin strongly supported.

I made my first close contact with him soon after I entered Parliament. I had spoken on a platform in Barking in support of a bus strike; the speech received some publicity. This led to a note from Bevin asking me to see him. I went to Transport House and received a firm dressing down! MPs should keep out of industrial disputes. They were for union officers and shop stewards to deal with. By intervening in matters they could not be fully informed about, MPs could seriously damage industrial negotiations. When a union wanted some matter raised in the House, it would approach MPs.

I have always followed his advice.

There were only seven sponsored TGW MPs in the 1935 Parliament and not many other members of the union. I was, therefore, invited to group meetings and took up points concerned with pubs and eating places. From time to time Bevin came and discussed matters he wanted raised in the House.

The Agricultural Insurance Bill, 1936

Then there came the Unemployment Insurance (Agricultural) Bill which was introduced on 6 February 1936. In 1920 the agricultural workers had been omitted from unemployment insurance at their own request. With the coming of the slump they had changed their minds. Bevin had worked on a farm as a boy and his union had many agricultural workers. In combination with the Agricultural Workers' Union, he had negotiated with the Tory Minister of Agriculture and the National Farmers' Union and had agreed a special scheme for farmworkers, foresters and a number of similar groups. This entailed lower benefits and lower contributions than those for other industrial workers. When the government introduced a Bill on those lines, it had been strongly attacked at the PLP as not being good enough. Whilst giving the Bill a critical welcome in the House, the PLP had abstained when the ILP opposed the Second Reading.

Bevin was furious; he was being stabbed in the back. His good name as a negotiator was destroyed if he could not deliver the goods when he signed an agreement. He issued a dictat to all sponsored TGW MPs to vote for the Third Reading whatever the PLP decided to do.

Nye Bevan strongly attacked his action at the PLP. Parliament was not a mere rubber stamp for agreements reached outside. It must be free to alter and amend such agreements. It was finally decided, in view of improvements made in Committee, to support the Third Reading, which passed in the end without a vote. However, new Standing Orders were passed at the PLP to the effect that no outside body had the right to mandate an MP on how he should vote. He was to be responsible only to the majority vote of a PLP meeting.

Soon afterwards the TGW approached me to become one of their sponsored MPs. I referred the matter to my Constituency Party, recommending that I should not accept the offer. I was unanimously supported by my party in view of Bevin's recent action.

Bevin in Parliament

Bevin was never very happy in the House. He hated criticism and showed his irritation when it was made. Frequently he put his brief on one side, especially after he became Foreign Secretary, and poured out an ungrammatical torrent of words. Hansard usually recorded his prepared speech.

When the Churchill government was set up, a National Opposition gradually came into being to criticize the government, led by Shinwell and Earl Winterton, who had failed to get the posts they had sought from Winston. Known as Arsenic and Old Lace, after characters in a play then running, they did a useful job ventilating grievances, often in secret sessions.

All the Ministers and their PPSs sat on the government side of the House, as the majority of Tories continued to do, but the majority of Labour MPs continued to sit on the Opposition side. This annoyed Bevin, although he accepted the fact that Creech Jones, his PPS, after sitting behind him for his questions, crossed over to the Opposition benches to fire questions at the Colonial Secretary!

After the publication of the Beveridge Report on 2 December 1942, widespread discussion about its proposals developed both at home and in the forces. A three-day debate started on 12 February 1943, which was opened by Arthur Greenwood, who had set up the Beveridge Committee in 1941 and been sacked by Churchill early in 1942. What had started as an exploratory debate developed into criticism of the government as it progressed. Attlee, Bevin and Morrison failed to head off a revolt of the PLP, despite Bevin's arguments that it would amount to a vote of censure on Labour Ministers. With only three dissentients, the PLP decided to support an amendment expressing 'its dissatisfaction with the now declared paper of H M Government towards the Beveridge Report . . . and urges the reconsideration of that policy with a view to the early implementation of the Plan.' This, moved by Jim Griffiths, was pressed to a division and was defeated 335/119 with most of the Labour MPs not in the government voting for the amendment and with 30 abstentions.

This certainly placed the Labour Ministers in a difficult position. Bevin challenged the PLP to expel him. For over a year afterwards he refused to attend PLP meetings. It was reported that he had gone to Arthur Deakin, his successor in the TGW Union, and suggested that the union should disaffiliate from the Labour Party; Deakin, however, had stood up to him and told him not to be a fool.

There was a strong streak of anti-Semitism in Bevin. I remember him saying at a meeting with his union MPs that he would take special care to see that all Jews who could serve would be called up to fight Hitler. He did not hide his anti-Zionist sentiments when dealing as Foreign Secretary with the future of Palestine. Like many of his Foreign Office advisers, he believed the Israelis would be defeated when the Mandate ended in 1948 and wondered where Jewish refugees from Palestine could be settled.

His hatred of Morrison was profound. Suggestions were canvassed by George Brown and others after the disastrous winter of 1947 that he should take over the Leadership. However, he recognized his limitations and gave loyal support to Attlee through all his difficulties.

Morrison's beloved LCC

Herbert Morrison made his mark in the House of Commons and on the London public as Minister of Transport (1929—31) when he launched the Bill to nationalize London Transport which became law in 1932 after the Labour government fell. He made a bigger impression on London Labour supporters when he turned down all offers of remunerative business appointments on losing his seat in 1931 and returned to his job as ill-paid secretary of the London Labour Party, which he had first become in 1915.

In this position he had built up Labour as a viable opposition on the London County Council and led it to victory in 1934 when he became Leader of the Council. I first came into contact with him soon afterwards. At the London Labour Party Conference he had been asked to have the books used in LCC schools checked for bias. He wrote to me and asked me to become one of a committee of three to look into the matter. All with such complaints were asked to contact us. At once allegations of bias were received from the Roman Catholic

Bishop of Southwark about history books used in council schools. We then discovered that he had already got the preceding Tory council to remove all references to 'Bloody' Mary from such books.

The practice of the LCC was to allow the publishers of school books to display them at an exhibition from time to time where teachers could visit and choose what they wanted. We found little evidence of bias, political or religious, but many textbooks were out-of-date and funds were insufficient for the purchase of books. Morrison willingly accepted our proposals.

My next contact with him was during the LCC elections of 1937. Labour had — to everyone's surprise — won control of the LCC for the first time in 1934 and the Tories were now making every effort to recapture it. Charles de Peyer, a Fabian Civil Servant, secretly provided £1,000 towards an election broadsheet designed by Michael Higgins, a lay-out man for the *Daily Herald*, whose work had greatly impressed him. Morrison, as a result, invited me to join an Advisory Campaign Committee which included Maurice Webb, an outstanding election organizer, and Clem Leslie (Mr Therm of the Gas, Light & Coke Co.). We four met daily for ten days before the election in Morrison's room in County Hall. I noticed its walls were hung with the originals of Low's cartoons of him.

Morrison's work on the LCC had won widespread acclaim, and financial support came from a number of individuals outside the Labour Party, including some directors of Marks & Spencer and Montague Burton.

The Campaign Committee planned a series of posters, newspaper and billboard adverts and a series of meetings in different parts of London dealing with local, London-wide, and national issues which were likely to appeal to local audiences. Press releases were carefully handled. Every Tory move in the campaign was assessed and countered. There was no doubt that Morrison led the campaign brilliantly. He knew his London and fought to make Londoners proud of their city by voting Labour. (He also got them to pay higher rates!)

Housing was the main priority in his appeal. He won the Jewish vote by his strong opposition to Fascism and he especially cultivated the women's vote. Much was made of the fine work done by Somerville Hastings and his colleagues in overhauling the old Poor Law hospitals. I was interested, however, to find that he did not consider education to be an election winner and did not push it. The decision to defy the Tory government and go ahead with rebuilding Waterloo Bridge without government assistance made a deep impression on the Cockney electorate. Labour returned to power with six extra seats.

His failure to become Leader

A typical Londoner, with plenty of Cockney bumptiousness, he put up the backs of many Labour supporters from other parts of the country. He undoubtedly resented what he considered to be their 'provincial bias'. He put down his lack of success at the election of the Parliamentary Leader in 1935 to this. When the wartime National government broke up in 1945, he at once made it known that he would stand for election as Leader when the new Parliament met. Like most other prominent socialists, he expected that Labour would win many seats but did not expect a landslide majority.

The one body that had expected a victory was the Central London Fabian Society which had hired a small hall near Leicester Square for a celebration on the evening after the results came out and had invited Attlee, Morrison and myself as Fabian Secretary to say 'a few words'. When the news of the landslide came through, Labour headquarters called the victors to a meeting in Westminster Central Hall where they duly acclaimed Attlee, Morrison and other prominent people as they arrived. Churchill had conceded defeat and Attlee set out for his first visit to the Palace.

When I arrived at the Central London Fabian meeting later that evening I was at once met by Herbert Morrison, who pushed me 'into the gents' to talk to me privately. 'We cannot have that man as Prime Minister, the new PLP must first have a chance to choose a new Leader.' I said I sympathized with him but no one would want to discard a Leader who had just led the Party to such a remarkable success. Surely he must see that. He continued to argue furiously. I don't think he ever forgave me for telling him this obvious truth!

An emergency meeting of the new PLP had been called at the Beaver Hall the next morning to confirm Attlee as Leader, so he could go ahead and form his government. I waited to see if anyone would put forward Morrison's name. No one did; Morrison clearly showed his disappointment.

As Leader of the House in the Attlee government, Morrison was a great success. When, however, he took over as Foreign Secretary (March–October 1951) he was a disaster.

Not a statesman!

I was an elected Member of the London Labour Party Executive, representing the Fabian Society, from 1942 to 1947, during which time I saw much of Morrison's influence on that body. Despite his active membership of the War Cabinet and the handing-over of the secretaryship to Donald Daines during his absence, he always kept a close watch on London affairs. He had systematically sought to buy up the South Bank from County Hall eastwards towards Blackfriars Bridge and arranged to dump the blitz debris there when cleared on to sites where the Festival Hall and National Theatre were later to be built.

The creation of a green belt around London was another imaginative idea. The LCC over three years agreed to provide £2,000,000 of grants to local authorities to buy land on which no building was to take place. I mobilized the Councils of Dagenham and Romford to take over from the Crown Lands the Dagenham Corridor between them to be developed in due course as an open space.

His policies were continued during the war under Charles Latham, who had taken over the leadership of the LCC. A break came, however, when Latham and his colleagues began to discuss London after the war. A report was drawn up by them for extending the boundaries of the LCC roughly to the area later fixed for the GLC. When this came before the EC, Morrison vigorously opposed it. His sole consideration was electoral. He did not think Labour would have a majority in the wider area. Latham fought back: Labour must seek the best administrative area for London and fight to take political control of it. He finally beat Morrison by a majority of one. Morrison at once announced that he would come to the Annual Conference of the London Labour Party and attack the proposal. Latham then climbed down and withdrew the report. Later, when Nye Bevan drew up his National Health Bill, which entailed taking over all local government hospitals into the National Health Service, Morrison alerted the London Labour EC and encouraged them to seek to retain the LCC control. When a head-on battle seemed likely, I suggested Nye Bevan be invited to a meeting of the EC. He came and won them over completely! Morrison was not present!

As time passed I, like Hugh Dalton and others, ceased to be an enthusiastic supporter of Morrison as I realized his limitations. Attlee was resolved to hold on until a possible Leader of a younger generation had arrived. He was encouraged in this by Nye Bevan and his friends who thought the longer Attlee remained the greater would be Nye's chances. Meanwhile Hugh Gaitskell was establishing himself. I remember one day in 1955 lunching at the same table as Hugh Dalton, Jim Callaghan and Arthur Moyle, Attlee's PPS. Dalton suddenly said to Moyle: 'You can tell your boss he can now resign. We have it all tied up for Gaitskell.' Within a month Attlee resigned and Gaitskell was elected Leader. Morrison could not believe that he would not secure the post. He appeared dumb-founded when the figures were announced showing how badly he had done. He took the result very badly and refused Gaitskell's plea to help him by continuing as Deputy Leader.

Morrison showed himself a good 'Tammany Hall' boss but failed to develop into a statesman. He was adept at organizing elections, particularly in the London area. He had a very high standard of political probity. Councillors were strictly forbidden expenses within the LCC area and only allowed them when on LCC business outside. The LCC Party, once it came near to power, was able to recruit many able people to run its committees. It had a very high proportion of married women, retired men and trade union officials whose unions allowed them time off for LCC business. It had a much more middle-class membership than the PLP at that time. It was also much more strictly whipped!

In the national and international field Morrison did not develop the broad vision and understanding his admirers had expected and hoped for at the time of the Spanish Civil War. I remember the mother of an active councillor in Barking who had come from Lambeth telling me when I was singing Morrison's praises 'He used to speak on our street corner and never had anything worth saying; he is just good at answering hecklers.'

He remained the bright, bumptious Cockney. But London owes him a great debt.

Some sources

Christopher Mayhew
Michael Stewart
Charles de Peyer
W.A. Robson
Hansard

16
A Junior Minister, 1945-46

Dagenham, 1945

For ten years without an election owing to the war I served as MP for the ever-growing Romford constituency, which reached 220,510 electors[1] in 1945 when it was divided into four seats. All four Labour parties invited me to continue as their MP. After some thought, I decided to accept Dagenham's invitation, despite my initial backing from Barking. The principal reason was that I had always got on well with the Dagenham party, which was a happy and tolerant party, whereas the Barking party had been a quarrelsome one – particularly in the immediate prewar period. Secondly, most of those who had been active in my WEA class had by now either left the district or dropped out of active politics. I have never regretted my decision.

During the war I got to know and respect Bob Crane, who was the principal Dagenham representative on the Romford Division Party Executive, and made him my Dagenham Liaison Officer, which he remained until his death in 1974. We became close friends. When the 1945 General Election came, he was appointed agent. After his death he was replaced by Len Collins as Liaison Officer.

This first election in Dagenham as a separate constituency was run very smoothly and efficiently and we won handsomely. After the poll had closed the enthusiastic Young Socialists carried me shoulder high to the station, down the Heathway. The count did not take place till three weeks later, to allow the service votes to come in. The result was announced to a waiting handful by the Mayor about midday from the steps of the Civic Centre, as results coming in from neighbouring seats showed that a landslide was in progress.

In the course of the Election I had won an unusual libel action against Quintin Hogg. Michael Foot had written a devastating attack on the record of Chamberlain and the prewar Tory government, called *Guilty Men*. Hogg had written a reply *The Left is never Right*. On reading a review of this book by Beverley Baxter, I was surprised to find I was attacked for having made a pro-Hitler speech in Parliament. On checking Hansard, I found that whoever had done the devilling for Hogg had turned over two pages and credited me with the speech of a pro-

Nazi. I received an apology and considerable damages. All unsold copies of the book had to be withdrawn and the defamatory pages removed.

Following this landslide, Attlee offered me the Under-Secretaryship for the Dominions. Addison, the Secretary for the Dominions and an old friend, was Leader of the Lords. I therefore spoke for the Department in the Commons and was generally put in charge by him. It was not a department I would have chosen, but seemed to have scope for useful work.

I acted as a link with the various self-governing dominions, then all white. I found the Canadians as a whole both charming and self-possessed. They were delighted not to be taken for Americans. The Australians, in contrast, were inclined to be brash and assertive. I well remember entertaining Sir Keith Murdoch, the newspaper magnate, who wore a well-laundered white shirt. He opened our conversation at lunch by saying 'I suppose you wear coloured shirts because you couldn't get good starch in wartime.' I fear I replied, 'I have always worn coloured shirts since my student days as I think them more attractive.'

Newfoundland

I was given special responsibility for Newfoundland and the three South African territories then called Bechuanaland, Basutoland and Swaziland, which were largely hemmed in by the Union of South Africa. The British High Commissioner for South Africa was responsible for supervising the government of these three territories.

Newfoundland had become a self-governing colony in 1855 and had been largely ruled by the Water St merchants of St John's who controlled its fish trade. Having few trading connections with Canada, it had rejected proposals to join the Canadian Confederation in 1869. Economic difficulties from 1918 onwards, particularly during the slump of 1929—32, led to a threat of bankruptcy and a demand for the end of 'Responsible government'. This resulted in 1934 in the setting up of 'Commission government' under which Britain resumed control of the island and its dependency of Labrador. The Commission, which consisted of three Newfoundlanders and three British under an executive governor, set out to modernize administration and improve services. This needed considerable financial help from the British government and increased taxation of the better-off in the island.

The coming of the war improved the market for Newfoundland's fish and paper, and the American bases brought money into the country. Funds became available for improving hospitals, schools and constructing Gander Airport and new roads. Greater prosperity was at once followed by a demand for a restoration of self-government. This was the problem to be faced in 1945.

The Water St merchants demanded a return to 'Independent Responsible government.' Many, particularly the fishermen in the outports, the loggers and workers in the paper industry, were strongly opposed to any return to the kind of government that had existed before 1934. In the Dominions Office there was a fear that 'Responsible government' could well lead once more to bankruptcy and the need for further financial assistance from Britain. I was one of those who saw the future of Newfoundland as being the tenth province of Canada and sought to persuade the Canadian authorities to offer inclusion within their social services and to develop stronger economic links — particularly in the development of the iron ore and hydro-electric resources of Labrador. In the meantime, I encouraged the Commission to spend the surplus built up during the war on raising the very backward living standards and social services.

To plan the future arrangements were made to elect by adult suffrage forty-five members of a convention. I decided that Labrador should be represented, although it had not had a member in the former Newfoundland Assembly. This provided a precedent followed on all future occasions. Only 20 per cent of the electorate troubled to vote for the Convention, which had long and acrimonious discussions over eighteen months (1946—8).

I continued to be interested in Newfoundland after I left office, when I visited the country and wrote a book about its problems. After two referendums had been held in the summer of 1948, Newfoundland decided on an 80 per cent poll by a majority of close on 7,000 to join Canada. The capital St John's voted 2 : 1 for 'Responsible government', but was outvoted by the outports, the loggers and paper towns, which welcomed the chance of inclusion in the Canadian social services which Newfoundland could not have provided on its own.

The inclusion of Labrador was an important factor, despite its small electorate, in getting the result accepted, as almost 100 per cent of the votes there were for union with Canada. Without its vote the overall majority would have been seen as highly marginal.

Southern Africa

The South African territories provided considerable problems. When the Union of South Africa had been set up in 1910 it was widely assumed that these three British protectorates would be transferred to the Union in the near future. However, during the debates in Parliament it was strongly urged that this should not be done without consultation with and the consent of their inhabitants. Whilst this did not affect the legislation, both government and opposition were clearly influenced by the tenor of the debates.

General Smuts had brought South Africa into the Second World War on the British side against considerable opposition in South Africa. The people of Basutoland had become maize eaters before being driven into their mountains by the Boers. Maize could not be grown in Basutoland; they grew wheat and exported it to the lowlands in return for maize. In 1945 there was a failure of the maize crop in South Africa. We, therefore, had to persuade Smuts to send coal to the Argentine in return for maize which we could then sell to the Basutos.

Smuts felt he had us over a barrel and demanded the cession of the territories in return for the services he had rendered Britain in the war and now over the maize.

I strongly resisted his moves and adopted delaying tactics whenever he raised the question, ascertaining that there would be strong opposition in the territories to any such proposal and telling him it would be strongly opposed if put before Parliament. I soon found that Smuts, for all his alleged 'liberalism', was strongly racist in his attitudes to South African questions, although sympathetic to British imperialist ideas at the world level, which explained Churchill's enthusiasm for him.

Then there came a very difficult question of conscience for me to decide. A Boer farmer some three years before had brutally murdered his white mistress in Swaziland. Being a wealthy man, he had used every legal delaying device to avoid hanging. The case finally came to me. The civil servants strongly recommended a reprieve, partly on the grounds that the case had kept him in suspense for such a long period, but mainly on the grounds that no white man had been hanged in South Africa for over fifteen years, although many blacks had been, and that if he were executed it would have dangerous repercussions on the relations of South Africa with Britain.

I strongly oppose the death penalty; on the other hand, I strongly favour racial equality. After careful consideration I decided to allow the law in Swaziland to take its course.

My opposition to his policies irked Smuts and he sent a personal note to Attlee asking for a change of Minister — in other words, he asked for me to be sacked. Attlee fell in with his wishes. Addison expressed his deep regrets to me at my departure.

At the time no explanation was given me. Many years later Harold Wilson found the relevant correspondence when researching for one of his books and informed me.

So ended my short period as a Junior Minister (May 1946).

Some sources

Ted Hennem
Sir Harold Wilson

17

The British–Yugoslav Parliamentary Group

Preparing the way for his attack on the Soviet Union early in 1941, Hitler attempted to neutralize the Balkan and Danubian powers. Prince Paul, the Yugoslav Regent, feeling himself under threat from Germany, Italy, Hungary and Bulgaria, decided to avail himself of Hitler's approaches, hoping thus to obtain some measure of security. After doing his best to play for time, he finally sent his ministers to sign an agreement in Vienna. Yugoslav opinion, already outraged by the Nazi treatment of Czechoslovakia, surfaced in Belgrade with a coup. This was widely assumed to have been inspired by the British government anxious to bring Yugoslavia into open opposition to Hitler. A new government was set up under General Simovic and the young King, Peter II, nearly 18, was declared of age. The deposed Prince Regent was bundled out of the country into British custody in Kenya.

Churchill was delighted at this defiance of Hitler and declared that 'Yugoslavia had found its soul.' He suggested that a British–Yugoslav Parliamentary Group should be set up to establish friendly relations between our two countries. At a meeting of MPs, Lord William Scott,[1] a Tory MP, was elected chairman of such a group and I was elected secretary. When part of the government in exile arrived in London (June 1941) our committee acted as a liaison and had regular meetings with them to discuss their various problems. A great deal of strain developed between the Serb and Croat members of this government when news came through of the Ustasha murders of Serbs in Croatia and Bosnia. We were continually fed by them with reports of the activities of the Chetniks and particularly of Mihailovič, who was made a member of the government in exile.

Gradually, however, news began to trickle through about the partisans and their exploits in fighting the Germans and Italians. More disquieting was the news of conflict between Chetniks, Ustashas and partisans. On 27 January 1943 I asked the Foreign Secretary whether 'discussions had taken place during the last six months with the Soviet government upon the unification of the various insurgent forces in Yugoslavia in a common fight against the enemy'. Eden replied 'Yes, Sir.' At that time we believed the partisans not only to be in contact with the Soviets but acting largely under their direction. On 24 February 1943 it was

90

reported in Parliament that Mihailovič, had collaborated with the Italians in Herzegovina.

Early that spring Churchill asked Tito to receive a British mission. Contact was established and Churchill was greatly impressed by the large number of German divisions being held down by the partisans. Disillusion with Mihailovič's activities mounted and critical questions about him were asked in the House.

One morning in February 1944 Lord William Scott told me that he had a very important statement to make on the authority of the British government to the members of the government in exile at our meeting taking place that day. Churchill, he said, was to announce in Parliament on 24 February that the British government had decided to transfer all support from Mihailovič to Tito because he alone was fighting the Germans. Pandemonium broke out and we were submitted to a barrage of questions, most of which Scott could not answer beyond saying that British officers had investigated the position in Yugoslavia and the British government believed their reports and had decided to act upon them.

The government in exile had brought with them a considerable number of advisers and assistants. Within a fortnight following Scott's announcement most of them had transferred their allegiance to the partisans. Amongst them was an able and enthusiastic young royalist. Many years later, when visiting a hotel on the Adriatic coast for an evening drink with some Parliamentary colleagues, I was greeted by the manager with a hug and kiss on both cheeks as he said 'How nice to see you John, after all these years'. I could not think where I had seen him before until he said over a drink 'I always was a good Communist, you know'. Then I remembered the enthusiastic young royalist. Somehow I think he was a Vicar of Bray rather than an under-cover agent!

Scott and I subsequently met and advised a number of the exiled Yugoslavs individually, but our group no longer acted as an official liaison with them. We met Velebit, Tito's representative, when he was in London, and obtained information from him about the partisans and developments in Yugoslavia. After the war was over, it was decided to reconstitute the Parliamentary group. Ernest Bevin and the Foreign Office at first believed that the break between Tito and Stalin was a 'put up job' and discouraged our efforts. Help and encouragement was given by Velebit, who had returned to London as Yugoslav Ambassador (1952—56). I happened to be in Belgrade with some colleagues and was present with our Ambassador, Sir Charles Peake, when members of the Yugoslav government accepted, for the first time, an invitation to a reception he gave. Peake also encouraged the reconstitution of the group. Ultimately, with the help of Fitzroy Maclean the Foreign Office were persuaded to drop their disapproval. He acted as Chairman and I continued as Secretary of the group, becoming Chairman in 1960 when the group became affiliated to the Inter-Parliamentary Union.

Some sources

Hansard
Velebit

18
A Double Agent

Early in 1946 I was approached by a young constituent working at Ford's, who asked me to take up the case of his father, George Dace, who was imprisoned in France as a traitor and was in danger of execution. It appeared that Dace had acted as a double agent, having been forced by the Germans to work for them; he had himself then contacted Allied Intelligence and supplied them with valuable information. In the immediate aftermath of liberation he had been seized by outraged local residents and narrowly escaped immediate execution. The police had arrested him and transferred him to Dijon for trial. The son alleged that, although the family had approached the British Embassy in Paris, he had been left without adequate legal defence at his trial. I, therefore, asked the Foreign Secretary, on 22 July 1946, 'Why no assistance had been given to Mr George Dace, a British subject honoured by Lord Montgomery for his help to the Allied Forces, who was condemned to death on July 20 at Dijon for alleged assistance to the Nazis during the German occupation?' Noel Baker replied,

> Our Ambassador in Paris satisfied himself that Mr Dace was provided with legal aid and that he had adequate opportunity to prepare and conduct his defence. Until Mr Dace has exhausted his legal remedies our Ambassador cannot properly take any other steps on his behalf and the question of diplomatic intervention does not therefore arise. The Ambassador, however, has been instructed to watch the case closely. Mr Dace has the right of appeal and I think my Hon. Friend may be assured he will exercise that right.

I further asked, 'How is it that despite the relatives' request to the British Consul to intervene to provide assistance to Mr Dace no action was taken?' Noel Baker added, 'I think we have done everything we properly could under the customs of international relationship.'

This question and answer received wide publicity in the French press, both national and local. There was criticism at British interference and a vigorous campaign was organized against Dace. Dace appealed and the death sentence was commuted to life imprisonment.

His relatives were far from satisfied as Dace suffered severely from dysentery in prison. I, therefore, pursued the matter and the case was again reviewed by the Commission des Graces in Paris. To speed matters up, on 13 January 1949, I asked, 'Why has there been six months delay in forwarding the records in the Dace case to this body and when will action be taken?' MacNeil replied, 'I have carefully examined this question and I cannot agree there has been delay on HM Government's part. Further copies of the relevant documents are being provided for the French authorities.'

On 30 March 1949, I asked, 'What public funds had been spent on the Dace case and to whom have they been paid?' Mayhew replied, 'Special expenditure amounting to some £120 has been incurred in connection with this case. The main items are the travel and subsistence expenses of witnesses, including certain testimony taken on affidavit in the USA and the cost of special journeys made by officials in connection with the case.'

After further pressure and as a result of the review of his case a conditional discharge from jail was agreed but he was expelled from France (1951), accompanied by his wife who could speak no English. The son who asked me to take up the case had earlier left Dagenham. Following the usual practice, however, I continued to follow up this case once I had embarked on it.

According to his story, George Dace was born in 1886 and worked at the Great Dunmow, Essex, post office as one of two male clerks before the First World War. He was a territorial and was called up in 1914; at the post office's request he transferred to RE Signals where he served throughout the war. Whilst he was away his wife went off with his male post office colleague and left him to care for three young sons.

He did not take his discharge until 1920 as he sought a transfer to avoid contact with his former colleague. This was refused and he then resigned 'from his established position'.

He then returned to France and subsequently married a French woman at Peronne who helped him bring up his three English-born sons. The youngest became a French citizen at 17 and served in the French Air Force. As such he flew to England in 1940 and was shot down over Liverpool. Dace's wife inherited a farm and he also became manager of a local cinema and ran a bistro. His business associate Deguise was aware of his frequent visits to England to enlist in the Officers' Emergency Reserve. Deguise occupied his office in Peronne, when Dace fled the oncoming Germans in 1940, and looted the premises, destroying a legal agreement to repay a debt of 35,000 francs lent to him by Dace in 1938. Dace had taken his family and fled south returning to his daughter-in-law's farm in Normandy after the armistice had been declared.

Dressed as a mechanic, he sought early in 1941 to cross into the Free Zone, but was arrested by the Germans at Moulins and 'thrown into a filthy stinking prison'. During his interrogation he was confronted with precise details of his prewar life which had apparently been supplied by Deguise who had alerted the Germans as to his proposed departure. He was thus faced with the choice of being shot as a British spy and reprisals against his family, or becoming their agent. Meanwhile Deguise, whom he now believed to have been a German agent since before the war, took over and ran his business, taking over his liquor licence.

Dace appears early to have decided to become a double agent, giving some information to the Germans but early establishing a contact first with the French Underground and providing a Colonel Celestin Perrin with valuable information (1941–4), and then in 1944 with the 'Sussex' Information Service of British Intelligence. He was contacted by a Lieutenant Monestier who had been dropped at Evreux, with short-wave transmitters, to locate V1 launching sites and provide information about the Seine Valley.

It was thought the Germans would make a stand to prevent an Allied breakout from Normandy. The Germans were short of petrol and had difficulty in bringing up reinforcements. Dace claimed that the information he collected and supplied to Monestier enabled the RAF to bomb seven V1 launching sites and to destroy the boat bridges and barrage at Poses and the locks at Conflans St Honorine, Paris. The destruction of these led the level of the Seine to drop by 10 to 12 feet. The enemy's pontoon barges were left high and dry on the mud, thus cutting their lines of communications for reinforcements. The destruction at Conflans St Honorine cut off the ammunition supply line for a hundred or more barges coming down the Northern Canal via Campeigne and then up the Seine to Muntes and Rouelles. To collect the necessary information, Dace organized his own group of seven young Resistants to report to him. Monestier was most appreciative of his services and sent him the following message hidden in a messenger's boot: 'Je vous signale que vos renseignements sont considérés en haut lieu TRÈS IMPORTANTS, very good work'. Unfortunately Monestier was captured and shot by the Germans 24 hours before the liberation of Paris.

The British Official Postwar Investigation Report (27 January 1949) stated that:

> The importance of Dace's work as an Allied Information Agent is further established by the following:–
> (a) On the 26/8/44 he was urgently summoned to the Headquarters of Field Marshal Montgomery, in order to give the necessary precisions for the Seine crossing by the Allied Forces.
> (b) By the glowing attestations given to him by Lt Col M Henderson, Chief of 'Sussex' Information Teams of IS.
> (c) By the testimonial which the Attaché Militaire of the British Embassy, on behalf of the War Minister sent to the Dijon Court on 18 July 1946. This document mentions the enormous services rendered by Dace by sending from France information of the greatest value to Intelligence Service.

This official report also confirmed that from June 1944 to the Liberation, Dace hid and fed four Allied airmen.

Dace never made any attempt to disguise the fact that he had been a double agent. As such, I saw from some of the evidence submitted against him, he had betrayed a number of French to the Nazis. This they found difficult to overlook. On the other hand there is little doubt of the great services he rendered to the Allies, particularly in assisting the breakout from Normandy which certainly saved many lives.

Dace and his family believed that he was not adequately supported by the Foreign Office during his trial. It certainly had to tread very carefully in view of the strong French evidence against him.

The British authorities were ungenerous in stating that he had only been an unpaid assistant to Monestier and in denying him any financial payment for his services. The French naturally gave him no compensation for his loss of jobs and property in Peronne, where Deguise was acquitted of any collaboration with the Germans and retained what he had taken during the war.

Dace settled down at Hemel Hempstead where he started a new life, becoming a local Conservative Councillor (1959–62). After the death of his French wife he married again in 1956.

As he aged he came to me again to try and sort out his social security and pensions problems and to try and reopen some of his earlier grievances. He died in 1972 aged 86.

Some sources

Dace correspondence
Hansard

19

The Battle for the
Legitimacy Act, 1959

For many years a ballot had been held each autumn for the right to introduce Private Members' Bills in the House of Commons during the current session. This started in November and terminated about the end of July with an overlap of a few days in October for outstanding government business. Some 302 backbench MPs entered for the ballot in November 1958. Six Fridays were allocated for Second Reading debates and four for later stages. Although twenty places were drawn in the ballot, only the first six could be certain of a full debate and a vote at least for its closure. MPs with a lower place were wise to attempt some minor non-controversial measure unless they wished deliberately to embark on a propaganda fight. Those in the first six might adventure with a Bill controversial across party with some chance of success. It has long been established, however, that all major legislation controversial between parties was the preserve of the government of the day. The odds are very heavily biased against the Private Member by the opportunities Parliamentary procedure provides for filibustering and in particular by the difficulty of getting the necessary one hundred MPs present to vote for the closure on a Friday afternoon when many MPs are away to their homes or constituencies. Governments normally can carry the closure, thanks to their whips, whenever they so desire; not so the Private Member, who can easily be torpedoed by a handful of keen opponents and is only likely to be able to mobilize his one hundred for a closure on a major issue like capital punishment or divorce law reform.

Having won the third place in the ballot in November 1958, I looked around for a Bill sufficiently controversial to be interesting and worthwhile, with some chance of passing into law through a Tory House of Commons. As soon as the list of those successful in the ballot is published a flood of possible Bills descends on the lucky MP from all the more active pressure groups: nearly everything that can be done to secure the welfare of dogs and horses in this country has thus been passed into law. I was told by a fellow MP that the Society of Labour Lawyers had, through sub-committees, prepared a number of Bills for Private Members which they thought worthwhile. This meant that such Bills had probably already been drafted by lawyers in a form reasonable for introduction in

96

the House — a very important help at a time when the services of Parliamentary Counsel were not normally available to Private Members. On inquiry from their secretary, Miss Jean Graham Hall,[1] I was told that a report proposing limited reforms in the legitimacy field had been prepared, and was being turned into a draft Bill by a sub-committee of three, consisting of Miss Graham Hall and two solicitors. I was delighted to learn this, as I had long been interested in the problem of the illegitimate child and had been one of the backers of Dame Joan Vickers's Maintenance Orders Bill.

I therefore decided to take up this Bill and on 12 November introduced for the First Reading 'a Bill to amend the Legitimacy Act of 1926, and to improve the law relating to children born out of wedlock in other aspects'. I had the great good fortune to secure the backing of Sir Robert Cary, a senior Conservative MP of standing, who agreed to second the Bill and was a tower of strength through all the forthcoming struggles. Among other backers were George Isaacs, Dr Barnett Stross, Geoffrey de Freitas and Charles Royle on the Labour side, and Dame Joan Vickers and William Shepherd on the Tory side.

This was to be a battle in which no help could be expected from an organized pressure group — often of great value in influencing other MPs and peers — for most of those suffering from such discrimination under the law were anxious to avoid any personal publicity. There was not even a 'Bastards Anonymous' to fight on their behalf.

The old law of legitimacy

The law of England on legitimacy before 1926 was clear and distinct. A child born in lawful wedlock was legitimate; a child born out of wedlock was illegitimate. But Roman law was quite different. It said that a child born before marriage could be legitimized by the subsequent marriage of its parents. That Roman law became incorporated into the continental systems but was not brought into this country. In 1236, at the Parliament of Merton, a proposal to make such a change was defeated despite the support of the Church. In 1926 the law was at last changed so that some children born before marriage were legitimized by subsequent marriage. However, during its passage into law, legitimacy was refused to all those born when one of their parents was married to someone else. This reduced the beneficiaries under the original clause by at least a half. The most important and controversial clause of my Bill was the proposal to remove this discrimination.

Eight Private Members' Bills had been introduced in the Commons and one in the Lords between 1920 and 1924 on the subject of illegitimacy; in each Bill the main clause aimed at legitimizing children whose parents subsequently married. Not one of them became law. Finally the House got irritated at this succession of failures. The government of the day was thus led to introduce its own Bill in the Lords, which became the Legitimacy Act of 1926. It was at the bidding of Dr Davidson, then Archbishop of Canterbury, that the clause excluding children whose parents were married to someone else when born was added. It was accepted by the government to speed the Bill into law. Among those who voted against Dr Davidson's amendment were Birkenhead and Haldane in the Lords, and in the Commons members of such varied opinions as Winston Churchill, Attlee, Neville Chamberlain and Ramsay Macdonald.

The subject was not again raised in the Commons apart from the odd question until 1954, when Reg Sorensen won a low place in the ballot and decided to amend the Act of 1926. This Bill failed to reach a Second Reading.

My Bill and its opponents

The main argument against my Bill in the Second Reading Debate on 30 January 1959 was its removal of Davidson's amendment. It was much the same case as that already set out by the majority of the Merton Commission on Marriage and Divorce (1955). The institution of marriage would be undermined, stated John Hobson; Sir Hugh Lucas Tooth thought the proposal did not go far enough as it would leave many still illegitimate — a hoary argument for doing nothing! In 1926 Douglas Hacking, then Under-Secretary at the Home Office, had said the Davidson amendment was necessary to protect a wife from undue pressure for a divorce from a husband who had had an illegitimate child by another woman he wished to marry.

The principal argument for the removal of the amendment was that it was wrong to punish children when they had done no wrong. Public morality was not strengthened by demanding that a guiltless child should go through life with a stigma just because one of its parents was married to a third party when the child was born.

It was pointed out that public opinion had changed. Already the law courts were hurrying through divorces if a child was on the way so that it could be born out of wedlock and legitimized by the subsequent marriage of its parents. *The Times* had reported a case where a child was born at 7.30 a.m. The divorce was granted at 10.00 a.m. and the court then held that it dated from midnight so that subsequent marriage could legitimize the child. It was the job of Parliament, not the courts, to bring the law into line with public opinion.

The second most important clause in my original Bill enabled the courts to give the custody and right of access to an illegitimate child's natural father if they felt this to be in the child's best interests. This was introduced largely to meet the wishes of children's departments in many large cities especially those with a big coloured population. It was quite common for a white woman living with a coloured man to desert her half-caste child. In many such cases the natural father desired the custody of his child especially if he decided to return to his country of origin. One of the other clauses aimed at making the position easier for a woman to claim an affiliation order if she was single at the time she made the claim and when the child was born; another clause attempted to restrict the publicity which the press can give to affiliation proceedings. Clause 5 of the Bill attempted to amend the Inheritance (Family Provision Act) of 1938 to give certain of its benefits to illegitimate children. The Bill was strongly opposed by a handful of MPs but secured its Second Reading by 45/4 with Government neutrality. Thirty-eight of the supporters were Labour. All of the opponents, including two tellers, were Tory. Supporters of the Bill had been asked to limit their speeches to enable a vote to be taken before 4.00 p.m. and so avoid closure unlikely to be obtained.

The Bill came before Standing Committee on 8 April. It had a possible member-ship of thirty-six; fifteen only attended that day. According to established practice, the main opponents on Second Reading were made members of the Standing Committee. In order to kill the Bill they organized a boycott in the hope that there would not be the necessary quorum present. This tactic had successfully killed Dame Joan Vickers's Maintenance Orders Bill two years before. However, R.A. Butler as Leader of the House had persuaded it to adopt new Standing Orders to reduce the size of the quorum necessary – fortunately for my Legitimacy Bill. If, however, the necessary quorum is not present at the appointed hour of meeting the committee cannot proceed to business until it is, and if it is not secured within twenty minutes the committee is adjourned. When the Chairman took his seat at 10.30 the quorum was absent. After a hectic 'chase around' by the Bill's supporters, we persuaded Eirene White to leave another committee of which she was also a member and the committee was able to start work soon after 10.30 with a few minutes to spare. As a result of the absence of its opponents, the whole Committee Stage of the Bill was completed by 11.39 that morning – in an hour and one minute!! The only Conservatives present were the Solicitor-General (Hylton-Foster) and the redoubtable Sir Robert Cary.

Much helpful redrafting and widening out of clauses was secured by govern-ment-inspired amendments, but the Solicitor-General insisted on the dropping of the original clause 5 (to amend the Inheritance (Family Provision) Act, 1938) as only touching on a much wider subject. To replace this I introduced a new clause to legitimize the children of void marriages where one or both of those taking part had believed it to be a genuine marriage. This carried out one of the few unanimous recommendations of the Merton Commission and was in line with Scottish law. It was added to the Bill.

The Bill returned to the full House for Report and Third Reading on Friday 8 May. At that time it was still possible at certain times of the day – and especially just after 1.00 p.m. on a Friday – to call a count and if forty MPs did not turn up within two minutes the rest of the business of the day was lost. Supporters had been forewarned that such an attempt to kill the Bill was likely and turned up in sufficient numbers when a count was called at 1.07. After that the Bill passed safely through the remaining stages and obtained its Third Reading with-out a vote in just over an hour. An amendment – to be discussed fully later –

was introduced by me and then withdrawn when it was made clear that I should lose the Bill if I persisted with it.

Trouble in the Lords

The Bill now passed to the Lords, where I was fortunate in getting Lord Chorley to sponsor it. Realizing the possible danger of an attack, similar to that of Dr Davidson from the current Archbishop of Canterbury, I wrote to Dr Fisher and asked if I could see him to discuss the Bill. To my surprise he wrote back to say he was a supporter of the Bill and would speak and vote for it in the Lords. 'Unlike Popes, Archbishops of Canterbury are not bound by the decisions of their predecessors. I cannot however speak for the other bishops who no doubt will take different views on the Bill.'

The Bill obtained its Second Reading without a division, but when it came to the Committee Stage on 2 July, Lord Conesford secured the defeat of the vital clause 1 by 27/9. Conesford and the Bishop of Exeter made very effective debating speeches against the clause. Denning and the Archbishop, who had made strong supporting speeches on Second Reading, were absent and no adequate reply was made. The debate petered out as the House emptied before the vote was taken, to the despair of those watching from the gallery.

What was to be done? Without this key clause the rest of the Bill seemed a poor reward for all the effort so far put in, even though it now passed through committee successfully. I contacted Lord Denning to discuss the position.

Denning was very keen to get the matter reopened. Under House of Lords procedure this could be done in the same Session (unlike the Commons). We got the help of Parliamentary draftsmen and put down the same clause in slightly different wording for debate on 21 July.

For nearly three weeks between the defeat of clause 1 and the proposal to reinstate it, an intensive campaign developed on both sides. I was approached by John Foster, a distinguished barrister and Conservative MP, to know what could be done to get the clause reinserted. He had been contacted by a well-known magazine publisher who would be legitimized under the clause. He was prepared to spend £500 for that purpose. I put him in touch with a firm of Parliamentary agents to plan a campaign. I agreed to write personal letters to all Labour peers, many of whom I knew, asking them to be there on 21 July. The Parliamentary agents agreed to send suitable letters to all other peers they thought to be possible supporters to ask for their vote. 'We have a card index of all peers, ticketed and docketed', I was told, 'and can send a very special letter to all with illegitimate children.' *The Times* came out strongly in support of the Bill as the day approached.

A full House awaited Denning's speech. After a lively and hard-hitting debate, his new clause, with amendments by Meston which brought it very close to the original clause, was put to the vote. Sir Robert Cary and I watched the scene

1 Oxford Union Society Standing Committee—June 1928

(Standing, from left to right) John Parker, (St John's), Stopford Brooke (Balliol) Ex-Treasurer, Alan Tory (St John's), Phelps Brown (Wadham) Secretary, Michael Stewart (St. John's), Brian MacKenna (New College);

(Seated, from left to right) Roger Wilson (Queen's) Librarian, Sir Herbert Samuel MP (Balliol), Aubrey Herbert (University College) President, James Maxton MP, Quintin Hogg (Christ Church) Treasurer (Hills & Saunders).

BRIGHTER SUNDAY!

Cummings

1953

4 *far left* 1966 A bust by
George Brooker,
Dagenham Councillor

5 *left* 1979 General
Election, Dagenham
(Bassano & Vandyke
Studios)

6 1979 Father of the House by Glan Williams, *Parliamentary House Magazine*

from the bar of the House with fascination. Citrine came up to me as he left the Chamber to say he had to go to sign some letters, but would be back for the vote which was due soon after 6.00 p.m. He returned just too late. An oral message came in for Attlee to say his wife was waiting for him. 'Tell her I can't come out till I have voted,' was his reply. To the last the sides seemed evenly balanced. Then the vote was called and the Archbishop led the way into the 'Contents' lobby. The vital clause[2] was reinstated by 83/64.

The Lords' amendments came before the Commons late on 28 July and were duly accepted. The government found the necessary time to complete the Bill's proceedings, as Private Members' time had long been exhausted.

In amending the clause concerning void marriages the Lords insisted on bringing the new English law on the subject fully into line with Scottish law. According to Scottish law the heir to a title or any other man wanting a male heir who found that his wife could not produce one could call himself Mr Smith, seek out a strong, healthy girl likely to be a good mother, marry her and then, when a son had been born, announce who he really was and arrange for this child to be his heir. The Lords' amendments made the same practices possible in England but applied only to those born after the commencement of the Act. This was a by-product of my Bill that I had not foreseen!

Two individual cases

As can be imagined, a flood of correspondence descended upon me when I announced my choice of Bill after the ballot. A few abusive letters attacked me for undermining marriage but the great majority were from those likely to be legitimized if the Bill became law. They vividly brought home the fears and anguish of those who sought to keep this disgrace, as they thought it, from those they loved or respected. Needless to say, they varied greatly in character. I give two very different cases. Soon after I announced my Bill I was approached by a successful London businessman. He had two children, a girl of seventeen and a boy of fourteen, who did not know they were illegitimate. The girl was about to enter for a scholarship at one of the women's colleges at Oxford. For this he believed she must produce a long birth certificate and so would learn her position. He told me that he had married a woman older than himself but it had not been sexually satisfactory so he had taken up with a woman of his own age who was the mother of these two children. Making conversation, I said that I thought marriage should be entered upon with the idea of it being for life, but that if it didn't work it was better ended. 'Not at all,' he replied. 'I don't believe in divorce. I am a churchwarden! It would have been most unfair to my wife if I had divorced her as she would have had no sex. So I spent the weekends regularly with her and the rest of the week with the other woman and her children. When my wife died I married the second woman. Your Bill will legitimize my children and put my family on a firm base.'

A more attractive supporter was an old colonel. His father had been a Scottish baronet who had got an Irish girl pregnant when he was 17 and had then married her. A son had been born who was brought up by the baronet's mother after the Irish girl had disappeared. Some years later the young baronet met and fell in love with another young woman and was anxious to marry. They took all the normal steps to trace the missing Irish girl, finally presumed her dead and got married. A son was born who became this colonel. Soon afterwards the original wife turned up and, being a staunch Catholic, refused a divorce. The couple continued to live together but decided to have no more children. Then the Irish wife died and the couple got married a second time and had another son. Because they were domiciled in England, English law governed their case. The first son, therefore, was legitimate, as was the third, but not the second. In due course the eldest boy died without heirs and then the father. The baronetcy therefore passed to the third boy. The father left a will dividing all he had between his two surviving sons, so there were no monetary difficulties between them. But the course of events had greatly disturbed the colonel. He had first learnt about his illegitimacy when he was a subaltern in the army and he was so upset by it that he had had a nervous collapse and had not been able to talk for a fortnight. He told me he had never discussed the matter with his own sons, but he had deep down a feeling that they resented his illegitimacy and could not accept that it was no fault of his.

When the campaign to get the vital clause through the Lords was hotting up, the colonel offered to come on a BBC television programme with me, anonymously, and answer questions about how it felt to be illegitimate. We met in the studio with the editor of the women's page in the *Daily Mirror* to be questioned by Ludovic Kennedy. After talking about suitable questions to be put, it was agreed that we should have a run through and then immediately afterwards go on the air. Opening, Kennedy asked the colonel, 'What does it feel like to be a bastard?' The old man answered very reasonably but as soon as we broke off he turned to me and said, 'I have never been called that to my face before. I will certainly not take part in this programme.' With some difficulty, and after due apologies, he agreed to go ahead on TV but went completely to pieces when questions were put to him. His pleasure when the Bill was passed was a delight to see.

A wife with a guilty conscience

During the passage of the Bill through the Commons I was approached by an East Midlands MP and asked if I could introduce an amendment to my Bill to meet the case of a constituent. This man, a county council clerk called Miller, had married at the start of the war, gone into the army and had been taken prisoner at Dunkirk, spending the rest of the war in a German POW camp. His wife had taken a civilian job at an RAF camp and in due course had an affair with a Canadian airman and produced a son. On going to register the birth she asked about filling in her husband's name as the father. She said she was told she could not do so as he was abroad, but that she should leave the place blank so that he could fill it in if he so desired when he returned. She wrote him about the child's birth and he arranged for his army pay to support it. On returning from the war he accepted the child as his son and he and his wife decided to make a go of it together. When the man came to see me he stated that he had grown very fond of the boy, now 16, and would not like him to know that he was not his father. Another child was on its way and he didn't want a mixed family, with one legitimate and one illegitimate — the facts would be bound to come out later and cause trouble, whatever efforts were made to keep the matter dark. He had been refused the right to fill the blank space on the boy's birth certificate as the local registrar held that this would be falsifying the records. A next door neighbour had been in the navy during the war and his wife had also had a child in his absence which was not his. However, the registrar had allowed his name to be entered as the father of the child on the grounds that his ship had occasionally come into Scapa Flow and so he might have come home for a weekend! In law, a husband is assumed to be the father of a child born to his wife and accepted as a member of the family unless he produces evidence to the contrary, or in a rare case such as this, where the registrar knows that the husband could not possibly have had access to his wife at the time of conception. I was not prepared to risk the loss of my Bill to try to cover such a small group.

I advised Miller to adopt the boy so as to remove any possible future problems. He and his wife were not willing to do so, as it would have made the boy aware of his illegitimacy.

Some years later when the boy, now a young man of 23, was in his last year at a teachers' training college, Miller urgently asked to see me to try to save his marriage. The second child had died soon after birth and Mrs Miller had developed an acute guilt complex over her son's illegitimacy. She had sought out the former Canadian airman who had settled in York, where he had married an English girl by whom he had had a son about the same time as Mrs Miller's boy. They had two younger children and were a happy family. Mrs Miller proposed that her husband should divorce her for infidelity. She then proposed to tell the ex-airman's wife — a very 'moral woman' she believed — who she was sure would then divorce her husband. Mrs Miller would then marry him and so legitimize her son!

At her request I saw Mrs Miller with her husband. All appeals to her not to break up two families made no impression until I pointed out that Mr Miller could not now divorce her for her infidelity as he had condoned her adultery by returning to live with her and accepting financial responsibility for her son. At Miller's request I later saw the young man when he was in London for an interview after taking his exams, and told him the whole story. He did not appear at all upset, said he was much fonder of Miller than of his mother and thanked me for stopping a family break-up.

A liberating Act

The Legitimacy Act (1959) was not only a big step forward in removing legal disabilities from the illegitimate, it was first of a number of leftward moves taken by the House of Lords in the field of social reform which took place in the 1960s following the first creation of Life Peers.

In the argument in favour of the Divorce Law Reform Bill (1969), it was a great help to its supporters to be able to point out that as a result of the 1959 Act the many couples who had embarked upon a common law marriage because one or both were not free legally to marry would be able to legitimize their children if the Bill passed. The Family Law Reform Act (1969) removed most of the disabilities in the way of inheritance by the illegitimate. This in particular enabled them to count as dependents under the Inheritance (Family Provision) Acts, 1938 and 1966.

The legal disabilities of bastardy have largely gone. But it will be long before the stigma disappears.

Some sources

Lord Denning
Judge Graham Hall
Hansard
Correspondence and interviews

20

On Delegation to Ethiopia, 1964

Early in 1964 I was asked to join a Parliamentary Delegation to Ethiopia. This land of Prester John, the mountainous Christian outpost in the Horn of Africa, had always interested me with its Monophysite church. The delegation was led by Charles Taylor, a Conservative. It included two other Conservatives, Col. Allason and Julian Critchley, Lord Walston and another Labour MP Wm Whitlock. We flew to Addis Ababa via Athens and Khartoum in an Ethiopian Airlines plane captained by an American.

We stayed at a large new hotel with a view of the Emperor's stables. Addis Ababa, which then consisted largely of ramshackle buildings spread over a hilly terrain, made a pleasant sight with its large number of eucalyptus trees from Australia planted by the Emperor Menelik[1] around the time of his defeat of the Italians at Adowa (1896).

Soon after our arrival we were taken to the British Embassy, a Georgian-style building erected early this century, and were welcomed by the Ambassador, John Russell, and his Greek wife, the 'Miss World' of 1937. Its outer walls were windowless, perhaps to avoid a possible shot through them from outside. Its garden was well filled with flowers and fruit trees all flowering and fruiting simultaneously. It was surprising to see apple and peach trees doing just this, though we were told that in that mountainous equatorial climate without any winter apples did not do well. Daffodils and rambler roses were out at the same time. Rose trees flowered continuously but soon exhausted themselves if not vigorously pruned. We were also told that being so near the Equator days and nights were nearly always the same length throughout the year with dawn around 6.0 a.m. and sunset around 6.0 p.m.

We paid an early visit to the Emperor Haile Selassie.[2] Appropriately, in view of his title 'the Lion of Judah', he had a number of lions caged near the entrance to his palace. He had been brought up to speak French and insisted on everything being translated into his own language, Amharic, to give him time to think, although his English was quite good. I told him that I had nearly run him down when he was a refugee in Bath during the Italian occupation and had crossed the road with his big umbrella on a wet day immediately in front of my car. His eyes twinkled at the memory.

He invited us to a reception partly in our honour and partly to celebrate the 23rd Anniversary of the liberation of Ethiopia. It was a great 'do' held in the Menelik Palace which had a fine wooden roof like a large English medieval barn. Dignitaries from all parts of the Empire were there, many in their local costumes.

The Ethiopians proper — a mixture of Semitic and Hamitic elements — varied in colour, some having much lighter skins than others, but most resembling the Emperor. Their features, like their language, were largely Semitic. Some of the Somalis were perhaps a shade lighter, whilst some of the Gallas and especially the peoples from the Sudan border were very dark. I sat at a table with some officers who had suppressed an attempted coup when the Emperor had been abroad. At the next table was the Indian Ambassador and his wife. The large tasty meal was served by waiters in European eighteenth century dress including powdered wigs, whilst some Ethiopian folk songs were performed. Suddenly the band struck up the Blue Danube, and I partnered the Indian Ambassador's wife in a series of Viennese waltzes to the surprise of the officers at our table who made clear their low opinion of Indians.

Whilst in Addis Ababa we visited the university and a large modern hospital. It appeared that these, although well run, had few schools or clinics to supply them. I was entertained by Richard Pankhurst, a history professor who was director of an Institute of Ethiopian studies and his wife who was University librarian, and their two young children. His mother, Sylvia Pankhurst, had embraced the Emperor's cause after his overthrow by Mussolini, and published a pro-Ethiopian anti-Fascist paper in London. She had subsequently gone to live in Addis Ababa to run a journal on Ethiopian culture, history and modern developments.

Our group divided into three. Taylor and Walston went to see the Crown Prince's farm whilst Allason and Critchley visited the military college at Harar. Whitlock and I decided to see something of the Highlands. The embassy provided us with a car and driver, and we set out for Dabra Markos on a Sunday morning on what was like a pleasant English summer day. We crossed a plain with cedars on the higher points. We passed a man and wife going to church. The woman, holding her umbrella to keep off the sun, was riding a mule whilst her husband walked beside. Not a likely picture for a Muslim country! Boys of about 13, clad only in a loose animal skin, tended large numbers of rather skinny cattle and chased an occasional rabbit. Suddenly we came to an escarpment. On one side of the road two boys' bare behinds stuck up as they looked at something down below; on the other side were the equally bare behinds of two gorillas also looking below!

We had come to the edge of the Blue Nile Canyon. Along the top were several small monasteries. The scenery was magnificent as we gradually wound our way down, crossed the river and ascended the other side. The plateau then continued and we arrived at Dabra Markos where we had been told we would be welcomed by the Governor. Apparently the message had miscarried and he had gone away. Our driver found us accommodation in a small private hotel built of sun-dried bricks. We went for a walk round the town whilst our hostess caught one of her chickens and wrung its neck for our supper. We returned as it got dark and entered to find our host and his son of about 14 nailing up the windows and doors with boarding. When our driver asked why he said: 'In case the Shiftas [bandits] come in the night.' After supper we went into an outhouse to sleep (I put some Flit round the metal legs of my bed, but was not invaded during the night). Our host sat on a chair outside with a gun across his knees — in case the Shiftas came — but soon fell fast asleep!

In the morning we journeyed on to Lake Tana, near the source of the Blue Nile, and visited a small market town where we were made very welcome. The people there had rarely seen a white man. We came across a family funeral with a child wrapped in a blanket being taken for burial. The weeping mourners resembled a biblical scene and one wondered whether they were all genuine or if some were paid!

After our return we all went south to the rift valley through which runs the Awash and visited a large sugar plantation at Wonji established by a Dutch company which had earlier operated in Indonesia. The river was fascinating with its hippopotamuses and small lakes. These were now used for bathing as the crocodiles had all been skinned for shoe-leather.

A large compound of bungalows was laid out for the sugar plantation. We were told that only four out of about a hundred executives living round it were Ethiopians, despite the firm's attempts to appoint them to such posts. Most educated Ethiopians it appeared preferred a job in Addis Ababa, whereas the Europeans seemed to enjoy life 'in the bush'.

We were told that there was little zenophobia amongst the Ethiopians, as, apart from the five years of Italian rule (1936–41), they had never been under foreign rule. The leading judge was a Maltese and there were a number of British, Americans and other foreigners on the university staff. Many Greeks, Armenians and Indians traded in the country. A large number of Italians appeared to have stayed on after the end of Italian rule, especially as garage proprietors and mechanics. Most of these had married local girls and had been nicknamed the 'copulatos', in view of their numerous offspring.

We were struck by the strong national pride especially in their historic churches with their attractive frescoes. A few of these, like the strip-cartoon paintings on canvas on sale to tourists, depicted the union of Solomon and the Queen of Sheba (who was believed to have ruled Ethiopia) and so gave rise to the imperial house (the Lion of Judah). Not only was there a large Jewish community, the Falashas, of Ethiopian origin, but the local Church appeared to have a number of Jewish traits. We were told that Ethiopians, both Christian and Muslim, traditionally do not eat pork.

Both William Whitlock and I appeared to have picked up differing viruses when in Ethiopia. I went down soon after the 1964 General Election with pneumonia, which was diagnosed as having been caused by an African germ, whilst Whitlock endured some months' blood disorder which could not be accurately diagnosed.

Some sources

Richard Pankhurst
William Whitlock
Julian Critchley
Lord Walston

21

My Relations with Ford's

The Ford Motor Co. (England) was incorporated in 1911. Their first plants were at Cork and Trafford Park near Manchester. It seems that their name first appeared on the Rate Book of the Romford Rural Council for a site near Dagenham Dock as early as 1912. It is to be noticed that Pritchett & Gold (now absorbed by Chloride Batteries) had transferred their works from Epsom to Dagenham Dock in 1911. The decision to make the change is thought to have been more than intelligent anticipation. However, work by Ford's on a major factory site near Dagenham Dock only got started in 1929.

At the same time as the commencement of production there, the Ford Company sought special powers for itself by promoting a Parliamentary Private Bill, the purpose of which, in the phrase used by the Essex County Council, was to enable the company to become 'an imperium in imperio' and thus to obtain a position similar to that occupied in Detroit as an incorporated town under the American system, giving the company wide powers that in Great Britain would conflict with those of local authorities.

Sir Percival Perry, the Chairman of Ford's (England) had been the founder and Chairman of Slough Estates Ltd and was still a director of that firm, which had bought the site from the government in 1925 to turn into a trading estate. It had been a Ministry of Munitions depot in the 1914–18 war.

In the course of the hearing in Parliament, Perry had cited Slough as a precedent, but this was rejected as a special case. There was strong opposition from the Essex County Council and the Dagenham and Hornchurch Urban District Councils to a 'Slough solution'. As a result, the Bill passed in 1932 just gave the company control over access roads and railways within its estate.

Ford's chose this site firstly because there was deep water there and boats could enter and leave their jetty at any stage of the tide. Secondly, Britain then being a free trade country, they thought it would be a convenient site for exporting, especially to northern and central Europe.

The building of the Becontree Estate by the London County Council offered the possibility of plenty of labour not only for their plant but for the Briggs Bodies, Kelsey Hayes Wheel Co. and Triplex Glass plants which were built simultaneously. However, there was a shortage of skilled labour and many were encouraged to move south from Trafford Park. Messrs Costain, then a Liverpool-based firm, built two large owner-occupied estates for them, one on the north side of the A13 opposite the works and the other nearby at Elm Park, Horn-church. At the same time there was a big turnover of tenants on the Becontree Estate, as many disliked the conditions which were very different from the street neighbourliness of the East End and were far from their places of work. The LCC therefore offered a number of tenancies to house Ford workers from the north but at higher rents than to Londoners. Many of the private houses became very crowded with single Ford workers seeking lodgings.

Henry Ford I had rigorously opposed trade unionism in all his plants, including Dagenham. The earliest attempt at unionization had been at the closely related Briggs Bodies. This had been led about 1934 unsuccessfully by the National Union of Vehicle Builders (now part of the TGWU). When I became MP for the area, I was invited to meetings of an AEU branch based at Romford which sought to organize workers within the plant. A good deal of feeling existed over the hire-and-fire conditions operating there, particularly at the discharge of older men who could easily be replaced by younger men as was the case during the 1930s.

Came the war in 1939; the workers in the 'Finance, the Foundry, the benches and offices' already numbered 12,000 by that date, of whom 4,000 belonged to skilled trades. There was already a large output of cars and tractors which steadily increased and became an important part of the war effort.

With the advent of Labour Ministers into the National government after Churchill became Prime Minister in 1940, the whole question of trade unionism at Ford's was opened up. Ernest Bevin, the Minister of Labour, insisted that Ford's should be fully unionized despite the opposition of the parent company in Detroit.

The breakthrough began with the wartime direction of Labour and the need to recognize the conditions of employment appropriate to the various grades of skill of trade unionists as required by agreements covering their respective occupations, when trade union members were directed to them. Difficulties in complying with this requirement occurred because of the two-tier system of wage bargaining prevailing in the engineering industry, where national and local agreements governed conditions of employment and working practices. In the absence of any form of shopfloor representation, the companies were compelled to enter into formal discussions with the trade unions. These were at first led by Walter Citrine, the Secretary of the Trades Union Congress. They were soon taken over by Vic Feather,[1] who had recently (1937) joined the TUC staff as head of the organization department. He worked in close contact locally with A.G. Pearce, the Secretary of the Trades Council (1937–42). As a result twenty-two different trade unions obtained members in the plant, although the AEU and the TGWU shared the largest number. It was a pity that one trade union for the industry, such as the Automobile Workers in America, could not have been created as it would greatly have simplified negotiations. However, a variety of unions had already come into being in other motorcar plants and it proved easier at the time to extend their membership to Ford's. Over the years there has gradually been a reduction in the number of unions with members in the plant.

Ford's had boasted that they had organized their labour on very different lines to those advocated by trade unions. Negotiations in time, however, led to the establishment of a proper National Joint Negotiating Committee. This produced agreed conditions for all Ford plants which worked smoothly throughout the war.

Despite being the largest employer in the area, Ford's held themselves very aloof from Dagenham as a community, in contrast to some of the other firms. As the local MP I had only two contacts during the war. I was invited to speak at the main plant to try to boost the National Savings Campaign early in the war. This obtained wide support amongst Ford employees. Ford's kept working right through the blitz and had a well-organized ARP (Air Raid Protection) team and fire-fighting service, manning two fully equipped fire-engines and a trailer pump. However, early one morning in 1943 when Mrs Lily Evans was Mayor, she informed me that the previous night there had been big fires at the plant following a German raid. The Borough Fire Brigade had driven up to offer their help only to be denied entrance. The German bombers had returned again and bombed the area on fire. The Mayor and I then visited the plant and it was agreed that the Borough Brigade should be allowed to help when there were bad raids in future.

During the war the redoubtable Mrs Evans, nicknamed 'the Duchess of Dagenham', was a tower of strength in the WVS (Women's Voluntary Service). In February 1943 they opened 'Forces House' to feed and accommodate servicemen on leave or in transit. She not only supervised the work, but lived there and did much of the cooking. Ford's sought at the end of the war to reward her by donating a Ford car. She showed her independence by selling it a week later and buying an Austin Standard!

Soon after the end of the war, in 1949, Ford's announced plans for greatly enlarging the Dagenham plant and employing another 10,000 men there. They ran into opposition from the Labour government which took the view that they would prefer another plant to be erected in a depressed area where housing, schooling and other services were already largely available rather than make increased provision for them locally. The Government would have no objection to any redevelopment at Dagenham provided approximately the same labour force would be employed. It thought it unwise for any community, such as Dagenham, to have 'all its eggs in one basket', but preferred a diversified local economy. George Isaacs (the Minister of Labour) and George Strauss (Minister of Supply) were invited down to Ford's to try and get them to alter this decision. George Strauss told me of their errand and said: 'Tag on, you will hear much of interest.' So I did. A dingdong battle took place over the firm's graphs but the Ministers remained adamant. Ford's thought it would be more economical for them to extend their existing plant; the Ministers insisted it was in the national interest that they should not. When the Tories came back to office in 1951

111

Ford's belatedly sought once more to change that direction, but without success. So, a new Ford's plant came into being on Merseyside at Halewood.

With the onset of trade unionism, the practice grew up of meetings from time to time between Labour MPs and shop stewards to discuss problems they wished raised in the House or with Ministers. As the MP for Dagenham, I have taken the chair. Although a majority of Ford workers have now moved out of Dagenham into surrounding areas, they continue to regard me as their MP.

In 1960 it was announced that Ford Motors, of Detroit, proposed to buy up the British minority shares in Ford Motors of Dagenham (they already held 55 per cent of the shares.) Selwyn Lloyd, the Chancellor of the Exchequer, stated that no application had so far been received for exchange control consent. As he refused to make any definite reply about whether he could make a statement to the House before a decision was reached, I moved the Adjournment of the House under Standing Order No 9. The Speaker refused, on the grounds that the Chancellor had not yet received an application for consent.

I found strong opposition locally to the proposal from the council, the trade unions and the Chamber of Trade. I therefore led a deputation from Dagenham Council to see the Chancellor. He took the view that, as the Americans already owned 55 per cent of the shares of the British company, they could already control its policy. They owned 100 per cent of the shares in their German and other subsidiaries. By acquiring the British shares, they would have no reason to discriminate against the British company in favour of the German or other subsidiaries. He was therefore going to allow the purchase to go ahead.

A lively debate in the House followed soon after. I stated that 'public relations had never been the strong point of the Ford Company. The way in which this news was broken to the British public and to the Ford employees was a very good example of these bad relations.' There were no sanctions to ensure the carrying out of promises that the majority of the directors would remain British and nearly 100 per cent of components in Ford cars continue to be made here. I thought some government-appointed directors were needed to safeguard British interests. I was followed by Godfrey Lagden, the Tory MP for Hornchurch, who had been well briefed by the Ford Company; he attacked me for 'carrying on a sort of running battle with Ford's for years.'

The acquisition of 100 per cent of the shares in Ford in Britain by Detroit was followed by an increase in the authority of Ford in Europe, which sought to co-ordinate production. Research staffs were cut as research was divided between Basildon and Germany. The same models were to be produced in different countries with the same components. All were to be produced where the firm found it most economical to do so. All the undertakings given to the British Government in 1960 were thus ignored. Such was the power of the great multi-national company!

The Ford Company long ignored the existence of Dagenham's MP. Suddenly to my surprise I was invited to see over their useful apprentices' school and found myself meeting some of the directors. After I had mentioned our lack of contacts, the firm introduced a series of annual meetings with MPs to brief them on the current position of the firm and development plans, similar in character to those given to shop stewards.

I had an amusing experience when I visited Ford's in the company of a Sudan delegation at the request of the Foreign Office. We went down the Thames to the plant by boat. A very lively man led the delegation. As we passed St Paul's he said: 'What is that?' 'St Paul's Cathedral' replied the Foreign Office representative. 'Why is it not in our itinerary?' 'We thought, being Muslim, you would not be interested!' 'I always like to see how the natives worship,' he replied. When we arrived at the jetty we started on a conducted tour of the works. After a few minutes he asked how long this would take. 'Half before lunch and half afterwards', was the reply. 'Get it all over in half an hour. One factory looks much the same to me as any other.' When we went into lunch with the Sales Manager he said: 'Where are the sherries?' 'Henry Ford laid down that no alcohol should be consumed at the plant.' 'I don't believe a word of it,' was the comment. In the course of the meal he stated that Ford sold a £1 million worth of cars, tractors and parts yearly in Sudan. He wanted an assembly plant put up — half the capital to come from Ford's and the other half from the Sudan government. In ten years he wanted it to manufacture there. He turned on the Sales Manager and said: 'Send someone to my hotel tomorrow who can take decisions, not just talk.' The Sales Manager looked horrified and said he would make inquiries.

What came of it I don't know. In the next revolution in Sudan this outspoken young man was bumped off!

I would like to conclude with a friendly story. At a social in the constituency, my wife and I were impressed by a young man who sang parts from operas. He told us he hoped for a singing career. A little later he told me he had won a singing scholarship at the Guildhall School of Music but it provided no maintenance. He was the eldest of a large family; his father was a labourer. I tried the Ministry of Education and every possible musical source in vain to obtain a grant for him. As he worked at Ford's I wrote to the Managing Director explaining the young man's case and asking whether the firm could act as a patron for him. A reply came back offering to transfer him to the Regent Street showroom and to fix his hours to enable him to attend the Guildhall School of Music. He accepted with enthusiasm and finally entered the Covent Garden chorus.

Some sources

Arthur G. Pearce (Secretary Dagenham Trades Council (1937–42))
Ford at War (1947) by Hilary St George Saunders
Danger over Dagenham (1947) edited by John F. O'Leary
Hansard
Dagenham Trading Estates Bill 1932
House of Lords Hearing: Petitions against from Essex County Council,
    Dagenham & Hornchurch Urban District Councils

22

The Search for Jessie Holliday

–A Historical Whodunit

When Beatrice Webb died in 1943 a fund was set up to commemorate her. This was contributed by members of the Labour Movement and personal friends. Winston Churchill was one of these. When the war was over, the Trustees, of whom I was Honorary Secretary, decided that a conference house for the use of all those engaged in adult education, especially in the Labour Movement, would be a worthy memorial.

Pasture Wood, a suitable country house near Dorking which could take up to 100 students, was acquired and renamed Beatrice Webb House. It is situated in beautiful surroundings in the Surrey hills. This proposal received her husband Sidney's blessing and their two elderly maids came over to the opening by the Prime Minister (Attlee) in 1947 and fully reported the proceedings to him.

When Sidney died some weeks later Barbara Drake, a niece of Beatrice and their executor, donated a number of the Webbs' possessions to the house including two large drawings of the Webbs. These were hung in one of the rooms and I fear I took little notice of them believing them to be copies. Some twenty years later my attention was drawn to them by an admirer of the Webbs and I had them cleaned.

It was now clear that they were original and unusual crayon drawings done when they were about 50 years old and at the height of their powers, whereas most pictures of the Webbs were done in their seventies after they had achieved fame. Who were they by? Their only signature was JH on the corner of each. Barbara Drake who had given them was now dead.

I unsuccessfully approached other relatives. Then I sought the help of the National Portrait Gallery and the Royal Society of Portrait Painters. The signature was unknown to them.

The back of each frame was then opened and inside each was found a faded typewritten note 'A crayon drawing by Jessie Holliday (later Mrs Dana) done about 1909'. One of the notes spelt the name 'Holiday': which was correct? This confirmed that they were done when Sidney was 50 and Beatrice 51. Who was Jessie Holliday?

I approached a number of survivors among people who had been active in the

114

Fabian Society, the Labour Party and the various women's movements of the time who might have known her, but without success. By chance I mentioned my search to an old friend, Surrey Dane, whose mother had worked for the Webbs in their campaign to break up the Poor Law after the publication of the Minority Report of 1909. He had long been associated with the *Daily Herald* and had been its Chairman from 1949—60 and a Vice-Chairman of its publishers (Odhams). We discovered much later that the Webbs had been so pleased with these two drawings that they had had them photographed and given signed copies to those who had helped in this campaign, including his mother.

Surrey Dane was keen to help and had useful contacts, including the editor of *Debrett*, once owned by Odhams. First an approach was made to the Royal Academy. Their records showed that Jessie Holliday had started as a student at the Royal Academy School of Painting in 1903 when she was 19 and had had a second term there between 1906 and 1908. She had exhibited a portrait entitled *Kathleen* in 1905 and in 1907 her picture called *The Reader* was accepted by the Royal Academy. After that there was no further record about her either under Holliday or Dana.

Next he examined a *Who's Who* of 1910 and found it contained two men who were artists and socialists, one spelt Holliday and another Holiday who might have been her father but neither had a daughter of the right age. Then he obtained a copy of Jessie's birth certificate which showed that she was born in Middlesbrough on 5 February 1884 and that her father, Henry Holliday, was secretary of an ironworks. There was no trace of her death certificate.

In the meantime I came across a genealogical dictionary which stated that Dana was an American name. Apparently a man named Dane had emigrated to New England in 1640 and had changed the last letter of his name to an 'a' and had many descendants. Only four subscribers of the name Dana appeared in the London telephone directory. Two of them replied in an American accent when rung up. A check on the Boston telephone directory showed thirty-seven Dana subscribers in that area. It looked as though Jessie had married an American.

To obtain further information I sent a letter to both the *New Stateman* and *Country Life*. The former refused to publish; the latter put it in on 13 June 1968. Headed 'The Art of Jessie Holliday', it described the crayon drawings of the Webbs and her career at the Royal Academy. It ended with the following plea 'Can anyone tell me whether she is still alive or any information about her subsequent history?'

The next day a letter was sent to me from a lady in Yorkshire who stated that she had in her possession two of Jessie's works:

a beautiful crayon portrait of my mother and a painting in oils of myself as a young girl. Otherwise I do not know much about her beyond the fact that she was a pupil of Sargent's and considered very talented. She came to my parents' home in Darlington about 1909 to do the two portraits. She was educated at the well-known Quaker school known as Polam Hall. She later

115

went to America to paint and married an American (the name Dana seems to ring a bell). She was quite a character and an ardent vegetarian and was drowned whilst bathing at a comparatively early age.

I next approached the Headmistress of Polam Hall School, who gave details of her school career and stated that their records showed that she had publicly announced in 1907 that she was open to receive portrait commissions, had married Edmund Trowbridge Dana at Cambridge Mass., USA, in 1912 and died 17 June 1915. She put me in touch with a school contemporary who paid tribute to her talent at drawing and sent me sketches she had made of girls and staff. Simultaneously Surrey Dane obtained a similar report of her early life but it gave the first name of her husband as Edward.

We next made inquiries at the American Embassy, the Museum of Fine Arts (Boston), the Archives of American Art (Detroit) and the Sargent School (Boston) but could find no trace of Jessie. On the offchance I picked on an Edward Dana from the Boston telephone directory (there was no Edmund) and asked if he knew anything of Jessie or her husband giving him all the information I had. After making a number of inquiries which were fruitless, he suggested that I contact the Boston newspapers and the *New York Times* for their reports on Jessie's marriage and death. The Boston papers were not helpful; they said their earlier issues were not indexed and they declined to do any research. They were not filed in this country.

The files of the *New York Times*, however, were at Colindale and my son examined them. These showed that Jessie and her husband, Edmund T. Dana, had jointly written their own marriage ritual (omitting the word 'obey'), which was performed in 1912 by a Justice of the Peace on the Longfellow estate in Cambridge, Massachusetts. Edmund was the son of Richard Dana,[1] a well-known Boston lawyer and grandson of a Richard Henry Dana[2] who was the author of *Two Years before the Mast* (1840); his mother was the daughter of Longfellow,[3] the poet.

Jessie's death in 1915 was first recorded as an accident whilst bathing but the next day the coroner stated it to be a suicide. Edmund had been working at the time at Minnesota University and in reply to a request to the *Minneapolis Star*, it sent Thermafax copies of their file cuttings on Mrs Dana's death which gave a sensational account of the tragedy.

This information was sent to Edward Dana who was then able to identify Edmund T. Dana and his family in the Dana genealogy. He had taken his PhD at Harvard in 1912 and got a post at a small college in Maryland, later moving to Minnesota University. Jessie had a son, Shaw Dana, who was born on 6 July 1914 (named after Bernard Shaw, he changed it to Dan Dana when he grew up). Eighteen years after Jessie's death, Edmund married a second time (in 1933) and had then moved to California to be near his son. After I had found Dan Dana's address at Los Altos, California, I wrote him a letter telling him of my search to date and asking for any further information of interest about his mother. His

116

wife replied stating that she had passed my letter to his father who lived nearby.

Edmund T. Dana sent me on 24 July 1969 a very full and fascinating account of how he met Jessie Holliday in 1910 at Llanbedr at a Fabian Summer School in Wales, where he had also met the Webbs and Aylmer Maude,[4] the translator of Tolstoy, but 'not Bernard Shaw who was Jessie's idol'.

In 1911 he had returned to England and saw much of Jessie. She was an enthusiastic supporter of the Food Reform Movement. Not only was she a vegetarian but she believed in only two meals a day and thought it harmful to eat more proteins and especially more carbohydrates than the system required. In fact she thought that most of the common diseases such as colds were the result of an excess of carbohydrates in the system.

After their marriage (1912) her husband believed that she was disappointed at the intellectual level they found at the small Maryland college where he worked compared with what she had been accustomed to in London. She longed for a child. 'She felt she knew the secret of life both as regards to food, physiology and psychology and that she could bring up a child who would really be something! (the age-long dream of mothers).' On account of the narrowness of her hips the birth had to be a Caesarian one. Her doctor disapproved of her ideas on diet but could not change her. He said she had built up no reserves and as a result was unable to breastfeed her baby. She became very depressed. Her husband was ill in bed with pleurisy whilst they were on holiday at Nantucket, Mass. She went for a walk before breakfast and her body was found floating in the sea. Despite the Coroner's verdict of suicide her husband was convinced after the doctors' examination that she had not drowned herself, but had so starved herself for years that she had died of heart failure and fallen into the water.

Edmund Dana possessed a book of photos of some of Jessie's English drawings especially those from 1909 to 1912. These included portraits of many distinguished people, particularly socialists, suffragists and other progressives. She did a remarkable water colour and many sketches of Bernard Shaw; Archibald Henderson[5] reproduced the water colour, *A Prophet, The Press and Some People*, in his first biography of Shaw in 1911. Hugh Dalton,[6] Aylmer Maude, William Archer,[7] Clifford Allen,[8] Mrs Blanco White,[9] and Sargent Florence[10] were among her sitters. Jessie also had some drawings accepted by *Punch* and said she was prouder of this than of having paintings accepted by the Royal Academy.

After reaching the United States, Jessie limited her work largely to members of her husband's family, doing a water colour of Alice Longfellow, the poet's daughter. She did a lively sketch of Norman Angell[11] when he was on a visit to America.

So Jessie Holliday had been found after two years' search! What a tragedy that her talent had been cut short so soon.

23

The Sunday Freedom Filibuster

During the winter of 1949 the English Table Tennis Association decided to hold their annual South of England Championship at Hastings on an out-of-season Saturday and Sunday. This they had done at various resorts for many years. Their application was granted by the Hastings Corporation and arrangements, together with publicity, went ahead. The Lord's Day Observance Society then stepped in and insisted that it should not be allowed to take place on the Sabbath. After legal consultation and the threat of action by a Common Informer the tournament was reluctantly cancelled with a heavy financial loss. This was possible because such activities were paid for by an entrance fee from all competitors.

Sunday Freedom Association set up

Kenneth Day, Hastings's Entertainments Manager, was so disgusted by this action of the Lord's Day Observance Society that he organized a public protest meeting at the White Rock Pavilion on a Sunday evening and invited 'Misery' Martin, the General Secretary of the Lord's Day Observance Society, to debate with Hannen Swaffer, a well-known journalist. 'Misery' Martin walked all the way from London to take part so as not to use public transport.

The meeting was widely attended and secured much publicity. Those present included representatives of the English Table Tennis Association, the Musicians' Union, and all the organizations connected with the theatre and music hall.

A constituent, a member of the Table Tennis Association, who had suffered from the ban on the Hastings Championship, approached me to support the creation of an organization to fight the Lord's Day Observance Society. I had been outraged in 1941 during the war by the action of Sabbatarians in the House of Commons when they had defeated Herbert Morrison's proposal to allow theatres and music halls to open on Sundays if local authorities agreed by 144/136. I therefore willingly agreed to act as Parliamentary Adviser to the Sunday Freedom Association when it was set up to secure the repeal of the

118

Sunday Observance Acts 1625—1780 in order that people could please them-selves what they did with their leisure time on a Sunday.

Within a few weeks of the meeting he had organized, Kenneth Day tragically died. The proposed organization nevertheless went ahead with the backing of those interested, with Bill Sensier acting as Secretary; Jack Warner, a popular TV star, agreed to act as President. As a past President of the Variety Concert Artists, he said he had first clashed with the Lord's Day Observance Society many years before over Sunday concerts for charity. 'I happened to be wearing a straw hat for the act I was doing at the time, and they said I was breaking the law by so doing, which certainly opened my eyes as to how silly the law can be over this particular matter.'

Shortly afterwards Herbert Morrison introduced his Festival of Britain Bill (1950). This was passed but a clause enabling an entrance charge to be collected at the Festival Gardens funfair was defeated (389—134) on a free vote. This was despite the fact that Lionel Heald, a leading Conservative lawyer, had pointed out that: 'In the Sunday Observance Act, 1780, we have an extraordinary and archaic provision. 57 funfairs are open on Sundays. To charge for entry is illegal. To charge for going on a roundabout is legal. There is only one body of people on whom the blame can be laid for this state of affairs and that is everyone who is an MP.'[1]

Despite the vote, roundabouts at the Festival Gardens continued to operate on Sundays!

My first Bill, 1953

I had raised the whole question of the obsolete character of the Sunday Observ-ance Laws earlier in that debate. In 1953 I won the third place in the ballot for Private Members' Bills and decided to introduce a Sunday Observance Bill to repeal existing legislation and allow theatres and cinemas to open subject to local option and a contribution to charity from profits; sports, circuses and funfairs were to be free from control in relation to Sunday opening. I had won an early place (30 January) in the ballot, which meant drafting a Bill for publication sometime before. The Sunday Freedom Association had no Bill ready, neither had any of the other interested parties. I had hurried consultations with the theatrical managers who were divided in their views and disliked the prospect of local option.

The Bill caused a considerable furore in the media and among MPs. It soon became clear my Bill had little prospect of getting a Second Reading, but many MPs said they would support a proposal for an inquiry into the Sunday laws. Unfortunately, I went down with flu a week before the Bill came up and got out of a sickbed to speak. I was, therefore, unable to rally support for an inquiry. The Lord's Day Observance Society organized a massive campaign against the

Bill. This took the form of getting a large number of churches and chapels to preach against it and to give away stamped addressed postcards at their doors to be signed and mailed to local MPs. A monster petition, said to contain 512,735 signatures, was presented to the House. There was no comparable propaganda on the other side. The Bill was defeated by 281/57. A proposal by Eric Fletcher that a Royal Commission be appointed failed by 172/164. The Welsh MPs at the last moment decided to oppose this proposal.

I received a large mail, mostly abusive (325 letters against my Bill, and only 85 for). One Christian gentleman wrote: 'May your eyes be gouged out and may I be there to see.'

The Bill, however, produced widespread discussion. There were a large number of debates on TV, radio and elsewhere, which showed up the fanaticism of the Lord's Day Observance Society's spokesmen such as 'Misery' Martin and Harold Legerton. I myself debated the issue at many university debating societies, including some in Wales, and found general support. The demand widened to include a growing number of sports which sought Sunday play and spectators. As an interested viewer of historic buildings, I persuaded the Minister of Works to open the Tower of London on Sundays in summer, and got it to open most other places in its care, such as Carisbroke Castle. The National Trust gradually found Sunday to be the most popular viewing day and sought to open its houses on that day whenever possible, as did private owners anxious to receive paying visitors. Lionel Heald went ahead and got his Bill through to abolish the Common Informer (1953); this cut the ground from under much of the work of the Lord's Day Observance Society. This went through despite his comment that everyone treated the subject like a red-hot poker.

Pressure on the Government to set up a Royal Commission grew, but without success. In 1958 Denis Howell, a football referee, moved a motion asking for a Select Committee to review the law on Sunday Observance. The Home Office thought such a committee would only reflect the cleavage in public opinion, but agreed if the House so decided. At the end of the debate the motion that the question be now put was carried by 54/31, but fell short of the necessary 100 to secure the closure. The question therefore lapsed.

Meantime, pressure also developed to extend the Sunday opening hours of licensed premises; the government, therefore, decided to extend midday opening from 2.00 p.m. to 3.00 p.m. This proved very unpopular with housewives because of the fear that the Sunday joint would be ruined and led the government to drop the proposal. I remembered that when I first came to London I frequently went 'to the pictures' on a Sunday evening only to find it too late to have a beer with my meal when I came out. I, therefore, suggested on committee that instead Sunday evening opening should be extended from 10.00 p.m. to 10.30 p.m. to enable drinks to be taken after the cinema or other entertainments. This was finally agreed on Report (5 June 1961).

The Crathorne Report

Further pressure on the Government finally led the Home Secretary (Butler) in 1961 to appoint a Departmental Committee to review the law on Sunday observance. The Chairman was Lord Crathorne (formerly Sir Thomas Dugdale) and four of its other seven members were drawn from the House of Commons; many shades of Christian opinion were represented, but no active reformers.

After three years of deliberation, its report appeared in December 1964. Evidence was collected from a wide variety of sources. Most of the Church bodies urged that the traditional character of Sunday should be kept for the well-being of national and family life. The LDOS wanted legislation strengthened to prevent evasions! TV, radio, cinemas and all sport should be prohibited on Sundays. There was, however, a wide acceptance that anomalies in the law ought to be removed. The Association of Police Officers stated that some aspects of the law were obsolete and difficult to enforce; this was bringing the whole concept of law into disrepute.

The recommendations of the Committee were more forthright than had been expected. It proposed the repeal of the 1625, 1677 and 1780 Acts and sought to make all entertainments permissible on Sundays which were allowed on week-days, except between 2 a.m. (3 a.m. in the West End) and 12.30 p.m.

On the question of sport there had been deep divisions of opinion among sporting bodies. Against any change in the law were the Football Association, the Football League, Rugby Union and the National Greyhound Racing Society; in favour of some relaxation were the Rugby League, British Boxing Board of Control, the Jockey Club, National Hunt Committee, the RAC, the Auto-Cycle Union and the English Table Tennis Association. The Crathorne Committee attempted a compromise! Sunday sport should only be prohibited if players and participants were paid for taking part. No betting should be allowed at race courses on Sunday.

The political situation was unstable as a Labour government had just been elected with a tiny majority and another election was likely at any time. A sympathetic debate in the Commons only took note of the report. The Home Secretary (Sir Frank Soskice) stated that legislation would have to come from private Members.

Willis's Bill, 1966

It so happened soon after that I led a Delegation to the Windward Islands, of which Lord Willis (Ted Willis), an old friend, was a member. We discussed the whole question of Sunday entertainments and he agreed to go ahead with a Bill in the Lords, which I agreed to take over if passed and try to push through the Commons.

After the 1966 election the Home Office was more sympathetic and gave

Willis the help of official draftsmen when he introduced a Bill (November 1966). It was limited to England and Wales and followed the Crathorne recommendations with two main exceptions. First, the starting time for events was to be 2 p.m. and not 12.30 p.m. Secondly, it contained no ban on professional sport. The Second Reading went through without a Division. On Committee stage, the only vote – to omit Wales – was defeated 28/9; on Report, the Bishop of Leicester tried to define more closely the type of 'spectacle' to be allowed on a Sunday. This was defeated 79/33. There was no time to take the Bill in the Commons; it therefore lapsed.

Hamling's Bill, 1967

Next session William Hamling took up the Willis Bill. He was ninth in the ballot and would have restricted time for the debate as the chair was certain not to accept a closure motion. For this reason the attendance at the Second Reading debate was thin. As 4 o'clock approached, I was on my feet discussing the origin of the Sabbath among the Jews in Babylonia during their captivity. I sat down a few seconds before the hour, having created the impression I was going to talk the Bill out. No one rose to continue the debate and the chair called a Division, when the Second Reading was carried (29/18). Our opponents were taken completely by surprise and could still have succeeded if they had remained out of the lobby, as at least 40 MPs must vote if a Division is to be valid.

With a sympathetic chairman, the Committee stage was completed in four sessions. A challenge to professional sport on Sunday was defeated by 11/8. Two amendments designed to check noise and defend the peace of worshippers were defeated by the casting vote of the chairman. The exclusion of Wales from the Bill was defeated 7/5, but a subsequent provision was added that there should be a local poll on the lines of the Sunday drinking laws. Meanwhile, a motion was put down on the Commons Order Paper urging the Government to bring in legislation on the lines of the Crathorne Report (i.e. the Hamling Bill minus professional sport).

On the Report stage, the Bill ground to a halt and was destroyed. Two whole Fridays were devoted to the measure, but little progress was made. This was mainly due to the fact that we sponsors could not muster the 100 votes necessary to get the closure on any amendment. The keen opponents numbered only 30, but this was enough to prevent progress. We could only rally about twice that number. A determined filibuster by Sir Cyril Black (the wealthy Tory Baptist) stopped the chance of further progress without government assistance through extra time, which was not forthcoming.

During the debates increasing concern was shown about noise and disturbance which might arise from professional sport on a Sunday, especially from football crowds. If there was trouble on a Saturday afternoon, why add to it on a Sunday? To meet this objection help was obtained from the Home Office to draft a clause to allow a local authority to apply to magistrates to prohibit Sunday use of premises for competitive sport if residents in the area had been unreasonably disturbed by such use on Sunday. A magistrates' order would have effect for three years.

My Second Bill, 1969

I drew the third place in the 1968 Private Members' ballot, but unfortunately chose the eighth and last Second Reading Friday in February 1969. This error was due to the hope that Willis would be able to get the Bill first through the Lords and then I could take it up in the Commons. I was not advised that this was not possible until it was too late to change the date for my Second Reading debate. Led by Sir Cyril Black, the Sabbatarians rallied strongly for the Second Reading debate. Every effort was made by bodies in support of the Bill to rally MPs and to counteract the pressure of the LDOS. The closure was carried by 113/84; the Second Reading by 104/95 and a motion to refer the Bill to a Committee of the whole House was defeated by 85/71. The small majority meant that supporters of the Bill had a majority of only one on the Committee and, as this was Denis Howell who had often to be absent on government business, we had a difficult time before us. The Bill excluded Scotland and Northern Ireland. None the less, nine Scots and seven Northern Irishmen voted against the Bill; the absence of Welsh Members was due to an arragement Hamling had made with them to stay away in return for a Welsh option clause. Taking English and Welsh Members alone, the vote for the Bill was 105/81, a much more substantial majority.

The Committee met twice a week. Excluding the Chairman, there were 19 Members — ten Labour and nine Tories. All Labour MPs save two supported the Bill; all Tories save two opposed it. A gigantic filibuster at once developed. It took nineteen sittings and over sixty hours to pass through Committee. Many of the sittings lasted much longer than the usual two-and-a-half hours; the nineteenth sitting lasted from 4.15 p.m. to 11.06 p.m. Despite the filibuster, the Bill emerged substantially unaltered save for the removal of the clause for local option for Wales, which opponents succeeded in defeating in the hope that it would lead Welsh MPs to vote against the Bill at later stages. The speeches of opponents were long and repetitive. A very incompetent and unsympathetic Chairman allowed them to wander far from the issue under debate and permitted new clauses — for example, to restrict pool betting on Sunday — to be introduced which were outside the scope of the Bill.

The filibuster succeeded in that by the final sitting — 15 July 1969 — all the time available for Private Members' Bills was used up. Douglas Houghton, the Chairman of the PLP, had successfully pressed for extra time at night to be found if necessary, to see Private Members' Bills through when there had been strong support shown for the Bill in the House. He urged the Cabinet that a similar course should be taken with the Sunday Entertainments Bill. Against this it was argued that the majority on the Second Reading had been small. George Thomas, the Welsh Secretary, thought it would damage the Labour Party in Wales at the next election. The removal of Roy Jenkins from the Home Office had removed a strong supporter from that position of influence. So the Bill failed to get the necessary extra time.

Why the Bill Failed

How came it that the Bill failed to become law when it had substantial support at the polls? The Gallup Poll had shown 64 per cent in England and 62 per cent in Wales in favour. Only in the older age group, those over 65, was there a majority against the Bill. This support at the polls was in striking contrast to Private Members' Bills on subjects as controversial as capital punishment, abortion and homosexuality, where Parliament had anticipated public opinion in its voting.

It has been my experience that where MPs have strong views on an issue, they vote in accordance with them. If they have no strong views, then they are influenced by pressure put on them in their constituencies. The vast majority of MPs were able to do whatever they wanted on a Sunday and did not themselves feel restricted by the obsolete laws. They were inclined to sympathize with those who feared a noisy Sunday afternoon.

Credit must be given to the LDOS for their fanatical devotion and energy in opposing any change in the law, particularly in the earlier stages of the controversy. Their opponents were not so well organized and sought different ends. The theatrical managers gradually came to support Sunday opening; actors remained divided, although it appeared that a majority of the younger ones were sympathetic. The cinemas faced with continued decline in audiences, wanted an abolition of local option restrictions on Sunday opening and of the 'charity levy' on takings on that day. Sports organizations increasingly came to the fore in the Sunday Entertainments campaign.

It has been suggested that the Bill would have gone through if the Crathorne recommendations to exclude professional sport had been adopted. This may well have been the case, but considerable trouble would have resulted. Every sport is affected by shamateurism. Large numbers of so-called 'amateurs' receive some kind of remuneration to meet their 'expenses'. Continual controversy would have arisen in many circles if the Crathorne proposals on this issue had become law. Quite rightly, the major sports organizations strongly opposed proposals they regarded as impossible effectively to enforce.

The main reason for the failure of the Bill to become law was the change in public opinion, which led to the increasing disregard of the Sunday laws. The law forbidding a charge for entry was got round. Motor racing at Brands Hatch was ruled illegal in a test case brought by the LDOS against the organization running it. By dropping payment for entry and introducing parking fees, the organization was able to continue its activities. Under royal patronage polo likewise covered its expenses from parking fees. Cricket, of the major sports, survived through Sunday play made possible by charges for programmes and parking. Rugby League did the same. As the law was 'got round', the pressure to alter it was greatly reduced. The main battle was transferred to the possible noise and rowdiness of football disturbing a Sunday afternoon — quite a different issue from the religious Sabbatarianism of the LDOS.

The change in public opinion has resulted from the decline of Nonconformity in Wales as well as in England. The number of churchgoers has dropped significantly and those who are devout Sabbatarians even more. The various Bills brought into Parliament since 1953 played a large part in the change of opinion about behaviour on Sunday. The media, particularly TV and radio debates, did much to alter public opinion on the whole question.

Changes of the law have continued. The Sunday Observance Acts of 1625 and 1677, which had been strongly supported by the LDOS, were quietly repealed in 1969 as part of the Statute Laws (Repeals) Act. The Cinema Act (1972) removed restrictions on Sunday opening. Hugh Jenkins's Theatres Act (1972) gave theatres the right to open on Sundays. An agreement still remains to be reached between Equity (the Actors' Union) and the theatre managers as to the terms on which theatres may open in London.

I made a last plea for my Sunday Entertainments Bill (March 1971) in the new Parliament of 1970 and lost the vote on a Ten Minute Rule Bill by 116/113. The need for such a Bill has now largely disappeared. Certainly there is no strong pressure for it.

However, the 1780 Act, forbidding a charge for entry, remains on the Statute Book. It remains a testimonial to British hypocrisy which refuses to bring the law into line with current practice, but prefers to 'get round' this Sabbatarian survival.

What a curious history British Sabbatarianism has pursued. Unlike Continental Protestants — even Calvinists — the British Puritans decided to attach the attributes of the Jewish Sabbath to our Sunday. Those who proclaimed the right of the individual to think for himself and worship as he pleased insisted on dictating to those who differed from them as to their behaviour on a Sunday.

Some sources

Sunday Freedom Association Minutes
Hansard
Bill Sensier
Lord Willis
Denis Howell
Peter G. Richards *Parliament and Conscience*

24
The Changing Commons

I first became an MP in 1935 and am the only one who has served continuously since before the War. I became Father of the House in 1979.

I have seen big changes during that time in the types becoming MPs. Despite the decline in the reputation of Parliament, I believe the individual quality and ability of MPs today is far higher than it was in the 1930s. Then there were many gaps on both sides of the House where knowledge was lacking. Nowadays on most subjects there are half-a-dozen MPs who can debate with some knowledge. Trade and industry, however, are fields in which knowledge seems most lacking on both sides.

Changes in personnel

The personnel of the House has greatly changed in character since the 1930s. On the Labour side the trade-union-sponsored Members were over half in 1935; they remained nearly half, with 131 out of 268 in 1979. The proportion falls whenever there is a Labour majority, as a large number of the safer seats are held by sponsored MPs. Of these some now appear to have had little previous connection with their sponsoring body. Miners and railwaymen formed a high proportion in the 1930s. With the drop in their industries, they have been replaced largely by engineers and 'white collar' workers sponsored mostly by the AUEW, general workers' unions and ASTMS. Miners had 16 MPs in 1979, compared with 32 in 1935 and 37 in 1950.

There were only 12 graduates out of 154 Labour MPs in 1935, almost all Oxbridge and public school; 53 university and polytechnic lecturers and school teachers with 33 managers and executives dominated the non-trade union element in 1979. They thus replaced the small businessmen (George Lansbury was a master builder) and small shopkeepers of the 1930s, who, apart from the small group of Co-op MPs (9 in 1935; 17 in 1979) formed so large a part of the PLP. Trade-union-sponsored MPs included many union officers. Jim Griffiths and Arthur Jenkins had been President and Vice-President respectively of the

South Wales Miners' Federation and took an active part in its affairs after becoming MPs. George Isaacs long continued as General Secretary of NATSOPA (National Society of Operative Printers and Assistants) after his election to the House. Today no union will allow an officer elected as an MP to continue as such, save in an honorary post, although a number of former union officials have entered the House.

The Conservative Party in the 1930s was largely dominated by the country gentry and farmers, retired military men and lawyers. There were some business-men, many of whom continued to run their own businesses. A number of firms welcomed an MP on their board, especially the larger family business, to keep them in touch with what was happening in the political world. There were many heirs to peerages.

Businessmen provided far the largest group of Tory MPs in 1979 with 188 out of 339 (82 directors, 52 executives, 17 underwriters, 12 in 'banking', 12 account-ants and 8 'economists'). But few seem to have had practical experience in large-scale industry. I feel that a large number of the young men from the City see Parliament as just a stepping-stone to be discarded on their way up if found an obstacle to their further advancement. There were only 14 lecturers and teachers and 25 farmers and landowners. In all, 204 out of 339 Tories came from public schools (1979); 50 from Eton.

No less than 102 lawyers (75 barristers, 27 solicitors) were elected in 1979 (70 Tories, 31 Labour). Lawyers are finding it increasingly difficult to combine their job with that of being an active MP. Many advise organizations and only appear in the courts when these are involved in litigation. The great days of F.E. Smith, Carson, Cripps and Patrick Hastings are past. Few MPs now go on to become judges. In contrast, journalists and authors (52) seem to flourish (31 Tory, 19 Labour).

Many Labour MPs, as in the 1930s, have had experience in local government and in trade union work, especially as research officers. Many others have worked for the Labour Party or the Fabian Society. A big increase has taken place in recent years in the number of Tory MPs who have taken part in local government and/or have worked for research bodies. In both parties it is an advantage to have worked for ministers or their shadows.

In 1979 433 of the 635 MPs were graduates; of this number there were 256 Conservatives (169 Oxbridge) and 165 Labour (58 Oxbridge). In the October 1974 election there were almost as many Labour graduates as Conservative. Many Labour MPs have also attended adult education colleges such as Ruskin, or been active in the Workers' Educational Association.

The number of women MPs remains low despite the advent of a woman Prime Minister. In 1935 9 out of 615 MPs were women. Only 19 (11 Labour and 8 Conservative) out of 635 were elected in 1979 (27 in October 1974), the lowest number since 1951.

The average age of MPs was much higher in the 1930s than today. Many trade union officials and business executives then 'retired' into Parliament in their sixties. It was thought their experience would be of value, but they found it difficult to adjust themselves to active politics. The average length of service today is just over sixteen years[1] compared with fifteen years[2] in the 1930s.

The few prominent businessmen and trade unionists who have entered Parliament in their prime have rarely been successful in the House. Ernest Bevin hated listening to criticism and Olive Lyttleton resented 'fractious opposition'. The majority of successful politicians need to enter the House in their forties at least — and certainly not later than their early fifties if they are to 'learn the job'. Most MPs are in those age-groups today.

During the whole period between 1935 and 1980 intensely strong feeling between the two sides of the House only erupted over the Spanish Civil War and the Suez Crisis. I can remember Philip Noel Baker being howled down as a warmonger when making a plea for collective security whilst Hugh Gaitskell's attacks on the Eden government were deeply resented. Labour MPs have felt strongly about the Trade Union Acts in 1972 and 1980 to the surprise of Conservative government supporters, but they did not respond angrily.

Co-operation between MPs

Despite the fact that they eat at separate tables, co-operation between MPs of different parties, when interested in the same subject, has always been a feature of Parliament. This has enabled a number of important Private Members' Bills to get on to the statute book. Joint pressure from both sides of the House has frequently been put on the government of the day. For example the Labour Arts & Amenities Committee found out that a site adjacent to the National Gallery was on the market. They approached the similar Conservative Committee and a joint deputation to Selwyn Lloyd, then Chancellor of the Exchequer, persuaded him to buy it. An extension was built some years later. As Chairman of a Labour Forestry Group, I have worked closely with Lord Dalkeith (now Duke of Buccleuch) and succeeding Chairmen of the Conservative Forestry Group to organize visits to forests and to press the need for more planting to diminish the need for foreign timber imports. The growth of committee work has greatly increased co-operation between their members in frequent attempts to get unanimous recommendations when reporting to the House.

The whole practice of Pairing, which makes possible activities away from the House, depends on goodwill on both sides. It has been interrupted from time to time when feeling has run high on some issue, but mutual convenience soon leads to its return.

New Members coming into the House are usually surprised by the friendly relations between Members across the floor. Patrick Cormack told me that when he first took his seat in the Chamber after his election in 1970 he sat next to Boyd Carpenter and, looking across at the Labour benches, remarked, 'It is good to have a look at the Enemy.' Boyd Carpenter replied, 'Those on the other side of the House are our political opponents, your enemies you will find are on this side of the House.'

The advent of the Social Democratic Party (SDP) and its alliance with the Liberals seems likely to create a powerful third force in British politics. This departure from the two-party system which has dominated the scene since 1931 could have a profound effect on the working of Parliament and the electoral system. I think, however, it is unlikely greatly to change the type of MP being elected or the relations between MPs of different parties.

Sartorial changes

Over the years the House has rather belatedly followed the fashions of the groups from which it has been drawn. Thus, in the first Parliament (1833) after the Reform Bill it still included three MPs wearing tie wigs.

The overwhelming Conservative victory in 1931 seems to have triggered off a return to Edwardian styles among its younger members wearing morning coats and sometimes bringing their top hats into the House with them. About 25 continued this practice into the Parliament of 1935. The vast majority of MPs, however, wore lounge suits, many double-breasted, with a pullover or waistcoat. Some, particularly among the older men and lawyers, wore black jackets and striped grey (pepper and salt) trousers.

I well remember on a number of occasions seeing in the evening around the coal fires in the lobbies and libraries groups clad in tails and white ties after dining out awaiting the final vote at 11.00 p.m.

This Edwardian picture died during the war. Crookshank was the last Minister to sit at times on the front government bench in morning coat with his top hat beside him.

After 1945 morning coats continued to be worn by a few on 'occasions' such as the opening of Parliament, or when they had attended royal garden parties or Ascot or on a budget day. The two MPs for the City of London continued to sit so clad on the front government bench until their seats were abolished in 1950. Churchill soundly rebuked one of the MPs who replied to the Address in 1945 for wearing a lounge suit. Major Milner, the tall Deputy Speaker, continued to wear his morning suit and so established it as standard wear for those deputizing for the Speaker in the Chair. He thus continued the conservative tradition which had originally led the Speaker in the early 1700s to continue to wear what had been the normal wear of the majority of MPs at that time.

From 1950 the *Times Guide to the House of Commons* has shown photos of successive MPs. The Speaker's library has a series of photos of the new intake of 1945. The Conservative Research Department has a collection of Election Addresses, mostly with photographs, for the 1935 and 1945 elections. The Labour Party Records Office has photos of a number of the unopposed MPs, of whom there were forty in 1935 and two in 1945. From these various sources it is possible to make some assessment of changing fashions. The high starched stiff collar, usually winged, was worn by about 108 in 1935 and about 40 in 1945. It then steadily declined to 19 in 1950 and four in 1955 and then ceased. They continued to be worn mainly by lawyers and ex-miners such as Tom Williams, who always wore one until his retirement. The majority of MPs moved over to coloured shirts, frequently striped, gradually getting more highly coloured, although for a time many wore turndown stiff white collars with their white or coloured shirts.

Beards were won by a few elderly members in the 1930s. Four were among the older Labour intake in 1945. The House then remained beardless until the early 1950s when Sidney Silverman grew one only to be greeted by Attlee with 'Move Previous Face'; it was not shown in his *Times* photo until 1959: three beards appear in 1964 and the number rose to fifteen in February 1974 and twelve in 1979. Most of these were among the younger Labour MPs, although there were three Conservatives in February 1974.

The moustache has shown a spectacular decline. It is not always easy to detect just how much hair adorns the male's upper lip, but the number appears to have dropped from about 207 in 1935 to about 116 in 1945, 79 (1950), 60 (1959), 27 (1970) and to 16 (1979). The great majority were Conservative MPs, mostly from the shires. There were about 138 in 1935, 74 (1945), 57 (1950), 42 (1959) but only 6 in 1979. Labour moustaches dropped from about 99 in 1935 to 43 (1945), 22 (1950), 16 (1959) and down to 9 in 1979. Leading figures, such as Attlee, Macmillan and Eden, all wore moustaches, which no doubt encouraged their supporters to do likewise. Many, such as Douglas Home, Harold Wilson, Hugh Fraser and Joel Barnett, dropped them in due course. Gerald Nabarro turned his into a veritable handlebar as a distinctive feature.

A few MPs, seeking to look 'distinguished', wore their hair on the long side. Lloyd George and Jimmy Maxton were the best known of these. With the 1970s a large number, especially of younger MPs, wore their hair longer.

When women first entered the House they followed Lady Astor in wearing black. A photograph taken at her 25th anniversary (1944) showed all the sitting women MPs who were there and most of the former ones so clad. However, Ellen Wilkinson, who was not present, broke away and introduced colour into her dresses, a custom which was gradually followed by other women MPs.

Some sources

The Times Guide to House of Commons (1979)
Butler and Sloman *British Political Facts* 1900–1979
The Register of Members' Interests
The British M.P. by Colin Mellor
Ulster Unionists included in Conservative totals
Totals include minority MPs
Peter Cozens

25

MPs' Salaries and Re-employment, 1979

From a debate on an increase in MPs' salaries — Hansard (11 July 1979)

When I first became a Member of this House in 1935 the salary was £400 a year. It was not considered a salary but was intended to meet the expenses of a Member. A large number of Members at that time either had a job outside or private means. As Sir Derek Walker-Smith has said, there were many Members who had private means and who could sit in Parliament because they had private means. There was a large number of farmers, a large number of lawyers, and there were many businessmen who ran their own businesses. Sometimes these businesses were big and sometimes they were small. There were certain exceptions. There were the sponsored trade union Members. In their case, the £400 was considered as expenses and they were paid a salary by the union, which also provided them with secretarial and research assistance.

A great many of the Labour Members who were not sponsored in that way were small businessmen. George Lansbury was a master builder. A great many Members had been set up in business, running small shops for the sale of cigarettes or as newsagents, or working for themselves in the building trade. Very often they had been set up in business by friends after having lost their jobs owing to a strike.

That was largely the way in which Parliament was financed in the 1930s. The salary was regarded simply as expenses. People had to have other jobs in order to earn their living while they were in this House. I had been Secretary of the New Fabian Research Bureau. When I came into the House, I at once went on to half-salary, £150 a year, which I received in addition to the £400 a year salary for Members. That was done so that I should have a reasonable amount of money on which to live. It was considered to be right at that time.

Two years later, Attlee, who was then the Leader of the Opposition, came to the conclusion, after discussion with many of his backbenchers, that 'salaries' ought to be raised because they were inadequate. He had budgets kept by various Honourable Members, such as Ellis Smith. They prepared a good many figures showing what were the expenses of Members. On the strength of this information, Attlee went to Baldwin, who was then Prime Minister, and asked for discussions. He agreed that the 'salary' should be raised to £600 a year, and that

131

the Leader of the Opposition should be provided with a salary of his own. Attlee had small private means. He could, therefore, only employ research assistants who had an income of their own. Baldwin agreed to the rise on condition that 'it would not bring clever young men like Dick Crossman into the House'.

With due apologies to Enoch Powell, I point out that there was no question of this matter being voted not to come into operation until after the next election. Parliament decided that it was right to make the changes there and then. The government put down a Motion, it was passed by the House, and it operated from that time onwards.

Having seen what salaries were like in those days, I support the present proposals put forward by the government to try to provide an adequate salary for Members, to enable them to do their job properly.

There is one important aspect which has been neglected in the debate so far. I refer to the 130 Members who ceased to be Members of this House after the last General Election. There were 61 Members who retired, and 65 Members who were defeated. Many of them retired on pensions which were provided by the House. I have the honour to be the Chairman of the Pensions Fund of this House. We apply the rules laid down for that fund as generously as we can in order to meet the needs of Members and of the widows of Members. But it is still a fact that the majority of Members sit in this House only for an average of sixteen years. Many young men and women, therefore come into this House and go out again. That point has to be borne in mind when we are thinking of the remuneration of Members.

To my own knowledge, no fewer than six Members who were in the last House are in receipt of social security payments. That is a disgrace to this House. There is certainly redundancy pay for three months when a Member leaves the House, but some better arrangements ought to be made to enable people to come into this House from all sections of the population – something that we do not have at present. It is necessary if we are to have a democratic House of Commons. It ought to be made possible for a young man or woman with a family to be able to take the risk of fighting a marginal seat, coming into the House, losing the seat at a subsequent election, and then trying to get back again. There are no arrangements to cover young men or women in those circumstances, and these ought to be made.

Lord Carr, who was a Member of this House and at one time Home Secretary, was asked by the Confederation of British Industry to chair a working party with the object of trying to find out whether it would be possible to get into this House more Members with practical experience in business. As a result of the inquiry, various recommendations were made to the CBI which were of very considerable importance. He took the view that all firms of any reasonable size should allow their employees to stand as Parliamentary candidates for whatever party they chose, and that time should be provided to enable them to do the work of a prospective candidate. He also suggested that at least three weeks' leave should be provided if they wished to fight an election. Most important of all, it was recommended that anyone who got into this House and subsequently lost his seat should be taken back into employment by his firm for at least two years. Obviously, anyone in such a position could not expect to be re-employed in the position that he might have attained had he continued with the firm. The working party felt that there would be no difficulty whatever in placing these obligations on firms employing more than 500 persons with the normal large turnover of staff.

There was nothing new about that. The railways had such a rule long before they were nationalized. Some Honourable Members may remember Archie Manuel. Before entering this House he had been an express engine driver. When he lost his seat he resumed his work as an engine driver, driving trains between Glasgow and London. Later he won back his seat and returned to the House.

Michael Stewart was a sixth-form master at the Coopers' School in the East End of London. The old London County Council had a long-established rule by which persons who had worked for the LCC and then entered this House could come back into employment again if they lost their seats. Michael Stewart always paid his contribution as a teacher to the pension fund of the Council. Had he lost his seat at any time before retirement age for teaching, he would have been able at once to resume his occupation with the Council.

I recall that Fred Montague, who was a Member in the 1930s, lost his seat in 1931 and was reduced to selling stockings in the street. That sort of thing is not to the honour of this House.

I think, therefore, that we ought to take up the question of ensuring that there is an obligation on all public authorities and large firms to take back into their employment any former employee who, having got into the House of Commons, later loses his seat. I do not suggest that people should necessarily go back into the job they held before becoming Members. This obligation ought to apply to all firms or organizations employing more than 500 people. It obviously could not be made to apply to small firms.

If we are to have a democratic House of Commons in which there are men and women from all walks of life — and particularly young men and women with families — we shall have to make arrangements of the kind that I have suggested. They should not have to worry all the time about what will happen to them and their families if they lose their seats. Some such law or rule should be imposed by the House. I look forward to seeing whether something of that kind can be referred to the Boyle Committee for suggestions. There has been much talk of the re-selection of Members of Parliament. It is more important from a democratic point of view to ensure that men and women with family responsibilities can come here — given the risk that they may lose their seats at the next election.

26

Forty-two Days in the
Soviet Union, 1945

**AN INTRODUCTION WRITTEN IN NOVEMBER 1975
TO MY DIARY**

I kept a diary during this visit. As we travelled slowly and comfortably in one of the former Czar's trains on the Russian broad-gauge track, there was plenty of time en route to write it up in my compartment between stops. On my return I showed a typescript of the full text to many Labour leaders including Clem Attlee. Attlee strongly advised publication, recommending, however, that I should cut out anything which might offend Soviet susceptibilities. This I did, and published a much-shortened, and very Bowdlerized version in September 1945. (Recently I compared this version again with the original contemporary typescript — the original seemed to be of much greater interest and therefore worth publishing.)

This Bowdlerization did not save me from Soviet disapproval even before the cold war opened. Soon after my visit I addressed a number of meetings in various parts of the country, giving what I considered to be a friendly account of what we had seen. Quoting Stalin's advice, 'Tell the truth about our country, we have many things that are good and many that are not. Tell the truth about both', I made a few criticisms. Immediately I was excluded from the Soviet Embassy's invitation list and, incidentally, have not been on it since.

Following up the talks which took place during our visit, the British Delegation strongly pressed a rather sceptical Foreign Office and Ministry of Education to prepare a scheme for fifty scholarships to be awarded to Soviet students each year at British universities, each lasting for three years. A reciprocal scheme was also suggested for British students at Soviet universities. No reply was received to the proposal or to the subsequent reminder; the Soviet government had no intention of allowing their students to learn anything about the West.

Around the same time I also got the London County Council to suggest a plan for twinning with Leningrad which was sent to the Leningrad Soviet; again no reply was received. This continues to be the standard Soviet way of saying 'No'.

Eighteen years later

I took a Fabian school of about thirty persons to visit the Soviet Union in the summer of 1963. We travelled out across Europe by train and returned on a Soviet ship through the Baltic. Most of our time was spent in Moscow and Leningrad, though we did spend some days at Yalta in the Crimea.

There had been enormous progress in reconstruction in the eighteen years since 1945; great office and residential blocks were rising everywhere in the suburbs of both cities and were replacing wooden buildings in the centre. Already the Stalin 'wedding cake' style was being replaced by the conventional western style 'matchboxes'. Crowds in summer clothes filled the streets in the warm weather. Most of the population seemed reasonably well dressed in the European styles common in London a year or two before. However, all the male members of my party (age range 15—70) were approached in the streets and asked to sell their clothes, many of which were far from new. For the quality of their material was well above that of similar Soviet clothes. Many goods were still in short supply, and queues for food and clothes could be seen in both Moscow and Leningrad. There appeared to be a shortage of sales points and no need for good window dressing or advertising. Yalta still had much of the charm it had had for Chekhov, with little new building. However the stony beaches were crowded, as with rising living standards many Russians sought a holiday at the seaside. Some of my group, including my son of 15, visited the Town Hall and discussed plans for its future development with the woman Chief Planning Officer. 'We shall construct seven large fourteen-storey hotels to accommodate the growing number of tourists,' she claimed. 'Where will they bathe', asked my son, 'as the beaches are already full?' Somewhat surprised, she could only answer, 'We shall have to create some more beaches'!

Thirty years on

I again visited the Soviet Union in 1973, 1974 and 1975, and formed a fairly clear picture of its achievements and of the way of life of its peoples. Besides again visiting Moscow and Leningrad each year (which seems to be obligatory in any tour) I visited the Transcaucasian republics including Baku and Azerbaijan in 1973, and led National Trust parties to explore the architecture of Georgia and Armenia in 1974 and of Uzbekistan and Tajikistan in 1975.

How do Soviet achievements impress a British socialist? Industrialization continues at a rapid pace and living standards are rising. More goods are available in the shops, although not always of a high quality and efforts are now made to display them more attractively in the shop windows. I was told that there was a three-year waiting period for a private car. Cars are certainly numerous in the streets of larger towns. Per household Moscow appears to have about a third of the number of cars as Greater London.

The fixing of wages and salaries, it appears, continues to be on similar lines to those generally existing during the war. Those doing dangerous jobs in mining and the chemical industries are well paid. The large body of 'educational workers' — 4 million strong — and inclusive of teachers, dons and university research workers, is well paid and a well-organized pressure group. High salaries at top levels are frequently obtained by doing more than one job. Wages generally are not high compared with western standards — women go out to work to augment the family's income whenever possible. Rents and fares on public transport, however, are heavily subsidized, as are seats at the theatre, cinemas and concerts and for general enjoyment of the arts. Equal pay for the sexes is the rule, but jobs where women predominate tend to be lowly paid. We were told that 80 per cent of doctors are women and that they are a relatively lowly paid profession.

The position of women has continued to improve in the last thirty years. They hold a large number of places on the local Soviets and appear to have a considerable say in local affairs. We did not meet many, however, in important positions. The most dramatic changes in the position of women have occurred in the Muslim areas. One has only to compare their position with that in surrounding Muslim countries to appreciate the advance made. The veil has finally vanished everywhere. It was of interest that a local guide in Tashkent complained that only men went to funerals even if of a woman and that the women were expected to prepare the food and drinks for the returning mourners. Much the same as the practice still operating in Ireland and rural Wales!

The predominance of youth in executive positions, so noticeable during the war, is no longer striking. The generation that then came to the fore appears still to hold many responsible posts particularly at the higher levels.

Housing continues to be a problem, although rents are low. High-rise flats are the norm in all large cities and many include a number of facilities like shops and nursery schools in some of the large blocks. However, they do not appear popular, especially in summer, and the affluent sector of the community follow the practice of generals during the war of obtaining a piece of scrub in the country at a peppercorn rent, and building there a wooden holiday 'dacha'. The country is so large that this does not so far appear to have created planning problems. General land nationalization has certainly been a boon in planning land use; a short visit to Kiev showed an imaginative townscape taking advantage of the natural bluffs, the Dnieper and neighbouring woods, in grouping the high-rise blocks and allowing town planning to be closely co-ordinated with the public transport system. Some parts of Moscow likewise utilize the river and Lenin hills in their layout, and every effort has been made to preserve, and where necessary to restore, the centre of Leningrad. However, I felt that much of the modern development was disappointing and rather pedestrian. We saw a large estate of individual but standard houses on an estate in Tashkent built by a housing co-operative with government assistance. These co-operatives appear to be growing up in a number of places as a result of the strong desire to avoid high-rise blocks, especially in the smaller and medium-sized towns. Cats and dogs — and in fact all pets — continue to be noticeable by their absence. There can be no room for them in the small standard-sized flats. Only in the countryside are dogs kept to care for sheep and for other utilitarian purposes.

Moscow, which we were told in 1945, was to be limited to a population of 5 million, already tops 7.4 million (1975) and is still growing steadily. It appears increasingly to be a city of civil servants as it is the highly centralized administrative centre both for the Russian Republic and the whole Soviet Union. When many of the old factories were demolished they were being replaced by residential quarters. One of our Russian guides commented that living standards in Georgia and Armenia were higher than in Moscow. 'Yet these were lands we had conquered in the past.' This appeared to be due in part to the more favourable climate in Georgia and to the energetic Armenian drive — with some help from Armenians abroad — to rebuild their nation on the limited area of Soviet Armenia.

The Uzbeks and Tajiks of Central Asia also seemed to be fairly well-off. Their high birth-rates — double that of the Russians — has led to a big increase in population there in the last thirty years, which is worrying the Russians as to what its political effects may be if it continues. There being plenty of room for expansion of population in Russia and the birth-rate there having dropped dramatically, there is no drive there for family planning. To start such a drive in Central Asia might smack of racism.

There is an obvious resentment against too much control from Moscow in all of these four republics. Whilst there is strong local patriotism, this co-exists with a strong Soviet patriotism. Georgians and Armenians realize that the Russian connection gives them security from Turkey, and the enormous developments that have taken place in Central Asia since the Revolution, and the fact that their cotton, jute and other southern products supply the whole Soviet market, have strengthened their connection with Russia.

An extensive air network links all parts of their enormous country, a sixth part of the world's surface. Goods continue in the main to travel by rail in large wagons, which seems economically sound given the large distances. I saw no juggernaut lorries and most of the roads could not have carried them. We travelled on one of the main roads from Leningrad to Moscow as far as Novgorod and found that a dual carriageway ended at the suburbs and continued as an ordinary tarmac two-way road (1975). A good road had been built from Erivan to Tibilisi but many places of architectural interest in that area we wished to visit could not be reached because the roads were in bad condition.

A good system of public transport with buses, trolley buses and trams operates in all large towns with low fares. Underground railways have been built not only in Moscow but also in Leningrad, Kiev, Tashkent, Tibilisi, Sverdlovsk and Baku. They make a big public contribution; the more recent stations are simpler than the rather elaborate early ones on the Moscow underground but not unattractive architecturally even if more functional.

The general impression in the Union as a whole is of an intensely patriotic and highly disciplined conservative society. Many of the features — good and bad

— that struck me as distinctive thirty years ago not only continue but seem to have strengthened. People as a whole appear to do as they are told. This has some advantages that should not be underestimated in that society at its present stage of development. Litter, for example, is absent from the streets and public places. Petty crime does not appear to be extensive. Queues are not only general but orderly.

Bullying, however, by minor officials throwing their weight about is patiently accepted. Bureaucracy is rampant. If a particular case does not fit into the rules laid down from above that is just too bad. For few appear to have the authority to set the rules on one side or to bend them to meet a particular situation or a hard case. All such problems are either ignored or referred upwards for a long-delayed decision. In fact, a visitor frequently feels that Orwell's *Nineteen Eighty-four* has indeed arrived.

Drunkenness still appears to be a major problem. Two of the women on our party in 1975 returned to their hotel room in Moscow to find a man in one of their beds, a full bottle of vodka in his hand with an empty one beside him. On each floor there is a woman with a drawerful of bedroom keys to deal out as required to staff or visitors. The drunk had apparently helped himself to a key when this woman was relieving herself. All the staff on the floor rallied to remove him, and were thankful that the visitors took the affair as a joke and did not report it. To try and reduce the problem the Russians have raised the price of vodka substantially over recent years, but the effect has been limited. Kavass, a very light kind of beer, is sold widely, but there are no pubs. The Russians are thus denied the pleasures of moderate drinking and of chatting and relaxing in company. In Central Asia however, Chinese traditions have created the teahouse where families and friends can meet together either sitting cross-legged around a teapot on benches in the park or indoors in winter.

Education continues to develop, with the university courses available being closely geared to the foreseeable needs of the economy. Students' grants (stipends or maintenance allowances), we were told, were received by 82 per cent. Much of the education system throughout is incentive based, with special paid holidays, higher grants and other privileges for the more successful. Co-education, which had been dropped during the war, has returned. Schools continue at all stages in their own language for the children of the various nationality groups in the Soviet Union wherever their numbers are considerable. Despite the fact that they also learn Russian in such schools, as the 'lingua franca' of the Union, many of the technical and administrative classes in these groups prefer to send their children to specifically Russian schools as we noted in 1945.

The majority of schools are comprehensive, but specialist schools continue to grow. We visited a school for 1,000 pupils (aged 12–18) in Moscow in 1963 where all the teaching was in English. Essays on how the summer holidays had been spent sounded interesting and well written when read aloud. The staff, few of whom had been abroad, spoke good, if a little pedantically accurate, English. A number of such schools exist, and one or two in other languages. Many of the pupils in such schools are boarders, as they draw on a large catchment area. In fact boarding is common for the secondary age group as parents may move around the country as they change jobs, but usually leave their children at this age to continue their education at the same school. In such cases the parents are charged boarding costs on a means-test basis. We were told of a highly specialist school for mathematicians in Central Asia drawing on able pupils from the whole Union. It was believed able mathematicians developed early and were stimulated by argument with fellow mathematicians. Selective entry is an essential feature of such schools. For example, children entering an English school of the kind described above must clearly have some English, and are likely to have parents who had been abroad or held jobs in trade or diplomatic fields. It still appears to be the case, as noted during the visit in 1945, that a career open to talent co-exists with certain advantages for the children of the ruling classes.

University students, if they do not live at home, sleep in large dormitories with little privacy. So far, this massing of many students together has not produced any student revolts of the character seen in many other countries. On leaving, they are frequently sent to fill posts in the more remote parts of the Union, extra pay being available in the less developed and more backward areas. In the Kurile Islands, teachers received 100 per cent higher salary than in a large city. The more highly educated thus have little initial choice of job or place when they start work.

Despite the fact that so much of the higher education is tailored to expected economic needs, there is a high cultural level among the population as a whole in most of the arts. This is particularly so in ballet, theatre, opera and music, all of which are highly subsidized by the state to enable cheap tickets to be given to the public. Folk dancing and folk music are widely encouraged in the different republics, and widely practised by amateur groups. The circus continues to be a popular Russian entertainment. Swimming and football are widely enjoyed, especially on summer evenings and in indoor stadiums. Ice hockey and skating have increased in popularity.

How far have cultural developments outside the Soviet Union had influence inside? 'Socialist realism' continues to be orthodox. In 1963, on visiting the Hermitage, we had great difficulty in seeing the Impressionist pictures. This year these were included in the official tour, and our guide commented upon them appreciatively. But notices had been put up to explain how decadent this art was. In 1963 youngsters came up in the street to ask if any of our party had some pop records. This year (1975) the blare of western pop incommoded foreign visitors in all the main hotels in the mistaken belief it encouraged them to visit the Soviet Union. Many Soviet citizens, however, danced there with enjoyment to music of the Beatles and other pop singers of a few years before.

The most impressive achievement in the Soviet Union in the cultural field has been the work of architectural restoration. When I saw the burnt-out ruins of Petrodvorets in 1945 and was told the palace would be fully restored, I was indeed sceptical. By 1963 the exterior had been restored, and in 1974 the finishing touches were being made to the interior decorations, fully restored to the original designs of the reigns of Peter the Great and Catherine II. True, the Russians had removed the pictures, furniture and even the parquet floors before the Germans arrived, and so could replace them. Ceiling pictures, however, had presented a problem which had been admirably overcome by asking the various Leningrad art schools to paint suitable pictures in the style of the period. The restoration of Pavlovsk, Paul I's palace, the Kremlin towers and cathedrals in Moscow, and the medieval churches and monasteries at Novgorod have all been carried out or are proceeding with admirable care and historical accuracy.

The same approach has been made in the other republics, where the churches and monasteries of Georgia and Armenia are being lovingly cared for. The only Hellenistic temple in the Soviet Union, in a remote part of Armenia, which survived the advent of Christianity by becoming a country palace of an Armenian king, had been shattered in 1679 by an earthquake. All the stones of its Doric pillars being on the spot, we were able to see the finishing touches being given to its re-erection. The famous Registan of Samarkand, that magnificent ensemble of Muslim Central Asian architecture, had been under restoration in 1945. Much more restoration has been done in the last thirty years. The pull of foreign tourist trade is likely to speed up further work.

How extensive is religious freedom? Here there appears to be a substantial difference between Russia and the other republics. In both Georgia and Armenia the local church is closely identified with their own nationalism; the cathedrals and main churches are in use for services and the state appears to support the maintenance of their structure. In 1973 we heard an admirable concert of religious music in a ruined church on a hilltop in Georgia as a cultural, not religious, event. In Russia, a large number of cathedrals and churches have been converted into museums. Congregations in open churches appear to consist largely of women and old men, although we had complaints that there were not enough open for the use of would-be worshippers — a difficult matter to judge as the Orthodox only visit churches on special occasions. The famous anti-God museum in St Isaac's Cathedral in Leningrad, which is mainly an attack on Rome and the Inquisition, had been relegated to the Crypt (1974) and the main museum in the body of the building had become a study of man and his religious beliefs through the ages. Fear of Muslim opposition to the regime and the changes it has effected and is effecting is strong. There is thus still a very high-powered attack on Islam in all the Muslim areas.

What of political freedom? It was not possible to discuss this with many during my visits. I formed a strong opinion, however, that the 'intellectuals' — using the word in its widest sense — tended to be as critical of government and indignant at limitations on their freedom as they had been under the Czar. Likewise, they had no very clear alternative to government policies. It was interesting to note that the only place where statues and pictures of Stalin could be seen were in his native Georgia, although our party were surprised in the marketplace of

Samarkand to be given pro-Stalin leaflets — presumably some local official held those views and allowed their circulation.

Anti-Semitism can be felt. Trotsky is always denounced as a Jew. Marx is never referred to as being one. When in Georgia, wandering round the streets at night, a number of us found a brightly lit building and thought it might be a bingo hall. To our surprise, it turned out to be a synagogue. Some function was just ending and we were welcomed in English by those who thought we were British Jews. These Georgian Jews appeared fairly prosperous and gave no sign of wanting to emigrate.

INTRODUCTORY NOTE
WRITTEN IN SEPTEMBER 1945
TO THE CAUSE OF ANGLO–SOVIET
FRIENDSHIP AND CO-OPERATION

Towards the end of 1944 it was decided to send an all-party Parliamentary delegation to the Soviet Union as a goodwill mission. This was to be representative of all broad sections of British opinion and was selected by Mr Speaker and the Lord Chancellor. Of the eight MPs and two peers, four were Conservative, three Labour, one Liberal, one Liberal National and one Independent. Two only of the party (Lord Faringdon and Wilfred Roberts) had been to the Soviet Union before — some ten years earlier.

The delegates had a wide variety of interests. Seven were university graduates and a large number had some connection with food production.

The party went out to USSR by the northern route (via Stockholm and Helsinki) and returned by the southern route (via Tehran, Cairo, Marseilles). The main delegation was forty-two days in the Union but some of its members had to return early.

Everywhere they went they received a very cordial welcome, both from the people and from government circles. Doors were opened everywhere and the members of the delegation were allowed to see whatever interested them. All of the delegates returned feeling that the friendships and contacts they had made and the knowledge they had acquired would strengthen Anglo-Soviet friendship. It is to be hoped that a return delegation will not long be delayed.

Here is a full and frank record of what happened and how it struck one member of the delegation. It is published in full agreement with Marshal Stalin's excellent advice on the best way to improve relations between our two countries: 'Tell the truth about our country. We have many things that are good and many that are not. Tell the truth about both.'

The following 'potted biographies' give some particulars of the delegation, including the author.

Right Hon Walter Elliot

Age 56. Leader of the Delegation. Conservative MP for Glasgow (Kelvingrove), (1924—45) and for Lanark (1918—23). Minister of Agriculture, 1932—6; Secretary of Scotland, 1936—8; Minister of Health, 1938—40; Director of Public Relations, War Office, 1941—2; Chairman of Commission on Higher Education in West Africa, 1944. A doctor.

Major Reginald Manningham Buller

Age 40. Conservative MP for Daventry since 1943. A lawyer. Parliamentary Secretary, Ministry of Works (May—August 1945).

Lord Faringdon

Age 43. Labour peer who has specialized in colonial and foreign debates in the Lords. Grandson of a railway magnate. A wartime fireman.

Tom Fraser

Age 34. Labour MP for Hamilton since 1942. PPS (Parliamentary Private Secretary) to Hugh Dalton, President of the Board of Trade, 1944—5. Joint Parliamentary Secretary, Scotland from August, 1945. A former miner.

P.W. Jewson

Age 74. Liberal National MP for Great Yarmouth, 1941—5. Lord Mayor, Norwich, 1934—5. Director of Jewson & Sons, Timber Importers (from USSR and other countries).

Commander Stephen King-Hall

Age 52. Independent MP for Ormskirk, 1939—45. Retired from the Royal Navy, 1929. Broadcaster and journalist. Founder of Hansard Society.

Lord Lovat

Age 34. Conservative peer. Head of Fraser clan, DSO, MC. Brigadier-General (trainer of Commandos), wounded during the invasion of France. Scottish Catholic landowner and farmer.

John Parker

Age 39. Labour MP for Romford, 1935—45 and for Dagenham since 1945. General Secretary, Fabian Society, 1939—45 and of New Fabian Research Bureau, 1933—9. PPS (Parliamentary Private Secretary) to Ellen Wilkinson (Ministry of Home Security) 1940—42. Parliamentary Secretary, Dominions Office, from August 1945.

Wilfrid Roberts

Age 45. Liberal MP for North Cumberland from 1935. An active supporter of the Republican side during the Spanish Civil War. A farmer and landowner.

Colonel Charles Ponsonby
Age 66. Conservative MP for Sevenoaks since 1935. PPS (Parliamentary Private Secretary) to Anthony Eden, 1940—45. Director of Companies; Chairman Empire Cotton Growing Corporation, etc.

Outward bound

Thursday 11 January
Arrived at Airways House at 8.30 p.m. Found that my baggage was the lightest of any of the passengers, amounting to only 16 kilos (about 32 lb). King Hall has the heaviest, having well over his 100 lb; he is taking pipe tobacco and other possible presents which he thinks he may find useful. All fitted out for air rig-out. Quite impossible to put on oneself. The zips very difficult to fit and result far too bulky for walking in Moscow — especially the trousers. Some members have decided to try to get thicker overcoats but I propose to make mine do — with an extra pullover if necessary. The fur hat with earflaps should do.

Friday 12 January
Breakfasted at Royal British Hotel (Edinburgh). Spent day shopping and looking round, catching 4.20 train for journey to Leuchers (Fife) airport. Accompanied Tom Fraser in great search to get a trench coat with fur lining. Tom saw the thing he wanted at Austin Reed's (37 coupons) especially for officers. Sale refused without coupons and special authorization from Board of Trade (Tom PPS to Hugh Dalton, the President of the B of T, so shop manager enjoyed being awkward). Went to local B of T office and phoned London. They gave authorization and promised to send coupons and letter, but manager proved adamant. Ultimately Tom got trench coat from another shop where manager was a friend of local B of T manager. Worst red tape — shown by Austin Reed manager.

  Got to Leuchars and dined at St Andrews (Abbotsford Hotel). Left for airport at 9.45 p.m. Two parties already been waiting since Monday to leave for Sweden. They finally went off to Gothenburg, but we had to return to sleep at hotel as Stockholm weather conditions reported bad. Much hanging about. Hope it won't be too many days before we can leave. Many Norwegians and Poles come on return journey to this country. Brimelow,[1] our secretary from British Embassy in Moscow, very interesting and instructive. Thirty-six mail bags for Embassy being taken with us. A great hold-up of mail to and from USSR. Housing shortage and conditions in Moscow reported very bad — including those for British Embassy. Little bombing; most damage from airraids followed freezing of heating apparatus after blast. Great shortage of vitamins in winter at all times but especially since war. Ponsonby taking out crate of apples for his daughter, who is working in Moscow for Ministry of Information.

Saturday 13 January

Had a good night's sleep and lazy morning at St Andrews. Left for airport at 2.45. Weather conditions reported good at Stockholm and we left soon after 4.0 in two planes. These were troop-carrying Dakotas. Much time was spent in getting into our rig. BOAC[2] staff assisted us like armourers fitting out medieval knights. First our ordinary clothing, then fur-lined tight-fitting trousers and jacket. Then the Mae West and parachute harness (with patent method of inflating first and getting out of second). Parachutes themselves put under seats. With considerable difficulty we rolled into our seats in the plane. We had been warned not to drink much beforehand as kit difficult to get off. We were all told a sad cautionary tale of a Swedish woman who could not contain herself and who froze to her seat. When they had removed her on arrival, her husband disgustedly pretended he was nothing to do with her. There was no heating in the plane (very different from peacetime saloon) but it was rarely below freezing point despite the heights we went. We sat in comfortable seats but could see nothing as all windows were blacked out. We made a very fast run with a tail wind, going 12,000 to 15,000 feet up when over Norway. Whilst over enemy territory all lights were cut to a dim. On nearing Stockholm we were not only allowed to light up but to remove blackout from windows. We were told that German radar was able to follow us throughout our route and that a plane could easily have been sent up to tail us and shoot us down despite our great height. Five planes *en route* to Sweden have been lost in the past two years. However, the Germans usually leave planes alone on this route and the British in return abstain from interference with German planes between Norway and Denmark.

The other plane had flown straight through at a low level. We had split the Parties between the two planes to avoid the risk of one of the Parties having to face an unfair number of consequent by-elections if one of the planes had been shot down!

Stockholm airport used extensively by both British and Germans; British Airways and Lufthansa actually having adjoining office rooms. The Swedes usually try to keep passengers apart, however. We drove through the town to the Ambassador's house (Sir Victor Mallet)[3] to a snack supper. Roads frozen and a sprinkling of snow but had not been a cold winter so far. Stockholm looked marvellous at night all lit up. The spaciousness of the roads and layout, the big blocks of flats over the water and the coloured signs were a delight. Electricity is cheap and the signs gay in colours without the garishness of those of prewar London. Very good reds and greens. Wood for fuel piled everywhere in the streets; town seems well off at first sight although am told cost of living is high.

We arrived at the legation to find first party tucking in to good smorgas (i.e. hors d'oeuvres), cold ham, a Swedish camembert, Ryvita, oceans of butter, snaps and beer — followed by oranges and grapes. Chocolates ad lib.

Sunday 14 January

Just getting light (late up here) as we arrived in Finland. Everything lit up by

144

snow — very plentiful here. We were greeted by Russian officers, British military mission members and some representatives of both the British and Soviet Foreign Offices. A good breakfast of caviar, sandwiches, Caucasus tangerines (with no pips — very good) and Russian tea in glasses with lemon and plenty of sugar. We were told that flying conditions were bad over Moscow, so a special train had been sent over the border to fetch us (it would take twenty-eight hours by rail to Moscow instead of four by air). Had a talk with a rather oily bald-headed Finn — was told afterwards by head of British military mission that he had been most anti-British during periods of the German alliance. One of the RAF boys on mission introduced himself as coming from Dagenham and asked after home. We then motored to the station. The train finally started about 12 noon Moscow time. We spent the day going slowly through southern Finland, getting to the new frontier after dark.

We discovered that this train had belonged to the Czar. It was well furnished and was used by our delegation throughout their visit. We had a staff of thirty, inclusive of the Soviet and British Embassy officials, railwaymen, restaurant staff and others thought necessary to look after the needs of eight MPs and two Peers. We each had a compartment in which to read and sleep; there was a bathroom with an attendant to scrub our backs and rub us down and a restaurant well supplied with food and drink. When we ran out of mineral water in Central Asia a plane was sent from Moscow to deliver a fresh supply.

After our experience of wartime rationing in Britain we were overwhelmed by the size of the meals. We informed our hosts that we were not used to such lavish hospitality. This, however, we found was a long-established Russian tradition and we were told the sad story of a Swedish prince who came to marry a Russian princess but had died of overeating during the wedding festivities before ever bedding his bride. We soon found that our visit provided an opportunity for those we met to enjoy a good meal, so we sat back to eat only what we wanted.

All houses were wooden in the Finnish countryside and most even in the towns. A wide variety of designs — most looking good but some shacks. Some good modern buildings in Helsinki, but town not well laid out compared with Stockholm. Very little damage from bombs although some houses burnt out. People looked healthy especially the children, but was told there was still a great food shortage. Official rations not enough and everybody supplemented them from black market at very high prices. It was a Sunday morning and church bells were ringing (a Lutheran country); many young people skiing or playing ice hockey. In country most walkers either go along on skis or else push something like a child's mailcart on runners. They frequently have a foot on one runner and hop with the other as British children used to do with scooters. The mailcart sometimes contains a child but often a basket for carrying parcels.

First Russian impressions

Our principal Russian host, a young man named Trukhanovsky, lunched at my table with Elliot (our first Russian lunch – dishes of caviar and butter to spread on white or black bread, three slices of ham, then a couple of boiled eggs, then a veal cutlet with carrots and sauté potatoes, then cheese washed down by vodka, white wine, mineral water and a sweet red wine from Caucasus like Marsala). He was specially educated at a training school for their Foreign Office officials and spoke English well (although he had never been to England). Full of hatred for the Germans and anxious to work with Britain and USA to prevent same happening again. Said Russia very interested in Pacific questions. Impressed by our account of damage done by fly bombs and rockets in London.

Had a lazy afternoon in my carriage reading and sleeping until summoned to a 'light' dinner (caviar, ham, bortsch soup, fish, meat and potatoes, cheese, fruit, vodka and sweet wine). Afterwards had a good talk with Faringdon, Fraser, Roberts and young Russian assistant (probably NKVD).[4] Latter tried to follow rather incomprehensible talk about British politics. Trukhanovsky then arrived and we had brandy with slices of lemon dipped in sugar. T very shocked by Faringdon. Could not understand his attacks on Churchill and the House of Lords. T surprised at talk of need for a 'revolution' in England. USSR had her revolution thirty years ago and it was not for export. Why was British constitution not written? Surely peerages were not bought and sold? (I am sure the good Walter would have thought Faringdon was letting the 'side' down if had heard him). I did my best to present a reasonable Labour view. And so to bed.

Monday 15 January

Awoke about 9.0 to find it was just getting light. Spent most of day passing through forests and clearings (mostly birch and fir but not so well kept as in Finland and little good timber near line – much obviously cut down during war). Part of this route had been conquered by the Germans. Wooden houses of all sorts, mostly small. No towns of any size. Meals alternated with talks. T had told Buller, one of the Tory MPs and King-Hall that if he (T) belonged to the British security force he would have Faringdon deported as a public danger. King-Hall replied that the Russian Security Police had once deported such a useful person as Lenin!

Had a further talk over lunch with Trukhanovsky about Britain. (Afterwards met in King-Hall's room to hatch plot of 'Left' to try to see more than the official twenty-one days' tour.) Have made great friends with Nina, a blonde bombshell, who is our principal waitress. She is continually bringing glasses of tea (chay) and trying out English words. Our waitresses are smart Moscow girls with very bloody nails – a great contrast to the village girls, who look very hale and hearty. Children covered with warm clothes at stopping places but all the boys seem to have extraordinarily dirty faces. Our old train attendant looks exactly like a Tolstoy character. Round fur cap, small grey beard and sunken eyes that look as though they never smiled – and would never complain.

Arrived in Moscow late in evening and lined up to leave the train for the official reception. Station hung with red flags and Union Jacks, and the Vice-

Mayor and many officials of Soviet Foreign Office together with British *chargé d'affaires* (Balfour)[5] there to meet us and British and Russian press correspondents, many arc lamps, photographers, movie cameras, etc. Went to hotel, where had a comfortable room with bathroom adjoining. We were asked down to have a cup of chay (tea), only to find a huge banquet waiting (we had already dined on train). We ate what we could and then heard a salute celebrating a victory on Polish frontier. Went out on a balcony of the hotel to see fireworks light up the sky. Most impressive to see Kremlin for first time in the snow by light of the green, red and yellow rockets. The boom of the guns alternated with the fireworks as the salvo was fired. And so to bed.

Tuesday 16 January

We shocked the hotel by insisting on a light breakfast. Then drove round the town seeing the Red Square, outside of Kremlin, and then went along river embankments. Many wide modern streets with new apartment houses and extensive offices along them. Dangerous for pedestrians to cross such wide streets as without 'islands'. Much warmer than we had expected. We were told it was a warm winter. All streets covered with snow and very slippery. All cars seemed to drive fast, however, and without chains. Town well lit at night.

We were then taken to see the underground and journeyed along it. They are rightly very proud of the fine modern stations. Big halls with bronze and other designs between the two platforms (used as air-raid shelters earlier in the war). Moving staircases much faster than in London. No advertisements anywhere in the town apart from a few in newspapers. This most obvious on underground where no notices even of theatres and cinemas. No smoking allowed on underground. Many women stationmasters in red hats. Enormous crowds travelling even outside rush hours (40 kopek fare takes one anywhere). Very interested in us, especially the children. Our first sight of Moscow humanity in the mass. Warmly clad but clothes often rather ragged, especially the children's. All with fur hats and high boots, latter usually felt. The front of first cars kept for women with babies. One drunk had to be removed from car we got in to return. He was deposited in corner of station and left.

About 12.30 we visited Shvernik, Chairman of the Council of Nationalities, and Andreev, Chairman of the Supreme Soviet of the USSR. Presented official messages from the Speaker of the House of Commons and Lord Chancellor on behalf of the House of Lords. Much photographing and movie cameras. These two speakers of their houses have many other posts. Shvernik is the government-appointed head of the trade unions in the USSR and Andreev is Minister of Agriculture.

In the afternoon we were taken to the Palace of Culture and Rest where a big exhibition of captured war equipment was laid out; this came from all over German-occupied Europe. A cold afternoon; this was nearly all in the open and it was snowing. In the evening we went to a film show given by the Committee for Film Production. Some good newsreels and the first episode of Eisenstein's

147

Ivan the Terrible. All very patriotic — which impressed Lord Lovat and other Tories. Theme of *Ivan* was that Russia was the Third Rome. It had some good battle scenes with the Tartars. Much was made of the friendly English trade mission sent to Ivan by Elizabeth I.

We also saw the British pressmen and asked and answered questions. They were not allowed near the front. Most were critical of our government at home. The *Times* man (Parker) was just back from Poland. He was very impressed by Lublin government.

Wednesday 17 January

After much discussion we appointed a sub-committee to propose an alternative plan to later part of our official tour. Brimelow, our secretary, agreed to put this up to the Russian authorities.

In morning we went to Kremlin to look round the palace. The old palace (c.1490) very interesting but the nineteenth-century parts very similar to Buck House.[6] The many cathedrals in Kremlin have delightfully exotic exteriors. Could not see inside as we were told they were being restored.

Talks in Moscow

Then went to an official lunch with the Soviet government. Molotov[7] and many high Soviet officials received us. Maisky[8] sat next to me, looking a little under the weather. The official uniform of the diplomatic corps (recently brought in for use inside USSR) did not suit him as it made him look fat. Lunch was not only good but interesting. Toasts drunk continuously between courses. First the Russians proposed one and then one of our people replied and proposed another toast. And so on right through the meal. Speeches thus kept short and on the whole lively. I replied to toast on foreign policy and proposed one on education. Maisky asked all about the British political situation, and when election was likely. Afterwards we went for coffee into adjoining room. Sat with Molotov and Faringdon and we were asked what was feeling in Britain about Greece. Later Elliot came and took Faringdon's place. We had a very frank and useful talk on whole question of relations between our two countries. The possibilities of a Western bloc were exhaustively gone into and then we went on to Poland, Elliot said that it was desirable to get a solution that appealed to all reasonable people in Britain including British Catholics on the Right like Lord Lovat, who was sitting near. (Molotov muttered something rude about Rightists under his breath.) He then said aloud, 'The Russians live rather nearer to Poland than the British Catholics and are rather more numerous.' He hoped for a satisfactory solution. He then told the following story about Stalin's and Churchill's last meeting. Churchill: 'We must get the Pope on our side.' Stalin: 'How many divisions does he command?' Just in the middle of a most fascinating talk when we had to go. The young Russian interpreters are extraordinarily good.

The lunch was between 2.00 and 5.00, which is the usual time here for such functions. In the evening to the Bolshoi Theatre to see a famous ballet, *The Fountain of Bakhcki Sarai*. It was the story of the kidnapping of a Polish girl for the harem of a Crimean Tartar chief and her subsequent murder by a rival wife. A Polish village was burnt down and cavalry charged across the enormous stage. The dancing was very lively and energetic, especially the Tartar dances. All the stars including the best ballerina from Leningrad were present. We sat in the old Imperial box where we received a big ovation from the crowd. We went behind the scene to thank the artists at the end. The huge men looked very hot and dripped with perspiration after their performance but the small ballerinas did not have a hair out of place!

We had long intervals during which we went for 'chay' with Maisky, Shvernik and other hosts. I have ruined my chance to see Georgia. Was introduced to Chairman of Georgian Soviet; Maisky was brought along to translate. He asked many questions as to why I wanted to go there. I suddenly remembered that he had been interested in my discussions with Beatrice Webb about Turkey and when I left I heard him hurriedly whisper something to the Georgian. (He probably thinks me a Turkish agent!) The audience did not appear to mind these long intervals when we were out. It was a first-class production — excellent theatre as well as dancing.

There were three salvoes tonight. News of fall of Warsaw and various victories been pouring in all the evening. Roberts and I walked to Red Square to see midnight salvo. Crowd appeared quite blasé about the victories. And so to bed.

Thursday 18 January

Went along to the university and were received by the Rector and colleagues. Asked a number of questions; were told that three out of four students now were women (owing to the war). Many of the ablest male students, however, were continuing their studies even in subjects not connected with the war effort. 'We cannot afford to lose our future seed corn', we were told. They worked on shift system owing to lack of accommodation. Quite a lot of students paid fees for the 'academic' subjects. Most of those from outside Moscow lived in digs. We then broke up and Roberts, Fraser and myself went to see some of the labs, where they were carrying out experiments with metal for war purposes. King-Hall asked to talk to students and, hearing a delighted row, we joined a class which he had taken over from the English Literature lecturer. He had constituted himself into a one-man brains trust and was answering a flood of questions from the British party system, to the war, to what girls were like in England. The English teacher translated very well. After Elliot had come in for a short time, four of us continued, supplementing King-Hall when we disagreed or wanted to add anything. K.-H. asked one bright girl what was the difference between a British dominion and colony and received the correct answer pat, saying that every 13-year-old learnt that. One rather aggressive boy was shushed by the class when he tried to ask awkward questions and finally asked why we were not doing more in the west. K.-H. gave a full reply about sea power and how Britain had used it. The boy replied that he could understand with his brain but his heart could only understand land power. We then had 'chay' with the professors and further talks. I sat next to a man with an enormous beard who said it was a camouflage to hide a war wound. He taught history and spoke good English. I tried out with both students and professors the idea of creating 'Rhodes scholarships' after the war with an exchange of students between our countries and found the idea very well received. Altogether we had a very impressive time and our party were all struck by the frank questions and answers and freedom of discussion. Apparently, we also made a good impression as we were not at all 'stand-offish'.

In the evening, I went to visit Mrs M's sister.[9] I found the flat, a central one, with a little difficulty. It was on the fourth floor in one of the new blocks. When I arrived, there was only a young girl of 17 who spoke little English. Later Mrs M's sister came in with a boy of 13, who spoke no English. I gave them the presents, which were very welcome, and stayed for 'chay', their evening meal, although I ate very little as their rations did not appear plentiful. Mrs M's sister worked in the day and the children were her niece and nephew (their father was at the front). The girl was at an art school and showed me some of her designs; the boy was still at school. They were thrilled with their cousin's Sacha's photo and were resolved to learn English so as to visit London and see their relatives after the war.

The flat appeared to be divided between two families with a common entrance-hall — used as an attic and general storeroom for boxes, etc. They appeared to have two living rooms for themselves, both with divans for sleeping. They had a lot of furniture, in fact, rather too much for the rooms. The meal they were having was some slices of very fat ham, pickled cabbage salad and bread without any fat, plus tea without milk or lemon but with imported American sugar. The bread was called white, but was very dark in colour and coarse. It obviously had a lot of rye mixed with it. A very different meal from those we are given officially! Soviet officials on a number of occasions have claimed that their people as a whole are now the best fed in Europe after Great Britain and the neutrals. Food, we are told, is much more plentiful in the countryside and small towns than in Moscow.

Moscow is very overcrowded, and was equally so before the war. It is intended to keep the population at about five million. A magnificent town plan exists and new industries are to be controlled, so as to limit the population, we were told. On being shown this plan, I felt that it really would be carried out and thought of the equally good plans for British cities which seem doomed to remain in great part only pious aspirations. 'In future, it is intended that each person shall have nine square metres when rehousing is complete. It will be very long before this is attained, however. The rooms are very high to allow for lack of ventilation in winter.' Far greater importance was being given here to public works, government buildings, new underground, libraries, parks, industrial plant, etc. than to housing.

Few flats have their own lavatories (usually one is shared between two or three families in the tenements) and only the rich have their own bathrooms. Most people attend public washhouses which exist in all quarters of the city. I saw one just before leaving. There were special communal washrooms, one for men and one for women. You first had a shower, collected a basin, then washed yourself all over and finally had another shower. Social evenings were spent with friends whilst soaping and chatting. Boys would push one another under the showers and flick one another with towels. Dad finally had his own up and scrubbed their backs and gave them the once over; they all scrubbed Dad's back and then all the family had a last shower before going home. Everyone brought their own towels and soap, and clothes were put in lockers. No doubt much the same happened in the women's rooms. I was told that the boys often got out of hand with so many older men being away and attendants had to chase after them and give them a friendly smack on the behind to keep them quiet. The Russians have the Muslim idea (no doubt passed on from the Tartars) that it is wrong to wash in still water. Hence they always had showers or rinsed in running water in a bath. Hence also the absence of many bath plugs noticed by Citrine.[10] Russians would not use them.

Friday 19 January
We first paid a visit to a special army school for aircraft communications where specialist officers were being trained. Most of them were NCOs with service who had been selected, but there were also a number of boys straight from secondary school. We divided up to see the school. I went round the dormitories and living rooms. Very crowded and beds one above another in tiers. One small locker each for all private belongings. Everything spotless and very efficient; slogans up everywhere; reading room full of improving literature. Communist Party branch meetings local to the school were advertised and a wall newspaper looked moderately topical, but largely improving. Elliot was introduced to four NCOs with many medals. One, a boy of 19, said he had been a chemistry student before the war and wished to take it up again as soon as possible. The three others, who were older, however, all wished to make a career of the army once they had become officers. Two had been tractor-drivers before the war and the third worked in a tax collector's office. The dining room was laid out very tastefully with tables and chairs for groups of four. The CO said that teaching good table manners was one of the important parts of an officer's training. Cleanliness was another and everyone had to have a bath first thing and was then inspected by his NCO to see if up to standard. We had a lunch ration which was quite good, soup, mince, onions and rice and compote, but not a lot for energetic men. We were told that the evening meal was bigger.

We all went along to an official reception later in the afternoon given to us by Shvernik and Andreev. After arrival, I went along with Hooper, Reuter's man, whom I used to know in Dagenham, to a room for 'top notchers' to eat. All guests were carefully shepherded into one of five rooms. (Hooper said he would not have been let into that room if not with me.) Litvinov[11] was one of the crowd. I had a good talk with trade union leader, Kusnetzov, who had been with a recent party to Great Britain. He said they had much enjoyed their visit. Most impressed by designs for Portal House and other houses, both temporary and permanent. Had brought all housing literature back with them and had translated into Russian. Thought some of the cottage plans might be used for rebuilding devastated villages and small towns. He was going to GB again for World Trade Union Conference. Also talked with Norwegian minister and a French journalist.

In the evening we went out to the Russian ENSA[12] theatre at Red Army House (for soldiers passing through). They had brought Alessandrev, their crack ENSA conductor, and best Red Army choir specially back to Moscow for our benefit. First-rate singing — Russian style — and some really energetic dancing finishing with the dance of the Don Cossacks. Four Red Army girls, almost the only good-looking girls we had seen so far, took part in the dances. We asked a number of questions during the interval about women in the services. They were entirely volunteers and some were in almost every branch of Service. There was a complete squadron of women in the Red Air Force, flyers and ground staff. In civilian life also there was no conscription officially, but a woman not working was entitled only to a dependant's ration. They filled every kind of post; even before the war women were doing jobs in the USSR which men usually did in Britain. The young women traffic police on point duty in the big cities particularly struck the eye. Six salutes tonight for a further mass of victories.

Saturday 20 January

Visited the Stalin Motor Works on outskirts of Moscow. Much of its suburban area a medley of unmade-up roads, wooden shacks and new factories (to be altered in plan). A huge plant well laid out with trees and shrubs along principal roadways. (Probably bigger than Ford's, together with Briggs at Dagenham.) Had a long questioning of the Managing Director — he'd been there ten years — with principal officers and shop stewards present. An old sailor of the Red Fleet during the Revolution and an obvious driver. Much equipment and many workers had been evacuated to the Urals when Germans were close to Moscow. A new factory had been built there and brought into production; workers living meantime in dugouts. Now they were building wooden houses for them. The original factory at Moscow had been re-equipped and was now about up to prewar production level.

The wages system was described to us in detail. We were told that piece-rates operate wherever possible; 70 per cent of all earners in USSR were being paid by some such system. A 'norm' was first worked out by a technician and was the amount of work which a reasonably good worker could do in a certain period. A standard wage was paid for this norm and bonuses given, rising rapidly according to the percentage by which it was exceeded. Many good workers could do two or three times as much as the norm and made high earnings. Special privileges in the way of rations and discounts at commercial shops were also available.

The manager definitely stated — in front of shop stewards — that the trade union took no part in the fixing of the norm, the basis of the whole wages system, although they might discuss general conditions in the industry with the government department concerned. Strict discipline was enforced by a committee, most of whom were elected by the workers in the factory, although a minority were nominees of the management. If a worker was slack he might first be fined and then have his rations cut. If these punishments did not avail, the director would be asked to send him for trial before the People's Court. If convicted, he might then be sent away on some unpleasant gang job in the wilds. The trade unions played a large part in encouraging production. There was no special production committee here. We were told it was not necessary as special technicians were now employed to look after production problems.

Went around works. Not so tidy as in Great Britain, although work appeared to be productive of results. I saw many women (some old) doing very hard manual work in foundry. There were foremen in special jackets with belts who appeared authoritative. Lorries were coming off the assembly line fairly quickly. I saw a design of a special one with tractor wheels at the back and skis to put under the front wheels for use in Siberia and places with heavy snow. I asked to see wall newspaper for one shop and after much agitation I was shown one for the week before. It seemed very formalized — almost entirely propaganda for increased production. Slogans appeared all over the place. At the principal entrance the following appeared: 'Discipline is everything, without discipline there can be no plan.' (I wondered what would happen if that was put up at Ford's!) Photos of best workers and records of 'brigades' were recorded on walls like House Cup honours at an English public school. We visited the canteen — much like an English one — then had lunch with Director and senior members of staff. I sat next to a young man in charge of examining mass production problems and of trying to solve them. He had full-time staff of six under him and was full of admiration for American production methods, but thought British old-fashioned and out of date.

There appeared to be quite a strong criticism of Communist Party members among technicians, administrators, etc. They were looked on as the 'good boys' who were always top of the class at school and in the good books of the authorities. Many were earnest and hard working, but not always the best at their jobs. There were some in every office and works often causing resentment in that they held down jobs they were not always the most fittest for. The Director said nothing at the outspoken criticisms at the lunch which many made of the Party which now had about five million members. Only five out of the twenty Russians present at this lunch were members and we were told on many other occasions by responsible people that they did not belong to the Party and that so far they had not found that fact any obstacle to advancement. None of the criticisms made were directed against the general line of government policy.

The trade unions appeared to be mainly engaged in administering the social services. There was no compulsion on workers to join them but they could only get 50 per cent of the Health Service benefits if non-members of a trade union. Practically everyone therefore joins.

An eight-hour day was worked; generally, there were three shifts. Much time was spent, out of work hours, on allotments in summer. This factory also had its own farm twenty kilometres away for supplying their canteens. We visited a very fine club premises after lunch belonging to the factory. It included library, dance hall, many children's rooms, music-rooms, etc. It was supposed to be limited to the use of factory workers and their families, but other children in the district used it.

In the afternoon we went on a shopping expedition and investigated the working of the rationing system. This seemed very complicated and strongly reinforced the 'reward of merit' which was the basis of the wages system. There were six main scales for rationing. The lowest was that for the non-worker, that is the old age pensioner, the woman who did not go out to work, even if she had a large young family, and the injured (if not as a result of war wounds). They get just enough to keep body and soul together. The heavy manual workers got more than the ordinary clerical worker. In general, however, the ration rose with size of income and importance of job. The highest ration went to generals, who had a very wide range of privileges. They were a very important group, as all heads of important arms factories were also given this rank.

Rationed goods were sold at low prices and usually bought at special shops. Any surplus of rationed goods, however, was sold 'off the ration' at commercial prices. To meet the lack of fresh vegetables and fruits in winter the government had mass-produced tangerines in Georgia. They were available one a week, with each ration book in Moscow, at a rouble apiece. A second one could be bought off the ration for ten roubles. Many foodstuffs in short supply were unrationed and available only for those with money at high prices. Collective farms in non-devastated areas thus did very well in meeting the needs of any nearby industrial centre.

Early in the war the government fixed the price of most goods in short supply. The law was widely broken, however, and the usual black market developed. To deal with this situation the government decided to 'nationalize the black market' and pocket the profits themselves. This policy had been a big success — for the government! Many workers had earned large incomes during the war and had got tired of investing in war loans. The commercial shops, which were opened to sell goods in short supply, quickly mopped up the surplus money about and brought down the price of non-rationed foodstuffs.

We visited one of these shops. I wanted to buy a present for my wife and found a bottle of scent which cost 500 roubles (about £10 at Embassy exchange rate). There were wonderful displays of furs, children's toys and musical instruments (most produced on the collective farms in winter). All prices were very high; yet there appeared to be plenty of buyers. Generals, stakhanovite[13] workers and other favoured groups were allowed considerable discounts at the commercial shops on all purchases.

The granting of privileges did not end at differential incomes and rations. The main theatres in Moscow and Leningrad are always full. Special booking offices had therefore been opened for generals and other officers respectively. They had the right to two seats each, which were bookable up to the day before the performance. The general public, booking through their trade unions and other organizations, took what seats were left. An officer had the right to walk to the head of any queue he joined. Both income tax and death duties were now low so that considerable fortunes could be passed on to relatives. The restoration of fees for various forms of higher education (accompanied though it is by scholarships for clever children) enabled children of moderate ability to qualify for good jobs which were beyond the reach of similarly able children whose parents could not pay for them. Those who could afford it could get a piece of waste scrub at a peppercorn rent with a long lease and build themselves a country cottage (dacha) to visit in summer. This policy of privilege seemed to be generally accepted. I asked one old woman whether she did not think it unfair that she should only get a dependant's ration whereas her son had a large number of privileges as a colonel. She said, 'No, not at all. He has done far more for the Soviet Union than I have ever done.' Stalin was said to see no generals get a lot of publicity in the press. He claimed full responsibility for military affairs and is always now referred to as Marshal Stalin.

Is this policy likely to have far-reaching effects in the USSR? Firstly, it must be remembered that any number of servants can be employed — if they can be found. But no one outside the family may be employed for profit. So long as this rule is rigidly enforced — as it is — the USSR will remain a socialist state on the economic if not the social side. Secondly, the educational system still in the main aims at providing a career open to talent. Thirdly, the end of rationing, when plenty returns, will modify the present position considerably. It is clear, however, that the present income and inheritance policy is bound to stratify the population into classes over a period of years if allowed to continue without important changes.

Left in the evening for Leningrad in the same train as before.

Leningrad after the siege

Sunday 21 January
Arrived in Leningrad and found comfortable rooms awaiting at the Hotel Astoria. Went on an official reception visit to see Mayor Popkov (Chairman of Leningrad Soviet for last seven years; now only 42; a very energetic young man who had led the town during the siege). This is definitely a young man's country and most of the responsible officials, especially locally, seem very young by our standards. He received us in the Smolny, now used as council offices — the former girls' school for daughters of the aristocracy, founded by Catherine II.

Later in the evening some of the party visited one of the churches (it was

Sunday) for the Orthodox form of Benediction and Evening Service. They were received enthusiastically by much-vestmented clergy in a magnificent interior. There was a small congregation present. We all went to the ballet (*Sleeping Beauty*). Technically a very finished production but not such a good story as the one we saw in Moscow. Again, given a big reception by the audience. In the theatres here there are always big halls where the crowd walk around between the acts and meet friends and chat.

Monday 22 January

Made a tour of Leningrad. The centre of the town was not much damaged, as the Germans had hoped to capture it and use it for winter quarters. The eighteenth-century part of the town is very well laid out in an excellent style with wide roads and squares. Saw the Winter Palace and went along the Neva which greatly improved the appearance of the city. Some cruisers lay along the quays frozen in. King-Hall went over one. Ice-breakers had recently been up the centre of the river. The Leningrad style is stucco colour-washed in bright colours. The re-colouring had already started on some of the palaces and apartment houses. The town should look very gay in summer when fully painted. The City Architect showed us the city plan and we then went to see new blocks of flats to the south of the city. There were more damaged by gunfire. Some of the new flats also to be colour-washed but of rather uninteresting 'classical style' — French Empire — which is now the official style here. Few good modern style buildings were evident here or in Moscow. The immediate post-revolution buildings were usually eccentric without being good. Some cottages were to be built on the outskirts; the total population was to be limited to three-and-a-half million we were told.

In the evening, we spent a very boring time visiting the War Siege Museum. Walter Elliot spent hours admiring guns whilst we wanted to get on. The city's relief from across Lake Ladoga, when frozen, provided the most interesting set of plans and photos. During the worst months of the siege daily bread ration reduced to a piece the size of two matchboxes, 30 per cent of this being wood pulp; soup made of glucose and laurel leaves was the main other food. (By the way, there were no cats and dogs to be seen here and practically none in Moscow, owing to shortage of rations.) Many gruesome stories were told of the siege. Over 200,000 died of starvation, although only about 8,000 were killed by enemy gunfire. There was also great shortage of fuel, yet none of the trees in central parks were cut down (the town Soviet said they must not be). The mayor had many of the old wooden houses on outskirts pulled down for fuel, and the forests north of the city — in front of Finnish lines — were also extensively cut. Leningrad was very proud of its resistance. A large part of the population — especially children — were evacuated. Most of the evacuees now back and a real housing shortage exists.

Tuesday 23 January

In the morning we motored south through the Russian and German lines. Here destruction was complete. Trees were practically all shot away in the woods and a suburb of 20,000 people was level with the ground. It was curious to see ruined tramcars almost all the way to Petrodvorets left along the track which ran beside the road, in groups (they ran in threes or fours) just where they were when the Germans broke through suddenly and cut off their electricity. They seem to have survived the gunfire much more than buildings, although some had been burnt out. Young trees were planted last autumn all along the main roads out (and many in Leningrad streets). We were told they took a long time to grow so far north and so were the first things to be thought about. None appeared to have been destroyed by small boys.

After passing the German lines we stopped some miles on and walked to see one of the gun emplacements from which Leningrad had been shelled. It was in a wood above a small stream and had movable concrete emplacements which swivelled round with the gun. All round were trenches for the infantry defence against possible attack from partisans and paratroops. It was a nice bright morning but quite cold enough even with fur boots, fur caps, ear muffs and thick gloves. What it must have been like for the German troops there when it was really cold one can imagine. The Russians had pulled up all German crosses and burnt them. They had erected occasional small stone obelisks with a red star on top for their own dead on the battlefield — usually buried in collective graves.

We reached Petrodvorets and were taken round the palace by the mayor and councillors. It was built by Peter the Great and was a very magnificent eighteenth-century showplace with well-laid-out gardens where Leningrad people came by boat in summer on a Sunday for the day out. The Germans had set it on fire when they left. Nearly all the houses in the town had been fired. Some of the inhabitants had been deported to Germany for labour; some had returned who had fled before the Germans or had been released when the Russians reconquered Estonia. These had either made some part of their homes habitable — or else had built covered-in dugouts below ground to live in for the winter. We were told the whole palace was to be rebuilt. It seems difficult to believe this possible, particularly so far as the eighteenth-century interior is concerned. They have already begun to restore the park for use in summer.

On our return we visited an electrical equipment works which had kept running all through the siege. It had received 230 hits and had kept up continual repairs. The Ponsonbys and I then visited the Pioneer House, which was an old converted palace. It made a very good youth centre and is used both by the pioneers (small children) and consomols (youngsters up to 17). We saw small girls doing ballet, a mixed troup acting and singing, girls doing physical training and boys boxing. They were just opening a big extension which would provide facilities for woodworking, engineering and learning about flying. We were told that similar smaller houses existed in various parts of the town and that members of this central house had to be chosen by the local leaders. If they did not attend whatever classes or activities they had put themselves down for their membership was soon cancelled. The supervision of activities and the teaching seemed mainly to be in the hands of adults; they were a very enthusiastic group.

In the evening we went to an official dinner with Popkov and the Leningrad Soviet. We were entertained by the stars of the Kirov Opera House — a first-rate performance. German music, whether by Beethoven or Strauss, appeared to have been banned since the war started. After Russian music the most popular was that with a southern influence — Carmen, Rigoletto, etc. Popkov was the life and soul of the party and certainly made it go. The train taking us back to Moscow was due to leave at midnight. He telephoned to have it postponed an hour at about 11.45. He ragged King-Hall about his teetotalism and ended up by getting him to drink a brandy, did a Russian dance with him and kissed him full on the lips in the Russian manner — just as we were departing! Popkov is a man with a future. When we left to catch our train it looked as though the party would go on till dawn. (He was shot with most of our hosts of that night by Stalin in 1949.)

Leningrad was less formal than Moscow but prided itself on having greater style. There is much rivalry between the two cities. The Leningrad people were very pleased to find that they had had our theatre programmes and menus printed in English as well as Russian — whilst Moscow had overlooked this. I suggested during the dinner that Leningrad and London might well establish some kind of friendly relations based on both being seaports and bombed cities, exchanging missions, plans for rebuilding, etc. The idea was very welcome. Popkov and the chief architects would obviously like to visit England after war.

Our return to Moscow

Wednesday 24 January
Journeyed back to Moscow. Went round in the evening and called on Mrs M's sister. She and the daughter were out. Only the boy, who did not speak English, was in, so did not stay. He was doing for geography prep a study of prewar Poland. I had a bath and went to bed early.

Thursday 25 January
We waited in Moscow especially to see Uncle Joe. In the afternoon went with Elliot to see Madame Saricheva, who was now in charge of education in Moscow, working for the local Soviet; she was previously Assistant Commissar for Education in the Russian Republic. She said that the Communist Party saw that general party policy was followed in the different republics and in particular that adequate schools were provided for the national minorities. Problems of evacuation of children from Moscow had been very similar to those from London. Most had now returned and she claimed they were all at school. Schools were run in two shifts; children attending either in the morning or afternoon owing to overcrowding in existing school buildings (many former schools being used for war purposes) and shortage of teachers. Teachers who took two shifts got

double pay. The legal school age was 7 to 17 but many now leave school before 17 to do war work. There were normally ten classes — one for each year of age.

We noticed later that some of the villages appeared to have as few as four classes. Many boys of 12 were at work but this could normally be during the half-day when not in school. In some of the devastated areas we were told it was the practice to put war orphan children to work when very young so as to earn their keep and help with war production or restoration of these areas. Many hostels had been opened for young workers. Education as a whole seemed better in the areas least affected by the war, although the reopening of schools was an early priority in restoration. There were many very large classes; Mrs M's nephew had 42 in his class.

The wishes of parents and children were overruled if they wanted a talented child to leave school early. A child had some choice in choosing the type of education he went on to but the teachers had a very large say in determining the child's future. Madame was an enthusiastic supporter of separate schools for boys and girls over 12 and the new policy was being put into force as rapidly as possible. She claimed that it was not only better when giving military training but it had been difficult to maintain proper discipline before. Boys were not only easier to handle when separated but worked harder if not diverted by the girls, especially the older ones of 16 and 17. Discipline was strictly enforced if necessary. For example, older boys could be put on 'guard duty' in full uniform for a period outside in the snow. Despite the war, Madame believed big improvements were taking place in technical and higher education. Every effort was being made to find and train talent for technical and administrative posts.

We meet Stalin; his visit to London

When we first came to Moscow we had indicated that we should consider it a great honour if Uncle Joe would see us. We went along to the Kremlin about 6.45 in the evening and were taken to his private flat. After shedding our coats we entered (the delegates and Balfour, the *chargé d'affaires*) and shook hands. Stalin was much shorter and more genial looking than I had imagined. His hair and moustache were now grey and he appeared very tired. Molotov did the translation. The walls were largely panelled with birch and there was a big wall map-case just behind our table. Stalin did not sit at the end of the table but a yard or so down. The meeting started very formally and went very stickily for some time whilst Elliot tried hard to make conversation. He said that Lord Lovat had been through D-Day and could give an account of the war in the west. Stalin answered that he would be pleased to listen if there were plenty of time. Elliot then complimented him on the recent Red Army victories. 'It is time someone else also got going,' was the reply. After this, at 7.15, it looked as though the meeting was going to end, as Uncle Joe pulled out his watch. Elliot said he hoped we were not detaining him. Stalin then smiled and said he could give us till 8.00 or possibly 8.30. He had been well briefed and knew all about us. After we had each been introduced by Elliot first he — and then we — put questions. At a previous meeting Molotov had spoken about the forthcoming Yalta Conference. King-Hall mentioned this and I saw a sudden look of fear on Molotov's face as though he had told us more than he should, but Stalin remained inscrutable.

I asked Stalin if he had ever visited Britain. Yes, he said, he had attended an International Socialist meeting in London at the Holborn Hall about 1907 at which Mussolini, then a socialist, had been in the chair.

He was obviously interested that I was Secretary of the Fabian Society and asked about its present activities. He gave us a great deal of information about the current Russian attacks. Asked by Roberts what were his (i.e. Uncle Joe's) suggestions for improving relations between the USSR and Great Britain, he said, 'Tell the truth about our country. We have many things that are good and many that are not. Tell the truth about both.' In reply to a question from Faringdon about the Free German Movement he admitted that it was a wartime expedient and would be dropped as soon as it had served its purpose. He strongly agreed with the idea of having some kind of Rhodes scholarship for Russian students to Great Britain and vice versa. We talked on till 8.00, when a salute sounded for the latest victory, and then left. He would be a difficult man to best; he is certainly all there.

A visit to Donbas

Friday 26 January

The party split up. Lovat went home to prepare a lecture tour in the USA. His wounds had been troublesome. Elliot, Ponsonby, King-Hall, Jewson, Brimelow and Lawrence were to go to Sverdlovsk, the centre of a big new industrial area in the Urals (now with about a million inhabitants). The rest of us (Roberts, Fraser, Faringdon, Buller and self) went to Donbas. My scheme for going on to Baku direct and there meeting the rest of the party after going through Georgia came to nothing, as I thought it would. We were all asked to be back in Moscow for the farewell reception — and could not very well decline.

We were taken during the morning to a cavalry school in Moscow and saw some very good riding. The Russians had only one such school before the war and had since opened two more. Cavalry had been used quite a lot as an auxiliary to their tanks in advance and for raids to set fire at nightfall to German-occupied villages during the winters early in the war. We then saw an amusing film of our delegation during the early days of our visit. We left in the evening on a special train for the Donbas.

Saturday 27 January

Trukhanovsky and Brimelow went with Elliot's party. We had a young man from the Russian Diplomatic Service (Okhov) who had spent three years in Denmark and had just returned from three years in the USA. He spoke very good American. His criticisms of the USA were very interesting, much more knowledgeable of and sympathetic to western ideas. He thought the Americans a very simple and uncultured people. How could anyone prefer the jitterbug to Russian folk dances? We visited a dance once or twice on tour, but never stayed a whole evening. Very like a wartime Fabian dance in its variety, but with local dances included. When the Russians talk of 'jazz' today they mean primarily the fast waltz! The quick-step, tango and slow waltz were also popular. Two years ago it was decided that the polka and mazurka should be taught to all officers learning dancing and I was told they were now becoming popular as all girls wanted to learn the dances the officers danced. The jitterbug is not considered suitable for officers.

Spent whole day in the train and got to Kharkov after dark. A deputation from the city soviet came to see us and told us of the destruction wrought by the Germans and by the fighting during the city's two liberations. We were asked how many relatives we had each lost in the war. None of us had so far. All of the Soviet deputation had. It was very embarrassing when its women members all burst into tears.

Sunday 28 January

Arrived two hours early at Stalino (now called Donetsk) after a restless night. Had asked for an extra blanket as it was cold and woke to find and kill about a dozen livestock of all kinds walking over me. Got some Flit from Wilfred Roberts and then returned to try to sleep (livestock finally eliminated after a two-night campaign!)

We were met by the Mayor and leading councillors (Mayor again an able young man — aged 30). Motored through area to temporary council offices some way from station. All large buildings had been burnt out with a few exceptions, and many of the cottages. The Germans appointed a special destruction corps when about to evacuate which did all its work in about a fortnight. The Russians had regained the town early in September 1943, and had carried out a remarkable amount of reconstruction since that time. Many of the flats and public buildings had their walls standing. These appeared in much better condition than walls of buildings burnt out during the blitz on London. Possibly the fire bombs created a greater heat than the flame thrower which was the Germans' principal incendiary here. They had already re-roofed many burnt-out buildings, using the existing walls, and were proposing to do the same with many others. Here again, first attention was given to public buildings. In fact one block of apartment houses which had survived destruction had had its inhabitants turned out to make way for municipal offices. Schools had been repaired and we were told all younger children were now attending, although not all age-groups. Out of 500,000 inhabitants before the war in Stalino, 100,000 had been murdered by the Germans, 100,000 deported for forced labour and 300,000 were now housed in the city as best they could. Many of these had been evacuated (especially skilled workers) and had now returned. In one mine shaft no less than 70,000 bodies had been thrown after being shot through the back of the head. In particular the wives and children of Red Army officers and of all responsible persons were systematically combed out and liquidated during the two years of occupation. The hatred against the Germans is naturally intense. We saw German prisoners employed in clearing 'war damage' guarded by Russian soliders against possible lynching by the inhabitants. Popular feeling was strongly Vansittartite.[14] Brailsford[15] is one of the most hated men in the Soviet Union, as his views on Germany had been much attacked in the Soviet press. (A great campaign against the Duchess of Atholl[16] was in full swing when we were in Moscow, because of her views on Poland — her support for the Republican activities in the Spanish war had been completely forgotten.) In the Donbas about 60 per cent of the population was Ukrainian and 40 per cent Russian.

We went out into the country and passed many mining villages. The steppe here is rolling, with no trees save where planted near streams or to form wind-screens to roads or railways to keep off snowdrifts. We were told that Germans had blown up most mine shafts and roadways leading to shafts. Only 20 per cent of prewar production had been achieved so far compared with 90 per cent of agricultural production in the district. It was going to take a long time to get production restored. The smaller mines were apparently the easier to get going; many new shafts were having to be sunk. We visited a big mine some miles out and saw the destruction effected by Russians on withdrawal, by partisans from local population (no cover so they had to disappear among residents) when Germans had almost got it started again, and then by Germans when they retired. Some of the more modern miners' cottages quiet well laid out with trees along roads and in small gardens, but the older cottages looked very slummy and badly built. Here most houses were built of stone with thatch or tiled roofs, although many older cottages were of a mixture of mud and stone. The roads were bad here by British standards even in the industrial areas, although the main streets in Stalino itself were good. Between Stalino and Makyeevka, a big industrial town about ten kilometres away, the road ran in three rough tracks as lorries went either side of the road when snow or mud made its surface bad.

We visited the enormous iron and steel plant at Makyeevka, which produced 10 per cent of the whole Soviet output just before the war. There was an amazing scene of systematic destruction, masses of girders and broken machinery every-where. In one small corner reconstruction had started and some foundries were working. They will have plenty of scrap at hand for a long time! We saw the architect and discussed the plan for rebuilding Stalino, a slight modification of the prewar development plan. The big blocks of flats and the parks would certainly be a big improvement on the sprawl of the surrounding old mining villages which were to be incorporated in Stalino, but the whole layout seemed very pedestrian and uninspiring (although a vast improvement on, say, Merthyr Tydfil). Pit heaps were to be left in the middle of parks, and streets were to look very much alike. Massive war memorials both to civilian and military casualties were to be erected. A competition had just been held and we saw the winning designs. Not very good. The Soviet Union having had no war memorials last time, save a few to revolutionary heroes, looked as if it was going the whole hog — in stone — this time.

In the evening we went to the theatre — the only important building not destroyed. The Germans had left it to the last, as they were using it, and the locals put out the flames. A modern building with rather elaborate classical internal decorations, completed in 1941. We saw a Ukrainian musical comedy. Some good Ukrainian dancing, but it dragged on for four-and-a-half hours with intervals and it was past 12.30 when we left after the heroine had poisoned the hero by mistake and then killed herself — all in a comedy!

Monday 29 January

In the morning, after donning miners' garb, we went down one of the pits that had been started. Much mechanized, but few safety devices (according to Tom Fraser). Many women and boys were working underground although we were told boys went below for only two hours a day instruction until 17. We were also informed that women would cease to work underground after the war. They all wore very warm clothing underground (according to British standards consider- ing how hot it was there). When coming up we asked to have showers in pithead baths, but were shepherded into an engineer's rooms (we never saw the manager), and brought bowls of hot water. We rather suspected that pithead baths did not exist — or were not in repair — as we saw many men, women and boys going back to their homes unwashed.

We were taken round by the Director of the local mining combinat (a young man of 33 brought back from the army, where he had been a colonel, to push reconstruction ahead). A combinat includes six or eight trusts (about 20 pits in each), which it co-ordinates. There were three mining combinats in Donbas. Miners were given double the ordinary pay of other workers and the Stakhanovites were able to earn very big incomes indeed (they found it difficult to spend earn- ings; there were big investments in war loans and many stories of the purchase of pianos and other luxuries when they could be obtained — at amazing prices).

Many of the best miners had been evacuated to Siberian and Kazak coalfields where they were likely to remain. New labour was being extensively trained for Donbas pits from local agricultural areas — especially girls. We visited one of the local hostels for girls in the pits. A pleasant common room but rather crowded dormitories. A small central table where they put photos of boy friends or families — so that all could share in them if they hadn't some of their own, one of the girls charmingly told us. The girls had nearly all come from Kolkozes (collective farms) and appeared to enjoy their new work. Most looked on it only as war work to be given up as soon as possible.

In the evening we were given a big chay by the Director of the combinat. He arrived rather drunk and embarrassed us by ignoring the local mayor — also invited. The local people put the head man of the oblast (i.e. province) near at hand to keep a watch on him. The Director had told us he was a Party man so he has probably got hauled over the coals for his behaviour! He put Tom Fraser, who sat next to him, in difficulties by continually asking him to down vodkas. We then saw an interminable film about life on a Ukrainian collective farm. It was a propaganda film in favour of hard work. The hero and the heroine each got the book-keeper to find out who earned the most and then set out to court! Our Russian guide commented that it was good propaganda for peasants, but not for the educated.

Tuesday 30 January

It was thawing everywhere and very muddy and warm — quite exceptional so early in the year we were told. We visited the Mayor, who had collected agricultural experts and administrators from the whole oblast. Most of the land round the pits was either in allotments or farmed by solkhozes (state farms). We were told that each Union Republic had its Commissar for agriculture who planned production for his state in consultation with all-Union authorities; quotas for crops then came down to oblasts and then to kolkhozes and solkhozes. There was no compulsion on kolkhozes to do as suggested, but they usually did. The kolkhoz was free to run its affairs, which it did through an annually elected committee and chairman. The state government, through its oblast organization, ran the machine motor tractor stations, controlled supply of seed, artificial insemination, irrigation, experimental stations, etc. It gave the lead and co-ordinated work of kolkhozes. Artificial insemination played a very big part and seemed long past the experimental stage.

Remarkable success had attended agricultural reconstruction despite enormous destruction of tractors by the Germans. Tractors were now being turned out in great numbers, but horses, oxen and other cattle had had to be used for ploughing and harvesting in the emergency. We were told that if this year's harvest was good the food position in all parts of the Union should be good. Only 30 per cent of the houses in the countryside in this part of the Ukraine had been destroyed by the Germans. As they were made of local materials there would be no difficulty in rebuilding them during the slack periods on the land. I asked about working hours in the kolkhozes, and was told that an eight-hour day in winter was normal. During sowing and harvest, however, they worked virtually all hours of the day. In the winter cattle were cared for and jobs of tidying up done as far as weather permitted. In this part of the Ukraine, where there was little rainfall, the snow was taken in from the roads and drifts nearby and piled in heaps on the fields so that it would melt slowly and water the land when spring came.

We saw the local miners' leaders. They had a very large number of full-time paid officials and few office-holders were still at their old jobs. As in Moscow, most of their work appeared to be taken up with the administration of social service benefits. Trade union contributions were 1 per cent of wages. These were not deducted, but were collected after payment. This covered the educational and cultural activities of the unions as well as the social service contributions.

There were standard national minimum wages and rations for each kind of worker in each industry throughout the Union (although variations as to norms, piece-rates, etc. as described before). In contrast to the position at the Moscow Stalin Motor Car Factory, we were told that the miners insisted on discussing the norm with the management very fully before it was fixed. Old age pensions and many other social services varied from industry to industry, but were related to earning capacity. The kolkhozes are expected to maintain their old and sick. The state pays only 5 per cent of the social services' cost; the remainder is divided 50-50 between the workers and industry. The trade union leaders here were not very exciting — one was rather old and deaf. We left in the evening.

Wednesday 31 January
On the train back to Moscow, we passed the big battlefield at Kursk where the land had been cleared for wheat-growing and an enormous park for broken-down tanks, lorries and guns had been created alongside the railway. There were Russian, German and other vehicles from all over occupied Europe, beside British and American ones sent to help USSR. The Russians had repaired or cannibalized all their own equipment but the rest had largely been left on one side. A few had been used for spares but most were waiting to be used as scrap. It was here that the Germans had made a big counter-attack after Stalingrad and been smashed by the Russians with enormous losses on both sides. Rolling tree-less country here looking under snow like the South Downs. The train stopped and we had a good look at the dump.

Back in Moscow again

Thursday 1 February
Arrived back in Moscow and met the other party who had been impressed by vast industralization at Sverdlovsk. It had been very cold and most returned with colds. As a result Tom Brimelow went to bed with flu and John Lawrence, the Editor of the *British Ally*, the British propaganda paper in USSR, took his place as Secretary for the rest of the trip. Lavinia Ponsonby, Colonel Ponsonby's daughter and one of Lawrence's staff, also joined us as his Chief Assistant. I was glad I went to Donbas.

Friday 2 February
We paid a visit to Andreev, the Commissar for Agriculture (all-Union). He is certainly one of the inner group in the Party and a up-and-coming man of about 45. He had two very competent assistants with him, both younger men, and confirmed points made to us by local agricultural people in Donbas. He believed that the Union could not have survived if collectivization had not taken place. It had enabled rapid adaptation of agriculture to meet war needs. Much new land had been broken in Siberia to grow sugar-beet, etc. Most of this would remain in

cultivation under other crops. Each new industrial area now had a surrounding belt developed to produce local supplies of vegetables, milk, etc. Many agricultural evacuees had been settled and would remain. A very large proportion of the livestock had been removed to avoid falling into German hands. After liberation many of these had been returned; some had travelled enormous distances on the hoof when returning. Farms in the non-devastated areas had contributed quotas of their livestock to help rehabilitate those areas requiring assistance.

In the evening we were given a farewell party by Shvernik. I sat between Sergeev, the Deputy Commissar for Foreign Trade, and General Shakharin, the Commissar for Aircraft Production, the one 38 and the other 40. After they had tried hard to make me drunk we settled down to an interesting conversation. I said we were much impressed by the youth of those in responsible positions. They said that they personally belonged to the middle-aged rather than the young group of those in important positions. No one in the Soviet Union seems able to explain clearly what happens to the older men, although it was suggested that they were pensioned off and their experience still used when necessary.

It appeared that development had been taking place so fast that places were easily found for all young men of ability. Sergeev said that he was a boy during the Revolution and got an elementary education, leaving school at 12. He then went to work in an engineering works and studied hard at night classes. When about 25 he was taken out of his job and sent for four years to the university — on the strength of his work at night classes and as a foreman in the shop. Then he was put straight into an important administrative post. This pulling out of able workers for further education appeared to be quite extensive. So far the tendency for the present governing classes to try to give their children a preferential start in life did not seem to have come into conflict with the attempt to find talent in the ranks of the workers. There certainly appeared to be room for all those with technical or administrative ability. A revolution in industrial administrative personnel appeared to have taken place in the previous ten years. Practically all of those in responsible posts had some kind of degree or technical qualification and had either come up through the education system or been given education later in life. They formed a pretty efficient, competitive, and somewhat ruthless class, who were very keen on discipline.

After the meal I had a talk with a Georgian from the Foreign Office and Mikoyan,[17] the very able Armenian, who is Commissar for Foreign Trade. He told us he was the only one of the twenty-seven Baku Commissars who escaped when the British landed there in 1919 and had had the rest shot. He had been out of town that day, he said. He is still a young man and obviously has a future before him, already being in the first half-dozen. He would drive a hard bargain. He tried to make Elliot merry by continually challenging him to sink cognacs. I found that he, Mikoyan, was responding in a very pleasant but weak blackberry liqueur! None of the Foreign Office men were present, as they were rumoured to have left for the meeting of Churchill, Roosevelt and Stalin in the Crimea.

Saturday 3 February

We lunched at Mikoyan's invitation in the cellars of the Wine Trust. Much sampling of the very many wines produced in the Soviet Union — mostly imitative of those in the west. Then off by train to Stalingrad (now called Volvograd). The country gradually got more and more treeless until we were on the open steppe. Sudden excitement as we saw a camel in a fur wrap pulling a sledge! Our first camel.

Stalingrad

Sunday 4 February

As we neared Stalingrad we saw gullies in the land where water was eroding light sandy soil. Then noticed large woods of young trees planted to check erosion. Few signs of fighting till right into Stalingrad, a long town stretching for miles on high ground along the Volga, but with no bridge over the river to the low-lying bank beyond. We were met at the station by Mayor and principal local people — a very tough set of the usual youth. Rather different in type from the fair northern and central Russians, being dark, with a touch of the Tartar about the eyes. After hearing an account of the German siege of the Russians and then of the Russian siege of the Germans, we went to see the city. Desolation was far more complete here than in the Donbas, as practically everything had been shot to pieces and little that was left was repairable. We drove in cars, part of the way being along the surface of the frozen Volga, to see the industrial plants in the northern part of the city. The Stalingrad Tractor Works were well on the way to full repair and so was the Metallurgical Plant. We were told production in both would soon be back to prewar. A vast number of the workers there were on repair work. I was surprised that one of the first buildings to be rebuilt was a hall that could be used as a theatre, a cinema or for meetings. I also visited one of the new schools and went over one of the reconstructed hospitals fitted up with equipment from Britain. All the goods sent out had 'G.VI.R.' marked on them — even down to the jerries. This hospital had only been reopened a few days and was mostly filled with maternity cases. All the staff were appreciative of the help received from Britain.

In contrast to all the reconstruction of industrial plant and public buildings, very little had been done in the way of housing — far less than in Stalino, which had been freed much later. There were a few new houses built for workers engaged on repair work but the vast mass of the population were living in holes in the ground covered with tarpaulins or in self-made shacks and even old railway trucks. The sandy soil was easy to work; it made the dugouts warm and dry in winter. The local soviet had banned certain areas for settlement which they intended to use for public buildings, apartment houses or industrial purposes. Plots had been allotted according to a plan in the hope that the temporary homes would be replaced later by more permanent buildings. A large part of the population had returned as there was plenty of work. It was difficult to conceive a British community allowing such a direction of building resources to 'public' purposes whilst leaving the greater part of housing provision to individual initiative.

We left in the evening for Baku.

Along the Caucasus

Monday 5 February

There was no direct railway from Stalingrad to Baku. So we travelled all day south-west to pick up the line from Rostov along the north side of the Caucasus. This was the line the Russians advanced along to roll the Germans up after cutting off Stalingrad. We went through flat steppe country, mostly under grass and not the plough so far as could be seen through the snow. There were occasional villages with a few trees and straight, wide unmade-up streets. We passed Gigant, which was for many years the largest farm in the world. Despite some reduction since, it may still hold this position.

I decided to join the party going to Central Asia by plane from Baku so as to see how some of the lesser nationalities get on in the Soviet Union.

Tuesday 6 February

By the morning we had started along the north side of the Caucasus, but scenery still flat as a pancake and Elbruz could not be seen as shrouded in mist. Later in the day it cleared and we had a wonderful sight of Kasbek and neighbouring mountains standing up out of the mist with the sun catching the snow on their summits. We stopped and got out at Beslan in the Ossetian[18] republic and were shown an account of our activities in the local Ossetian paper. Complete sheep-skin hats now appeared on some of the peasants and we visited a local market where peasants were selling their goods near the station. The most popular purchase was sunflower seeds which many Soviet citizens chew and spit out, keeping up a constant fire. It was very muddy, as thaw had set in. Some women asked when would the war be over. Despite the victories announced daily, there is widespread war weariness. One man hearing that Fraser was a 'deputy' complained that the quantity and quality of bread supplied to wives of Red Army men was scandalous, being 'full of bits of string'. On being told to approach either his deputy in the Ossetian Parliament or else in the All-Union Assembly, he said that was no use. Nothing ever happened if one complained to them, but if a British deputy said something to the authorities, something would certainly be done!

It was getting dark as we passed through the Grozny oilfields which were beyond the further limit of German advance. There had been little sign of damage in this north Caucasus area, save burnt-out stations and an occasional house without a roof or an armoured train or railway waggon bottom up beside the track. Railway sidings, however, were full of trucks from all over Europe, left behind in the rapid German retreat. Owing to the Russians' changeover of the track to their broad gauge when they advanced, these trucks would never move again! The rate of the Russian advance, like that of the German, had been limited by this need to change the gauge.

Baku and Azerbaijan

Wednesday 7 February

We arrived in Baku to find snow gone and glorious sunshine. Entrance to Baku was very unpleasant. First barren salt steppes, then derelict derricks, then such clouds of black smoke from oil refineries as would have shut out the sky even at midsummer. On arriving the only compliment Elliot could find to say to the welcoming Mayor was, 'What a beautiful sky you have.' We went to a comfortable Intourist hotel, driving through the city. Some fine modern squares and promenades with oleanders and Mediterranean pines along the Caspian. We passed through Liberty Square with a memorial to the 26 Commissars we were told the British[19] had had shot after their landing in 1919! We then spent some minutes in a room with a large mural depicting this scene before meeting the Azerbaijan government! At our first meal in Baku we fell upon plates of radishes, spring onions and tomatoes. The absence of fresh vegetables in most of the Soviet Union in winter is certainly felt when you have been accustomed to them.

Walked along the front in the sun. Beach a foot or so from shore black in oil. So bathing in warm weather is from piers or boats. No tides in Caspian. Large wharves for tankers. We were told that a third of Soviet merchant navy is on the Caspian carrying oil up the Volga to central Russia. Went for tour of city and saw some fine modern flats for workers on the heights above. Despite warm weather people looked less well than in Moscow or the countryside. Many children looked undernourished. Clothes rather more ragged here than elsewhere. People very free and easy. Men relieving themselves and playing jokes on one another as they walk along, whilst small boys take their trousers down in the gutters when they so desire. This may also happen in Moscow in summer, but it was too cold for such behaviour there in January. Soviet closets one of their weak points. In big towns rarely well kept and ill ventilated owing to danger of freezing. In country and quite large towns no water for sewerage but just ash closets with two holes in the ground. The stench in summer must be overpowering. Truly a tough people!

Baku has about a million inhabitants, having grown a great deal since the war; 40 per cent Azerbaijanis (Turks), 35 per cent Russians, 10 per cent Armenians. Some big textile manufacturers and the administrative centre of Azerbaijan, a republic with just over three million people (60 per cent Azerbaijans, 13 per cent Armenians, 10 per cent Russians). Many of the houses in old quarters were very slummy. A fine park with a view over city and bay in construction just behind the Intourist Hotel. Soviet parks are filled with plaster statues usually of Lenin placing his approving hand on Stalin's shoulder (occasionally one of Marx survives in the more remote places), or of young athletes or children. All very prim — even the cherubs wore small panties. Many trees were being planted along streets but many more were required if the city was to be properly beautified. Constant watering was necessary here if they were to survive. Industrial parts of city as bad in appearance as the worst old British industrial centres. Many new workers' cottages appeared to have been built right among the works.

Thursday 8 February

We visited the oil wells and lunched with director of the big oil trust (a young Azerbaijani of 32). Technicians in oil industry drawn from whole Union but a growing tendency here to draw on local people educated at local technical schools. We were told that many such preferred to send their children to Russian rather than Azerbaijani schools. A large area reclaimed from sea to sink wells but many derricks were now being sunk directly into the sea. Oilfield has a very ugly appearance. Was introduced to an old man — unshaven — who was described as a representative oil worker. He was a member of Supreme All-Union Soviet but appeared to do very little in that position beyond attending occasional meetings in Moscow.

The All-Union Soviet meets in a very fine assembly hall in the Kremlin. Its meetings are much more in the nature of public meetings than of debates, as the assembly is too large and all speeches are made from a pulpit. Many famous persons, such as Eisenstein, if members of the Party, are made deputies and wear the flag badge which shows membership. There are a number of working men from principal unions, but every effort is made to include famous actors, doctors, scientists, etc. They usually lead very active lives in their professions and could not be members if membership involved the kind of work done by an MP. Membership of the state and town soviets, on the other hand, appears to involve a great deal of work.

We had the rotund but active woman secretary of Azerbaijan Soviet attached to us, who went by the appropriate name of Fatima Ferrageva. She said she had worn a veil from 12 to 19 and had married at 16, without having seen her husband since he was a boy. She had educated herself since and was a strong advocate of women's rights. In the Azerbaijan Parliament there were 89 women out of a total membership of 300. She was very indignant that there were only 14 women in the British Parliament. The average marriage age among Azerbaijanis had now risen to 19 and would soon follow the average Russian marriage age into the early 20s. The Azerbaijanis — despite their Turkish language and some inter-mixture of Mongol blood — are on the whole Caucasian in type with dark hair; they frequently have the Caucasian large nose often described as 'Jewish'. We were told that some intermarriage with Russians is now taking place in Baku. In the evening we went to an operetta at the State Opera House. A very good production — story rather like *The Maid of the Mountains*[20] — based on local folk tales. The eastern style of music was modified to suit western ears. The singing and production were good as well as dancing. The women excel in this kind of dancing in contrast to the Ukrainian dances where men have the best parts. This local dancing was very fine and delicate compared with the bad Hollywood imitations of eastern dancing. We were introduced to the author and cast. We were told that we had been expected a day earlier. We asked how was it that we still had the best seats. 'That is no problem', we were told, 'when we have distinguished guests we take the best seats and those who have booked them have to come another night.'[21]

The local Commissar of Education told us that the running of theatres and operas cost yearly about 3,000,000 roubles, of which they received half back in receipts. Prices were definitely kept low and a government subsidy to 'culture' was expected The author had already received very large royalties. Big developments had taken place in the cultural field throughout all the trans-Caucasian republics.

Friday 9 February

We said goodbye to King-Hall, Buller and Jewson at our hotel, where they joined a number of visitors also waiting for suitable flying conditions. These included Air Marshal Tedder (1890–1967), who jokingly told us that the new jet 'flying fortresses' had been nicknamed by his airmen as flying fartresses. We were intrigued to see the Orthodox Patriarch of Alexandria, who was returning from Moscow, where he had been the guest of the Soviet government, loaded with icons and crosses as gifts. Very surprising in view of the small Orthodox community in Egypt consisting mostly of Greeks!

Elliot and Ponsonby decided to join the Central Asian party. After the recent disaster to the British party on the way to Crimea, Russians would take no risks about flying and insisted on our going round the Caspian by train to get there. In fact, very little flying takes place in USSR in winter owing to frequent fogs. Elliot and I paid a short visit to Baku University. Most professors were now Azerbaijanis. I had some fun talking to three intelligent girls in an English class.

En route to Central Asia

We left at lunchtime and travelled back north along Caspian coast, crossing the old wall from the Caucasus to the sea which was built to bar nomads from the north. After going through a very barren area we came to Dagestan, where there were many trees and orchards looking very like parts of Devonshire.

Saturday 10 February

Woke in the morning to find ourselves crossing the sandy Kalmuck steppe on a new line built during the war to link Astrakhan with Baku. It was covered with tussocky grass with occasional lakes where fishermen were dragging nets through holes in the ice. We stopped at a Russian village and had talk with a railway worker from Bessarabia who was living in a dugout in the sand. It was very clean and cosy inside.

The Kalmucks[22] had all been deported to Central Asia as it was thought they would sympathize with the Germans during their advance (they were the only Buddhists in Europe and almost pure Mongol in race). Russian cattle farmers appeared to have taken their place, though there had been a number of old Russian villages in this area.

A number of the peoples in the Soviet Union have been deported during the war. The Volga Germans, it was feared could not be trusted. The Crimean Tartars and some of the lesser people north of the Caucasus were removed as a punishment for collaboration with the Germans. The Crimean Tartars were sent to Uzbekistan (their language is very similar) and the others to various parts of Siberia and Kazakstan. On the whole, however, most of the lesser nationalities remained loyal to the Soviet Union.

In the evening we stopped and visited a Tartar village in sight of Astrakhan. Mud houses with doorless privies down the middle of the street but very healthy-looking people — especially the children. We had a fine view of the principal buildings of Astrakhan strung out along the river and crossed an enormous bridge (twenty-two spans of various sizes) over the Volga and then saw the sun set behind it — a wonderful sight. As we went over the central span a camel drawing a sledge drove underneath. The centre of the river formed a main roadway in winter. This bridge, we were told, was built in six months early in the war and was the main route by which the Russians got their forces and supplies across for the southern part of the pincer movement which cut off the Germans at Stalingrad.

Sunday 11 February

Woke up to find ourselves going northward to the west of Kazakstan through steppe country once more under snow. Stopped at an occasional village — they looked very prosperous in this area. Russians and Ukrainians seem to have filled up the Volga German territory. We passed a prison camp with wooden watch-towers, guards, machine guns and a high barbed-wire fence. Our Russian companions did their best to divert our attention from it.

Monday 12 February

Awoke some way past the boundary of Asia and Europe which is at Uralsk on the Ural river. Much of this country seemed fertile, although on the edge of the desert. There were many Russian settlers among the Kazaks. I was surprised to find the latter very Mongol in type; their children looked very Chinese. We had quite a long stop at Aktyabinsk, which has a chemical industry. Population had been almost doubled by evacuees. There were many Poles from east of the Curzon Line and Volga Germans here billeted on the people. Faringdon had a talk with a Polish Jew who had originally been deported further east. He was very unhappy

172

and said all the 250,000 Polish Jews in the USSR wanted to go to USA. They will form a big problem after the war as the Poles have made it very clear they do not want them back and the Americans are unlikely to want that number. Anti-Semitism is still a problem in the USSR as Hitler's propaganda had stirred up feeling particularly in the western areas where there was a large Jewish population. Many of those who fled were now trickling back but many of the refugees will probably remain in other parts of the Union. The Jews had caused a certain resentment as their ability has given them a high proportion of the administrative posts. Stalin's view that anti-Semitism would be terminated by the end of the capitalist system which would put Jews on terms of equality with non-Jews in the industrial and commercial field had not therefore been borne out.

Tuesday 13 February
Awoke just in time to see Aralsk, a wretched-looking fishing and railway town at northern end of frozen sea of Aral. Later passed many reed beds which were being cut for thatching and then along the frozen Jaxartes (Syr Darya). It was still very cold and there was little sign of vegetation far from the river. A fine red sunset over the desert.

Wednesday 14 February
Awoke in time to see Turkestan, the first Central Asian place of any size, watered from neighbouring snowclad mountains. Snow had melted here and desert looked very barren without a sign of life as the grass which follows the snow had not yet sprung up. Had a good climb up neighbouring hill when we stopped at a Kazak village and had a fine view of the mountains. Truk had great difficulty in getting us all back into the train on such an excellent spring day after being so long cooped up on the journey. The Kazaks wore very bright colours and the small boys had the front of their heads shaved and two little pigtails behind. Houses mostly built of mud with thatch and mud roofs. These seemed warm and comfortable. Large numbers of sheep, cattle and camels were kept on the rough herbage with good stocks of lucerne which had to be brought from irrigated lands.

Tashkent and the Uzbeks

Later in the day the land began to take on a green colour and we went through a belt of better grazing before suddenly entering the irrigated garden land round Tashkent, where we arrived in the evening and went to stay in two dachas – i.e. country houses – which were used by members of the town and Uzbek soviets. We gathered that these were mainly used at weekends in summer. There were lovely gardens filled with fruit trees, vines over pergolas and roses. Shaded platforms to sleep or lie upon were suitably arranged. Indoors they were comfortable – but only one lavatory-bathroom for each house and a most explosive sort of geyser over a furnace to heat the shower. It was sunny when we arrived but snowed each night so we spent the days splashing about in the mud caused by thawing snow.

Tashkent is a finely laid out town of about one million inhabitants (grown greatly since the war); 40 per cent of Uzbeks, 35 to 40 per cent Russians, and the rest other Central Asian peoples. It is the capital of Uzbekistan, a republic of six million people. Masses of trees have been planted everywhere both along the public highways and in parks and in the citizens' gardens. The town is very spread out, covering a vast area. Many of the inhabitants had small, self-built houses and gardens with three or four fruit trees which they could sit under in the great heat of the summer. Water channels went everywhere to refresh these, and there was an elaborate system of control to see that they all get their fair share of water. In the centre were the government offices and some flats. The old town of mud huts without gardens was rapidly being pulled down. A considerable amount of building was taking place despite the war which felt very remote here. There did not seem ever to have been a blackout. We finished the day by visiting the bigwigs. The chief of these was Yusepov who was the local boss, being Secretary of the Uzbek Communist Party and Chairman of the Uzbek Soviet. A man of 45, with completely clean-shaven head, looked like a benign Buddha. He gave the impression of remarkable drive and administrative ability. I asked if he were related to the murderer of Rasputin, only to be told it was a common Tartar name and some Tartars had invaded Russia and some Uzbekistan in the past The Uzbek Prime Minister, a young man in his early thirties, also appeared able but was obviously second string to Yusepov.

Thursday 15 February

We arrived down to breakfast to find glasses of yogurt, cream cheese and grapes and melon available. They dry these two fruits in the sun and then hang them in their dry cellars to keep right through the winter. It was the twentieth anniversary of the establishment of the Uzbek Republic (1925), following the reorganization of Central Asia after the Revolution. We first, therefore, visited the exhibition organized to commemorate this event. It consisted mostly of the story of recent industralization and irrigation. I was most interested in the big Fergana Canal which had already been completed and a scheme in prospect for running a canal from the Oxus through to the Jaxartes with a branch back to the Oxus from Bokhara. It was to be both a hydro-electric and an irrigation scheme – on the grand scale.

In the afternoon we visited the university for a talk with some of the professors and research students. Most of the students were on holiday, just having finished their exams. The majority of teachers were now Uzbeks although there were a considerable number of Russians. I had a chat with a Russian professor of mathematics who spoke English. He had been on the staff of the Russian University at Warsaw before 1914 and had been evacuated with staff to Rostov in 1915. After the Revolution he was sent to Tashkent (1920) and has been on its staff ever since. He said that when first opened they admitted practically any Uzbek who could read and write and who wanted to come. The university was thus full from the beginning. As time went on, however, and better material became available, they had raised their standards. There seemed to be a far less rigorous call-up of men students here among the former subject people than in Russia proper. At Moscow University there were three women students to every man. It appeared that men here got exemption for the period of their studies in a wide variety of subjects both of industrial and cultural value. Having started to create an intelligentsia, every effort was being made to develop it as rapidly as possible.

We also visited the Observatory, the third largest in the Soviet Union. A great deal was thought here of the astronomical studies of Ulug Beg, Tamerlane's grandson. A plaster cast had been made of him by opening his tomb and reconstructing his features from his skull. In the evening we went to an Uzbek opera, a charming and tragic love story based on a fifteenth-century poem by Mir Alister Navoi. The woman lead had a very good voice.

Friday 16 February
In the morning we motored out of the town to visit a kolkholz — the Red Uzbekistan collective farm — and were greeted by three enormous men with large fur hats, one of whom was the Chairman. We tramped through some of their fields, vineyards and orchards and then looked at their stalls and stables for cattle and horses which were grouped round a large yard. The animals looked quite good although the horses were very light compared with British farm horses. The stabling did not appear very warm for winter; during the night we were told a number of guards slept out in the stables on carpet-covered beds with rifles beside them, both to prevent theft and to care for the animals if necessary. Most of these guards were boys of 16 or 17.

The kolkhoz's clubroom was an amazing sight. On a low dais covered with carpets sat all the old men of the kolkhoz, who were past doing a full day's work, sitting cross-legged having their elevenses (bowls of green tea) and a chat, most of them in white or blue turbans and bright-coloured warm-padded dressing gowns. The old women did not have a similar meeting-place but, we were told, preferred to go to one another's homes for a chat. The clubroom was used for concerts, meetings and other entertainments as required; it had a good stage, wireless, some papers and a canteen.

We were then invited to a 'ploff', the Uzbek name for a feast. We sat cross-legged on carpets and cushions round an enormous table covered with very fat legs of mutton, ducks, chicken and all manner of fruit and sweets. There were no plates but we ate off large flat pieces of bread made to look like plates. The chairman broke bread with each of us to start the meal. I was offered a sheep's eye, which was considered a great delicacy. I swallowed it down like an oyster and tried very hard to look as if I had enjoyed it! Kebab — skewers with pieces of mutton on them — were then brought to us and the 'ploff' itself. This was composed of rice with bits of meat. The locals took up handfuls, squeezed out the gravy and then swallowed it in mouthfuls. Cups of sweet wine accompanied the meal which was terminated with green tea with sugar and milk or lemon. We did out best at the meal but they were very disappointed with our appetites. After it was over they presented us all with tippy tiacas, the small local skull cap still generally worn. The old men put the turban over it; the fur hats worn in winter are usually put on top of it. 'Tippies' are in a vast variety of patterns, often being very gay in colour. Elliot was also given a silk dressing-gown of the type worn outdoors by Uzbek men in the summer or on holiday. The Chairman put his on also and, after many hugs all round, we departed. The Chairman and members of his committee appeared quiet and effective.

Their kolkhoz had turned over largely to vegetable growing to meet the growing population of Tashkent but they still had a big cotton production. They had put more land under the plough and their production generally had increased despite their heavy loss of manpower owing to the war. Unlike Britain, agriculture lost its manpower in USSR to a far greater extent than industry. Most kolkhozes depended on the work of the old men, women and children with the great help of the tractor stations. The great success of the kolkhozes in the war on the smaller manpower may speed up the transfer of population to industry when the men come home.

In contrast to the good collective buildings put up directly by their own labour, the individual cottages with their surrounding plots did not appear in good condition. Most of them were the same mud huts which had existed before collectivization, scattered about without a plan.

Local dress in its bright colours, sometimes modernized in cut for women, was extensively worn especially in summer and on holidays. The men's workaday clothes, both in town and country, were largely the same as for Russians — khaki-coloured jacket and trousers, heavily padded with cotton wool in winter with tall felt boots and the usual European dress in summer but with the tippy or a cap with a very large peak on the head.

Some of the party then visited a textile factory, a very large mill making up the locally grown cotton for the Central Asian market. I visited the cotton research station. Much work had been done there to get a better type of cotton, and green- and brown-coloured types developed which could be spun for making into blankets without dyeing. We went some way into the country along very bumpy roads to make this visit. Ponsonby was very impressed and was anxious to establish contact between these people and British cotton research people. All the responsible staff here were Russian.

In the evening we saw an excellently produced and acted *Othello* in Uzbek. This gripped the imagination even though we did not understand the words. Othello himself had been a boy sweeper who cleaned out the theatre when his talent was first discovered. All the women, including Desdemona, wore blond wigs. The sound of waves and seagulls brought a realistic noise of the sea to an audience many miles from one. Shakespeare appears to be more extensively acted in Central Asia than in Great Britain today. Popular throughout the Soviet Union, his rolling rhetoric particularly attracts the new theatre public of Central

Asia which had no drama in their own tongue twenty-five years ago. Theatres here usually run a repertory of six or eight plays at a time. *Othello* had been running in such a repertory for five years, whilst *Hamlet* had a run of seven years and a new production was in prospect. We suggested to the director that Marlowe's *Tamburlaine the Great* would be very appropriate. He said that it had been considered but there was as yet no good translation into Russian and they had to re-translate everything from Russian into Uzbek! Here as elsewhere in the Soviet Union the theatre is immensely popular. There were eight theatres in Tashkent, including those in the Russian language and forty-five in the whole of Uzbekistan. These figures were exclusive of the kolkhoz halls which were sometimes used by visiting companies and more frequently by their own local talent. Cinemas, including the open-air ones, were rather more numerous but did not provide the same scope for national expression, as most films shown in USSR are either Russian or American. The local talent for acting, singing and dancing was found for theatres by innumerable competitions between local groups of amateurs. Those who had already arrived had to hold their places against new arrivals thus thrown up yearly. The result was that the small parts were very well played and productions remarkably finished.

Saturday 17 February
In the morning we visited a large aircraft factory mainly engaged in building transport planes. Most of the machinery and many of the employees had been transferred from Moscow and Kiev. It was intended to keep this plant here after the war. Most of the workers and all those in responsible positions were Russians or Ukrainians. Many local youngsters of school age were working especially at riveting — presumably in their period off school. As in all factories and public buildings in USSR there were masses of guards with rifles everywhere — both men and women. In the early days of the war such precautions against sabotage or paratroops may have been necessary but now it seemed a great waste of both man and womanpower. I even saw one man guarding a bust of Lenin!

We then went to lunch with the general in charge of the factory and the principal members of the staff. We were due to visit a nursery school and other educational institutions in the afternoon so were hard put to it by the general, who was determined to make it a real party and tried to make us sink vodka after vodka with toast after toast. His whole staff joined with him and when we insisted on standing up to go he produced bottles of champagne which were drunk standing. I had an interesting talk with a young lad of 21 who had just been appointed full-time trade union organizer in the works. He had come from Moscow with the plant and had fought in that city's defence as a civilian. He had not been allowed into the forces, being a skilled technician. Many of those present had never had champagne before and were soon very merry, practically detaining us by force. The general then began enthusiastically kissing Elliot and the other members of the delegation. I managed to escape by cowardly transferring myself into the ranks of the already kissed! Then the Uzbek Secretary of the works' Young Communist League, kissed the horrified Colonel Ponsonby full on the mouth and great comradeship and enthusiasm ensued. To our surprise, Lavinia, Ponsonby's pretty daughter, escaped with a gallant kiss on the hand from the general. In the USSR it is definitely considered the right thing for men to kiss full on the lips on all occasions where friendly emotion is displayed. It was only because we were foreigners that we had been let off lightly — so far. On the other hand, it is definitely indecent to kiss a woman in public unless one is engaged to her or she is a close relative! At last we escaped.

Some of the party visited the Industrial Institute. I went to a good nursery school for children aged 2 to 7 with Russians and Uzbeks mixed. A pleasant building with large tree-covered courtyard for use in summer and a staff of enthusiastic young teachers. Most of the time was spent in 'being prepared for school', which included learning the letters, being taught manners, dancing, singing, etc. We had a very good show specially put on for us with dancing by both boys and girls together in various national costumes. They then sang. The opening song was 'My brother is in the Red Army, I hope to join him soon' — from kiddies of 5 to 7. Other war songs followed. John Lawrence, our secretary, made a toy sword out of a sheet of newspaper and gave it to one of the small boys. The girl teacher of 19 rushed up and told the boy he must always remember to fight the Fascist enemy. Right through Soviet education, especially of course among the older boys, there is a very strong military bias. I have a feeling how-ever that there is a deep-rooted underlying dislike of war amongst the people of the Soviet Union and that the government have introduced the military bias to offset this feeling. It will be interesting to see how victory will influence edu-cational training. This was undoubtedly one of the best nursery schools, but they exist in all big cities on a voluntary basis. We were told many mothers working night shifts left their children to sleep at school the whole week, just collecting them for weekends.

We then went on to an Uzbek girls' school in the old slummy part of the town — with all ten classes, that is with girls aged 7 to 17. The headmistress was a young woman in her late twenties, with long black plaits right down to her waist, looking like one of her own senior girls. This is the fashion among Uzbek women if they have nice hair — especially among those of marriageable age. A common Uzbek saying 'The longer the plaits the smaller the brains' was not borne out in this case. We visited a number of classes and asked questions. Many in the top class wanted to be doctors; we were told that if they passed well in their examinations they would get the necessary facilities and financial support to do so. One of the girls who was asked if she knew where Britain was replied that it was an island on the edge of the Atlantic Ocean — a very suitable reply from someone in Central Asia; an efficiently run school. All the teachers were Uzbeks save two Russians teaching Russian and Military Knowledge respectively. The class taken by the latter (girls of 12–13) was being taught all about poison gases, their uses and how to deal with them!

In the evening we were taken to an Uzbek concert and sat with Yusepov, and the local bigwigs. It started, however, with a symphony which was too highbrow for me; it also did not interest the more musical members of our party. The composer conducted. There were some good folk dances, but the star turns of the evening were the acting of Tamara Hanum, an Armenian Gracie Fields,[23] in her Central Asian folk songs, and the singing of Halima Nasyrova, whose powerful voice was thoroughly at home in the high notes of the local music. A crowded and enthusiastic audience.

Sunday 18 February

We first visited a hydro-electric power station some way out of Tashkent which supplied the industrial needs of the district. It was part only of a much bigger scheme in construction and assisted also in irrigation. The main part of the equipment had been transferred from the Ukraine when the Germans advanced. We then visited a big chemical works which was largely engaged on war production, although also producing fertilizers for the local market; in the afternoon we looked round Tashkent and did some shopping.

An Usbek party

In the evening we went to Yusepov's official dacha for a farewell 'ploff'. It was a grand do. We arrived to find a skinned gazelle complete with horns and studded all over with white nuts, sitting on a plate in the middle of the table. It was so arranged that it nodded its head whenever you walked near it. On either side were enormous sides of meat and dishes of poultry. These last had the heads at one end of the plate and tail feathers at the other. They included swans, peacocks, pheasants, ducks and geese. Just as we had reached our first toast a live gazelle with very long horns[24] was led in and tied to a post behind the Chairman. It was about to have its throat cut in our honour (an ancient Uzbek custom), when our protests caused its removal, butting everyone violently.

Yusepov ran the party with great gusto, having Tamara and Halima and all the local talent present. Most of them sat below a large bowl of salt placed on the tables. From time to time he clapped his hands and summoned them to perform in front of us. As he was the chief patron of the arts and was responsible in particular for cultural activities, they fell over themselves to carry out his every wish. Tom Fraser, whose birthday it was, sat next to Halima, who got very affectionate on one vodka. Yusepov suddenly called on Tom to propose the toast of the ladies, which he did gracefully. Halima then jumped up to sing an impassioned reply, swinging a large plate round her head. We all expected it to crash at any moment on Tom's head. She finally smashed it on the table with a flourish, saying that thus did her love fly to Tom and all of us. She then fell flat on the floor and had to be carried out.

Yusepov interrupted or added to speeches both of Uzbek and British as the toasts went on. He then asked Elliot if the British government would arrange a season for Uzbek artists in London after the war (Tamara Hanum came over for short seasons in London and Paris respectively about 1930), and was very disappointed when told a firm promise was not possible. He was not a diplomat, he said, when Elliot tried to explain the capitalist workings of the British stage. Such an Uzbek season would probably be a paying proposition to Cochran[25] with a public tired of the typical American musical. Roberts, who sat one side of Yusepov, was in one of his mischievous moods. He asked Y. whether all these local cultural activities did not unduly develop nationalist feeling, but was then properly squashed with the reply that their form might be nationalist, but their substance was socialist — whatever that might mean!

In the intervals I had a talk with my neighbour, the Commissar for Planning who described himself as the local Gosplan man. He apparently was responsible for submitting plans for local economic development to Moscow for approval. He said that local industralization was to continue rapidly after the war based on hydro-electric power. He claimed that an enormous coalfield existed in Uzbekistan which would be as productive as Donbas if opened up. Only two pits were so far working and its development did not appear to be early on the list of priorities. While most of the Uzbeks drank wine in preference to vodka, this young man was proud of his Russification in this matter.

It was a most enjoyable evening, but the party finally ended and we left an hour late — the train having been held up. It was only 25 years since the last emir from Central Asia fled into exile. He had probably given very similar parties to important guests.

From Fergana to Bokhara

Monday 19 February
I woke in the morning to find the train travelling through the Fergana valley right up to the frontier of Chinese Turkestan. This area is in part very fertile irrigated land alternating with patches of desert. An important irrigation scheme was carried out here some years ago — the big canal being dug out by volunteers from the collective farms in a very short time. All land available was then flooded. Some of this then proved unusable as salt came to the surface. Smaller canals are now being built to enable this land to be systematically flooded to 'leach' out the salt. After lunching off the gazelle which had decorated the table the previous night, we arrived at Fergana, a town founded by the Russians on their conquest towards the end of the last century. It was well laid out with large trees. Many of the women here still wore the black veil which was pulled up from the back of the head and covered the whole face. It is very ugly and has been much attacked in government propaganda.

We visited an oil factory where cotton waste was exploited both to provide liquid cooking oil and soap. We also went to a Tajik school for a hurried visit. These people were the original Iranian-speaking people of Central Asia who have not adopted the Turkish language of succeeding conquerors. They are a majority in Tajikstan and a substantial minority in most of the large towns of Uzbekistan. The Central Asian Jews who speak an Iranian dialect also attend the Tajik schools.

We then visited a kolkhoz some miles from the town. It had some very fine collective buildings which had been constructed in 1944. The reconstruction of the village houses appeared to be in progress. We saw a fine new mud house in the traditional Uzbek style. No windows opened on to the road, but all the rooms faced on to a veranda which ran along one side of a tree-covered courtyard. The men's part of the house was still separate from that of the women and to go from one part of the house to the other you had to come out on the veranda. The owner and his two sons of 15 and 16 showed me their rooms. There was no furniture save a pouffe and masses of carpets on the walls and floor and some eiderdowns. Apparently all three males sat or slept on the floor with their heads against the pouffe.

There was a pleasant dining room for the whole family with similar furnishings. Shelves were let into the wall at different heights to place food on. There were some large bowls which looked as though filled with Devonshire cream which was turning into yogurt, a favourite local dish. Lavinia was allowed into the women's portion of the house and had some tea. It was similar to the men's room, but all the young children lived there. I noted that in spite of being a keen member of the Party, he still kept to these traditions.

We then saw a silk artel (producers' co-operative) in a small country town nearby. Some lovely stuff was being made, mostly by old men and children. The looms were crowded into some old mosque buildings and the work was very repetitive. I cannot understand the preference for handmade rather than factory-made textiles which some people have even in Russia.

Tuesday 20 February
We arrived early in Samarkand. We spent most of the day sight-seeing. First we visited the Registan — a fine square of mosques and medresses (Koranic schools). Then we looked at a good series of tombs of Tamerlane's period (1400 onwards). These had either been excellently restored or were in process of restoration — as was Tamerlane's tomb itself. Almost all of these buildings were in a local form of Muslim architecture and covered with decorative blue tiling. During his conquests Tamerlane carried off good craftsmen from all over the Middle East for his building activities. From time to time these had been much damaged by earthquakes. Their restoration was intended partly to encourage national traditions and partly to lay the basis for a future tourist industry. We were told that Tamerlane, when a boy, organized two rival gangs of boys to fight one another. When his gang won and captured the rival leader he asked his followers what punishment should be inflicted for defeat. 'Cut off his head', was the reply. So he did so. Tamerlane's mother is reported to have said on hearing of this that he would be a great conqueror! History does not relate what was said by the mother of the lad who lost his head! Samarkand is a large town of about 160,000 people,

with most of its modern buildings being connected either with its university or other higher education institutes.

Wednesday 21 February

We arrived in Bokhara, which until 1920 was the capital of a local emir who ruled a large territory with the assistance of a Russian resident, being in a similar position to an Indian prince under British rule. The town (about 60,000 inhabitants) had grown very little since the Revolution. We were shown plans for rebuilding its central areas, but little had yet been done in the way of reconstruction. We also went sight-seeing here and climbed to the top of a large minaret from which we had an excellent view of the irrigated plain around the town and of its quaint crowded streets. I walked round the roofs of a medresse, looking into the surrounding homes, which appeared very biblical in character. The emir's palace was partly destroyed in the revolution of 1920. After some severe fighting he galloped away with 200 horsemen to Afghanistan where he had recently died. Most of the horsemen returned when their pay gave out. His three official wives were sent after him a year later, but his sixty-three unofficial wives (concubines) were freed to find a new husband apiece. As there is a surplus of men in all these Central Asian states, the abolition of polygamy proved very popular! The emir's two sons were sent to Moscow to school. We were told one had become a successful engineer and the other an industrial technician — a better fate than that of a penniless pretender in Afghanistan.

We went out for dinner to the emir's summer palace, now the dacha of the local Soviet. This was some miles out of the town and was a hideous construction of 1911. It was amusing to come across massive brass bedsteads of the type lately in fashion with Blackpool landladies in the midst of all this eastern splendour.

The people here looked European in appearance, although not of course in dress, many being light in colour. The Uzbeks are the people of the irrigated lands in contrast to the Tajiks and Kirghiz of the mountains and the Kazaks and Turkomans of the steppes and deserts. In and around Tashkent the Mongol element in the Uzbek population is large, but it is thin elsewhere. The Uzbeks have a strong national consciousness and are much the most important of the Central Asian peoples.

Turkomans and Finis

It being our last night on the train both the Russian and British members of our party were anxious to have a celebration. After Elliot had been safely seen to bed all jointly embarked upon the finishing up of the supplies of champagne, which would otherwise have been returned to stock. I arrived in search of a glass of tea to be offered a bowl of champagne. One of the Russians, who we believed to be a member of NKVD (Political Security Police), had always spoken to us through an interpreter; with champagne aboard he blossomed into excellent

English. The next morning there was some dispute as to whether the number of bottles of champagne which had been left at the beginning of the previous evening was 35 or 50. It was rather an academic argument!

Thursday 22 February
Woke to find we were well across the Oxus in the middle of the desert, having already passed the Merv oasis. The snow-covered mountains on the Persian border glittered in the sun, as we gradually approached them through occasional oases where streams came down from the hills ultimately to lose themselves in the sands of the Kizil Kum Desert. We arrived at Ashkabad in the early afternoon, a fine modern town of over 300,000 people, the capital of Turkmenia. A former frontier post, it had grown tenfold since the Revolution, having asphalt streets lined with trees and modern buildings. As in Baku and Tashkent, about 40 per cent of its population was of the local national republic, and 40 per cent Russian and Ukrainian and the rest being of other Soviet peoples. We met the local leader, an active little man, and some of the commissars who created a good impression. The Turkomans are a little over a million strong, living around the Kizil Kum Desert. They are tall and dark, being rather Persian in appearance, due no doubt to the custom of raiding into Persia to carry off wives before the Russian conquest in the 1880s. One of the commissars told me that Turkomans did not like their own girls, but found other people's girls very attractive. In the evening we saw a locally written opera.

Friday 23 February
We went some miles out of the city into the foothills of the border mountains to visit a kolkhoz. The collective farms here contained both mountain pastures above and desert below, with a rich strip of land watered by mountain streams between. This farm was planned as a large estate with big orchards, vineyards, etc. Close by were the barracks of the Soviet frontier guards and also the citadel of Nissa, the old Parthian capital, which had been partially excavated. It was a beautifully warm day with spring in the air; we lunched at the kolkhoz. The Turkomans keep up their national dress which is in very bright colours. Their women never seem to have worn the veil save in the form of a scarf across the front of the chin. The men were very fond of wearing either big busbies of sheepskin or else fur hats of the astrakhan type with the top pulled out either side. Coats are worn in bright red or similar colours, especially when on horseback. We then visited a 'horse factory' on a state farm. The Turkomans are good horsemen and we were shown some graceful animals. The riders all wore national dress in their displays. In the evening we had an even larger official dinner than usual. When we thought we had finished, a steak with fried eggs on it appeared! We were well entertained by the local talent.

Saturday 24 February
We woke early, intending to depart by plane for Tehran, only to find it snowing

hard. After a restful morning many of us visited the local museums. There was an excellent display of carpets, an important local product, each of the Turkoman tribes having evolved its own standard designs. We then entered an artel (a producers' co-operative) where women in national dress were making carpets by hand. It seemed very slow and primitive even when in bright surroundings. We were told a carpet factory to replace the artel had been under consideration when the war started and would be built as soon as possible. Practically all carpets were bought by the government for export. Later we visited the Commissar for Water, an important member of the Republic's government. He explained that a canal from the Oxus to Merv was already half completed. Other plans were under consideration, including one for sending part of the Oxus back along its old course to the Caspian. Some of us visited the more recently completed flats. They were all built, but all fixtures had not been completed owing to the war and evacuation had made them very overcrowded. A Russian boys' school was also visited. Many had come with their parents when industries had been transferred. There were a large number of boys in khaki uniform, who we discovered to be war orphans, being cared for in 'infantry schools' — in reality orphanages. They came to the ordinary schools for their schooling. In the evening, we went to a local ballet which was put on especially for our benefit. It was a pleasure to see. The production was not finished, but was extraordinarily lively. Here in Turkmenia there has been a similar cultural development to that in the much more populous Uzbek neighbour.

Friday 25 February
Raining when we awoke and it looked as though we should have to stay another day. It cleared late and we visited the street market. Then came a hectic message to say that flying was OK and we hurriedly left for the airfield. Rising abruptly from the plain, the Russian machine wound through the mountains and then across the rocky Persian plateau to Tehran. The country looked very bleak and desolate with occasional small pits (they were part of the Carnet irrigation system). Small pits are sunk along a route and then connected underground to lead water where required. We arrived in the evening and were distributed among the principal members of the embassy staff.

We had been forty-two days in the Soviet Union.

27

Obituaries–Three Friends

OTTO CLARKE (SIR RICHARD), 1919–1975*

As an old friend who shared a flat with him at 12 Great Ormond Street, for four-and-a-half years just before the Second World War, I should like to pay tribute to the important contributions Otto Clarke made to the Labour Movement before his wartime entry into the Civil Service, and his subsequent successful career in that field. Richard was called 'Otto' by fellow students, when a left-wing member of the Cambridge Labour Club, because he appeared short-sighted and wore glasses of a German model at a time when Hitler was climbing to power. He greatly impressed Colin Clark, then lecturer in Statistics at Cambridge, who brought him into the New Fabian Research Bureau, which was actively engaged under the leadership of G.D.H. Cole, Hugh Gaitskell, W.A. Robson and Leonard Woolf in rethinking Labour Party policies and trying to work out detailed practical ways of carrying them out.

Otto was elected to the Executive of the NFRB in 1934, and served as an active member until its taking over of the older Fabian Society at the beginning of the war when he entered the Civil Service. He was particularly interested in the hitherto vague plans for extending nationalization when a Labour government should come into office. His book *The Socialization of Iron and Steel*, which he wrote under the name of Ingot and which was published for the NFRB by Gollancz in 1936, had a big influence in persuading the Labour Party and leading trade unions of the need to include this industry in the field of public ownership and the form its nationalization should finally take. Its detailed analysis of the industry and its problems and of its international ramifications foreshadows the kind of study he later carried out when dealing with problems in the Civil Service.

A keen member of the Holborn Labour Party, Otto was one of the six Labour members elected to that hitherto 100 per cent Tory Council in 1937 along with George Wansborough, Ena Chaplin and Bill Shebbeare, another journalist, who was killed at the Normandy landing in 1944; to the fury of the Tory majority,

---

* *The Times* declined to publish this, 24 June 1975.

who consisted mainly of businessmen commuting to the suburbs, they insisted on evening meetings to ventilate their constituents' problems. A keen trade unionist, Otto was elected Father of the *Financial News* chapel, which post he held until leaving the paper. He was a good speaker and gave me considerable help in the 1935 General Election in Dagenham where his sister was a school-teacher.

He met his first wife, Joan Simeon Clarke, at Holborn Labour Party meetings. She became Research Secretary of the Fabian Society soon after their marriage in 1939. He undoubtedly helped and advised her in many of the research projects she initiated and in preparation of the evidence given by the Fabian Society to the Beveridge Committee which had such a big effect on its recommendations.

Unfortunately, the marriage broke up and Joan married Wenzel Jasch, Sudeten German Socialist leader, then in exile in Britain, before he returned to Germany to enter the Hessen government after the war.

Otto never lost touch with his socialist friends, although undoubtedly he moved very much to the right politically, during his Civil Service career. One of his sons became the left-wing Secretary of the National Union of Students.

GAVIN FARINGDON, 1903—77 *

Lord Faringdon
Active in Labour Causes

Lord Faringdon, a Labour peer who played an active role in many of the early causes of the Left, died on January 29 at the age of 74.

Mr John Parker MP writes:

Gavin Faringdon was born in 1902 and succeeded his grandfather, the first Baron Faringdon, CH, a railway magnate, who had been a Unionist MP, and was created Lord Faringdon in 1916. Gavin's father died in 1922 and after an education at Eton, McGill University, Montreal, and Christ Church, Oxford, Gavin inherited the title and estate on the death of his grandfather in 1934.

In the early 1920s he was a somewhat notorious member of the 'Bright Young Things'. By 1934 he had become keenly interested in public affairs and joined the Labour Party, giving substantial help to Dr Addison (later first Viscount Addison, KG) when he was elected in a by-election that year as MP for Swindon which then included Faringdon in its constituency.

At first, he was a nervous and rather indifferent speaker. He came to help me in the large Romford division in the 1935 General Election. My agent sent the 'noble lord' to speak to the commuters in snobbish Upminster, thinking they would be impressed. A young Oxford student, Bill Nield, later the distinguished

* Published in *The Times*, 2 February 1977.

civil servant, Sir William Nield, arrived to find the crowded meeting out of control with Gavin trying to quell noisy interrupters with 'Shut up, shut up!' Nield seized Gavin by the seat of his trousers, pulled him down, and successfully took over the meeting.

Meanwhile, having inherited Buscot, he restored this eighteenth-century house internally and externally, demolishing the Victorian wing his grandfather had added for his large family. He later made arrangements for the house to pass to the National Trust.

A keen supporter of the Spanish Republican cause during the Spanish Civil War, he flew its flag whenever appropriate. Also a strong pacifist, he reconciled his conscience when World War II came by joining the Fire Service and giving sterling service during the blitz in London, Bristol and other large cities. In his fire brigade uniform, with Faringdon, the name of his local branch, written across his chest, he frequently attended the House of Lords and Fabian committees when in London. I accompanied him on a Parliamentary goodwill mission to the USSR in January—March 1945, when we toured around in one of the Czar's old trains, a party of eight MPs and two peers, serviced by members of the Soviet Foreign Office and the British embassy. Lord Brimelow, later head of the Foreign Service, was our secretary.

Gavin emphatically stated his views to the Russians at meal times, making clear his disapproval of many of Churchill's prewar policies. Our leader, Walter Elliot, was informed by the senior Soviet official present that we had a dangerous Trotskyist in our ranks who would certainly be incarcerated if a Soviet citizen. However, in due course, his idiosyncrasies were accepted. He had brought his fire brigade uniform with him and spoke with authority about fire-fighting in the blitz. As a result he was asked officially to inspect the fire brigades of Moscow, Leningrad and other bombed cities.

Gavin became an active Fabian, being either elected or co-opted to its executive committee (1943—69) serving in due course as its vice-chairman. His main interest was in colonial and international affairs, and he became chairman of the Fabian Colonial Bureau, 1952—58. For many years he acted as host at Buscot to many Fabian specialist groups including that under Crossman, which produced the latest Fabian Essays.

The last important conference held there was in 1970 after the fall of the Labour government to discuss its shortcomings. Those present included many former ministers such as Crossman and Wedgwood Benn and their advisers such as Lords Balogh and Kaldor. He acted as host for many years at his Brompton Square flat after annual general meetings. Already suffering from cancer, he retired in 1970 and was made a Fabian vice-president.

Gavin also played an active part in London government, being an elected LCC councillor (1958—61) and an alderman (1961—65). After the creation of the GLC he became a member of its historic buildings committee.

He was a kindly man, finding a home for Susan Lawrence, an early Labour stalwart in the House of Commons, after she had been bombed out. When a boy in the Fabian Bookshop got married to one of its office girls Gavin learnt that they could not afford a honeymoon. He promptly invited them to spend a week in his absence at Buscot, gave them first-class railway tickets and sent his Rolls Royce to fetch them from the station. He arrived back on their last evening to drink their health in champagne and wish them luck.

MARGARET COLE, 1893–1980*

Dame Margaret Cole
Distinguished Fabian
and Educationalist

Dame Margaret Cole DBE, who died yesterday at the age of 87, was an outstanding Socialist writer and educationalist. A collaborator with her distinguished husband, Professor G.D.H. Cole, who died in 1959, in much of his political work and in the writing of detective stories, she was a personality in her own right, making as distinctive a contribution to a happy partnership as Beatrice Webb did to Sidney Webb.

Born in 1893, she was the daughter of a Cambridge don, J.P. Postgate, who 'ater became Professor of Latin at Liverpool University, and a sister of the author, Raymond Postgate. As she states in her autobiography *Growing up into Revolution* (1949), she was unhappy at Roedean, but blossomed out at Girton, where she acquired an interest in politics and took First Class Honours in the Classical Tripos.

After a short period as classical mistress at St Paul's Girls' School, she became in 1915 the paid Assistant Secretary of the Fabian Research Department, which later became the Labour Research Department when the links with the founding Fabian Society grew weaker. Here she met and married G.D.H. Cole, the Honorary Secretary. Together they played an active part in the exciting left-wing politics of the day. Growing more and more out of sympathy with the Labour Research Department which passed increasingly under Communist influence following the foundation of that party in 1920, both of the Coles severed all connexion with the LRD in 1925. In that year G.D.H. Cole returned to Oxford as Reader in Economics; at their house in Longwall Street, Margaret acted as a successful hostess to the early meetings of the 'Cole Group', a weekly gathering of the cream of the Oxford Labour Club upon whose successive generations Cole had such a profound influence.

Tiring soon of Oxford, where she never really felt at home, Margaret Cole insisted on taking a house in Hampstead to which Douglas returned for weekends from his rooms in University College. She now gave such time as she could spare from bringing up a son and two daughters, to adult education and writing.

The failure of the second Labour government led the Coles to take the initiative in organizing a series of weekend conferences at Lady Warwick's house at Easton Lodge to discuss a practical approach on Socialist lines to the problems of the day. Those taking part included such diverse figures as Ernest Bevin, Leonard Woolf, Attlee and Addison, and younger men like Gaitskell and Evan Durbin. Much of the organization work of such conferences and of the New Fabian Research Bureau which grew out of them fell upon Margaret. From 1935 to 1939 she was the Hon Secretary, first of NFRB and then from 1939 to 1953 of the revived Fabian Society which was in effect taken over by NFRB.

Here she was a driving force in getting voluntary research done which made possible much of the legislation carried through by the Labour Government of 1945—51. She edited many of the books resulting from Fabian activities such as *Twelve Studies in Soviet Russia* (1932), *Democratic Sweden* (1938), *Evacuation Survey* (1940), *Our Soviet Ally* (1943) and *The Webbs and their Work* (1949).

Margaret Cole had always been fascinated by the Webbs even during the conflicts in Fabian circles between the Cole and Webb generations. This ripened into a warm affection for Beatrice Webb in her old age. She assisted in editing the second part of Beatrice's diaries — *Our Partnership* (1948) and selected the quotations for two later volumes in 1952 and 1956. The *Story of Fabian Socialism* (1961) was a new and lively appreciation of the great role in British politics played by the small society to which she had devoted so much of her time and energies. Attlee's comment on reading it was that she was extraordinarily fair to all those who took a different view in controversies in which she had taken an active part. From one who knew how keenly she could fight for her views this was indeed a compliment. She was made President of the Fabian Society in 1963. Her biography of her husband appeared in 1971.

Her interest in education led her to become a member of the LCC (later ILEA) Education Committee and Chairman for many years of its Further Education Committee. She was an LCC Alderman from 1952 to 1965.

Sharing as she did so many of her husband's interests, she not only looked after him during the many years when he suffered from diabetes and continually overworked, but she complemented him in much of his work. Her commonsense, zeal for accuracy in research, and stablizing influence were not only an invaluable help to her husband, but to all organizations with which she was connected.

She had been appointed OBE in 1965 and was made DBE in 1970.

* Published in *The Times*, 2 May 1980

Notes

1 Why politics? Why Labour?

1 N.P. Birley (1891—1980) Headmaster King's College, Canterbury 1927—35; Merchant Taylors (1935—46).

3 Oxford politics in the Late 1920s

1 Joint Parliamentary Secretary for Agriculture in Churchill's wartime government (1940—5).
2 Dr James (1844—1931); President 1909—31.
3 Michael Stewart, Labour MP 1945—79; Foreign Secretary 1965—6, 1968—70.
4 Brian Roberts, Editor *Sunday Telegraph* 1966—76.
5 Ivor Thomas, journalist and conservationist; Labour MP 1942—8; Tory MP 1948—50.
6 Lord Diplock; judge 1968.
7 Philip Guedalla (1889—1944); author.
8 Dingle Foot (1905—78) Liberal MP 1931—45; Labour MP 1957—70; Solicitor-General 1964—7.
9 Richard Acland; Liberal MP 1935—45; Labour MP 1947—55.
10 Lady Lloyd George's Diaries 3 Feb, 1927.
11 A.L. Rowse, historian.
12 E.F.M. Durbin (1906—48), don; Labour MP 1945—48; drowned.
13 Dr Joseph Wells (1855—1929); Vice-Chancellor 1923—6.
14 Dr McGrath (1839—1930); Provost Queen's 1878—1930.
15 Frank Lee (1900—55); railwayman; adult education lecturer, Northampton.
16 *Isis* 3 November 1926.
17 John Simon (1873—1954); Liberal MP 1906—18; 1922—31; National Liberal MP 1931—40; Foreign Secretary 1931—5; Lord Chancellor 1940—5.
18 Oswald Mosley (1896—1980); Tory MP 1918—22; Ind MP 1922—4; Labour MP 1926—31; Fascist leader.
19 Dr Pember (1862—1952); Vice-Chancellor 1926—9.
20 A largely honorary post mainly concerned with conferring honorary degrees.
21 For the earlier history of Oxford socialism see *Red Oxford* (1930) by Maurice Ashley and C.T. Saunders.
22 27 January 1926.
23 Proctors were responsible for maintaining order among students.
24 Margaret Cole (1893—1980); author, wife of G.D.H. Cole.
25 Quintin Hogg, barrister, Tory MP 1938—50; 1963—70; Lord Chancellor 1970—74; 1979—.
26 Colin Clark; Labour Candidate 1929—35; Australian civil servant; Oxford don.
27 James Meade; Professor Political Economy, Cambridge.

28 Lord Addison (1869—1951); Liberal MP 1910—22; Labour MP 1929—31; 1934—35; first Minister of Health.
29 University seats had proportional representation. Their franchise varied. Oxford, at this date, had a contracting-in a graduate electorate.
30 Roger Wilson, Education Professor Bristol 1951—71.
31 Osbert Lancaster; artist, writer.
32 Lord Boyd Carpenter; Tory MP 1945—72; Minister.
33 Miss L.S. Sutherland, Principal Lady Margaret Hall.
34 R.B. Haldane (1856—1928); Liberal MP 1885—1911; Lord Chancellor, 1912—15, 1924.
35 Lawrence Housman (1865—1959); author; artist.
36 Gilbert Frankau (1884—1940); author; journalist.
37 *Isis* 26 May 1926.
38 George II, King of the Hellenes 1922—3; 1936—41; 1946—7.

6   Contacts with the Oxford Group Movement

1 Founded by Frank Buchman (1878—1961), an American.

8   The New Fabian Research Bureau, 1931—39

1 Pulled down in 1948.
2 Economic historian.
3 Labour MP 1945—64; Lord Mitchison (1964—70).
4 Assistant Editor *New Statesman*; Head Social Science Dept, LSE.
5 Later a civil servant.
6 Granddaughter of Joseph Chamberlain; married Frank Pakenham, later Lord Longford; author.
7 Later international civil servant.
8 Liberal candidate 1910; Labour MP 1935—40; Independent Labour MP 1940—50.
9 General Secretary Iron & Steel Federation 1917—36.
10 Transport & General Workers' official; active in WEA.
11 LSE Professor and long-standing Fabian; founder *Political Quarterly* (1930) Joint Editor 1930—74.
12 Labour MP 1929—31; 1936—70; Minister; Chairman Labour Foreign Affairs Committee 1951—70.
13 LCC educationalist; niece of Beatrice Webb.
14 Later Madeleine Robinson, distinguished magistrate.
15 Publisher (Hogarth Press); husband of Virginia Woolf.
16 LSE dons; Greaves became a Professor.
17 Later Lord Chorley; active in National Trust.
18 Later Sir Ivor Jennings, Vice-Chancellor Cambridge. He told me my father had taught him at Bristol Grammar School and had caned him for 'fooling about'
19 Both Labour MPs later.
20 Labour MP 1940—48; journalist.
21 Later Sir Frederic Osborn, estate manager Welwyn Garden City; town and country planner.
22 Destroyed in the war (1941).
23 Granddaughter of C.P. Scott, editor *Manchester Guardian*, later Honor Croom, economist.
24 The May Committee recommended cuts that had largely been carried out by the National government after 1931.
25 Later Chairman, Countryside Commission.
26 Later Sir William Nield, civil servant—Permanent Secretary.
27 MP, Wolverhampton West 1945—50; Principal, Ruskin College, Oxford 1950—79.
28 Killed on the Republican side in Spanish Civil War (1938) after writing for NFRB *The People's Army*, a short book on Spain.

29 Later Bursar, Christ Church, Oxford.
30 Married Ivor Bulmer Thomas MP, conservationist.
31 A merchant banker.
32 Later Sir Richard Clarke, civil servant — Treasury.
33 Later Sir Geoffrey Wilson, Chairman Race Relations Board 1971—6.
34 Economist, became Baroness Wootton.
35 Labour MP 1945—50; 1955—67.
36 Labour historian and journalist, brother of Margaret Cole.
37 Author, wife of Dick Mitchison.
38 Labour MP 1945—50; 1951—74 Junior Minister; Liberal Candidate 1974—9; Lord Mayhew 1981.
39 MP Colchester 1945—50; later General Secretary PO Engineering Union; became Lord Delacourt Smith; Minister.
40 Article in NFRB *Quarterly* (June 1934) 'The New Deal & Social Reform'.
41 Economist, became Baroness Jackson of Lodsworth.
42 Later a civil servant — Treasury.
43 Niece of Maynard Keynes.
44 Alderman LCC; Investment Trusts; City Editor, *New Statesman* (1913—31).
45 The original of 'Enery Straker in Shaw's *Man and Superman*.
46 Began as an office boy (aged 12) and ended as a scrutineer.
47 John Ramage took his place at many of the talks.
48 Solicitor; Labour MP 1945—70; became Lord Fletcher.

9   The late 1930s

1 Wickham Steed (1871—1956) former editor, *The Times*.
2 Given by him to National Trust (1947).
3 Later Lord Cherwell (1886—1957); Personal Assistant to Churchill; scientist.

13   Some wartime activities

1 Later Lord Montevans (1881—1957).
2 Rt Hon. Charles Key (1883—1964); Minister of Works (1947—50); MP 1940—64.
3 Both were subsequently ennobled by Attlee (1945).
4 Owen Sheehy Skeffington (1909—70); later an Irish Senator.

14   Attlee (1883—1967) and Churchill (1874—1965)

1 Sir Archibald Southby (1886—1969); MP Epsom 1928—47.

16   A junior Minister, 1945—46

1 For the new constituencies of Romford, Barking, Dagenham & Hornchurch plus the Warley ward of Brentwood.

17   The British-Yugoslav Parliamentary Group

1 Lord William Scott (1896—1958); MP Roxburgh and Selkirk 1935—50.

19   The battle for the Legitimacy Act, 1959

1 Now Judge Graham Hall.
2 The Labour Whip reported that 40 Labour peers attended; 34 voted for and 2 against.

20 On delegation to Ethiopia, 1964

1 Menelik II, Emperor 1889—1913.
2 Haile Selassie, Emperor 1930—6; 1941—74.

21 My relations with Fords

1 General Secretary of TUC 1969—73.

22 The search for Jessie Holliday — A historical whodunit

1 Richard Dana (1851—1931).
2 Richard Henry Dana (1815—1922); author and lawyer.
3 Henry Wadsworth Longfellow (1807—82).
4 Aylmer Maude (1858—1938).
5 Archibald Henderson (1877—1963); American author and don.
6 Hugh Dalton (1887—1962); don; Labour MP 1924—31; 1935—59, Minister.
7 William Archer (1856—1924); drama critic; translator Ibsen.
8 Lord Allen of Hurtwood (1889—1939); Chairman first Labour daily; chairman ILP 1922—6.
9 Amber Blanco White (1887—1981); author, lecturer.
10 Sargent Florence (1890—1982); lecturer (Economics) Cambridge 1921—9; Professor (Commerce) Birmingham 1929—55.
11 Norman Angell (1874—1967); journalist and lecturer; Labour MP 1929—31; wrote the antiwar *The Great Illusion* (1910).

23 The Sunday Freedom Filibuster

1 Sir Lionel Heald (MP 1950—70) Attorney General 1951—54.

24 The changing Commons

1 Figures supplied by the Fees Office (1979).
2 Estimate J.F.S. Ross, *Parliamentary Representation*, p. 40.

26 Forty-two days in the Soviet Union

1 Lord Brimelow born 1915; Head Foreign Office staff, 1973—5.
2 British Overseas Airways Corporation.
3 Sir Victor Mallett (1893—1969); Minister Stockholm 1940—5; later Ambassador in Spain and Italy.
4 Formerly known as OGPU (Political Security Police).
5 Sir John Balfour (born 1894); Moscow 1943—45; later ambassador Argentine and Spain.
6 Buckingham Palace.
7 Molotov (born 1890); Soviet Foreign Minister 1939—49; 1953—6.
8 Maisky (1884—1975); Soviet Ambassador in London 1932—43.
9 Mrs M. and her husband were distinguished Russian émigrées resident in London.
10 Sargent Florence (1890—1982); lecturer (Economics) Cambridge 1921—9; Professor
11 Litvinov (1876—1951); Soviet Foreign Minister 1930—9.
12 Entertainments National Service Association (ENSA).
13 Those with large outputs — and therefore with large earnings!
14 Lord Vansittart (1881—1957); Foreign Office civil servant (1928—41); strongly anti-German.

15 H.N. Brailsford (1873—1957); left-wing journalist.
16 Duchess of Atholl (1879—1960); known as the 'Red Duchess'.
17 Anastas Mikoyan (1895—1978); Foreign Trade Minister 1939—49.
18 The Ossetians are descended from the Alans, who were driven into the Caucasus by the Mongols.
19 We later learnt that Dunsterville (1865—1946), the British commander (Kipling's Stalky), had handed them over to their Social Revolutionary opponents who had shot them.
20 A popular British musical comedy (c. 1918).
21 When a return visit was paid to Britain by a Soviet party we booked for them the best seats at Covent Garden and the Old Vic. At the last minute the visit was postponed a week. We then got the best seats available, but our guests could not understand why we could not put them into the very best seats as they would have done.
22 The Kalmucks were allowed to return in the late 1950s; their autonomous Socialist Republic was re-constituted in 1958 with a population of 41 per cent Kalmucks and 46 per cent Russians (1974 census).
23 Gracie Fields (1898—1979); actress.
24 On my return I told Naomi Mitchison (born 1897) of this episode. 'Pure Homer', she replied, 'You should have let them go ahead.'
25 Sir Charles Cochran (1872—1957); theatrical manager.

Index

FABIAN NEWS

11 DARTMOUTH STREET
LONDON SW1   01-222 8877

JANUARY 1988
No.1 Vol.100 10p

Chairman's Message

NICK BUTLER

After a hard decade, what the Fabian Society (and the Labour Party) needs most is a degree of intellectual self confidence. Despite all the defeats and setbacks, we need to reaffirm that both our objective—a socialism of equity and justice in an open society—and our methods—gradualism and reform—are as correct now as they have always been. Electoral defeats have delayed or halted progress but they have not invalidated our cause. Despair for Fabians, as for Christians, would be the ultimate blasphemy.

To revive self confidence must be the prime objective for 1988. From that starting point I offer a number of assertions which between them provide an agenda for the year ahead.

- that socialism for Fabians is not an academic study or an intellectual pastime but a practical process of change and reform. The socialism of academic lectures and learned prose is valueless if not linked to the implementation of ideas. We are not a cosy discussion group but a political society whose goal is to achieve the progress we debate and to translate into reality the plans we publish;

- that collective action, however unfashionable, is still the only means of creating a more equal and fair society, and that individualism will always favour the strong over the weak, dividing society from within and promoting conflict and competition over the values of cooperation. For us the task is to promote once again the benefits which follow from the creative use of public power;

- that Fabianism is not, and should not be, exclusively British. In "a beautiful, dangerous world" socialism in one country is a false goal. We must seek out and join forces with those who share our basic beliefs wherever they are;

- that Fabians must distinguish ends from means and recognise detailed policies as no more than means—tools, often to be used experimentally and to be discarded if they fail. Although our goals remain valid and unchanged, the means and the detailed policies can and must change with time and circumstances. Politics reflect the priorities of the

Continued on page 8

Can governments manage the economy?

Jim Tomlinson

Preface by Bryan Gould MP

Tract 524, £1.50

From the 1930s, the most striking feature of the development of advanced capitalist countries was the rise of national economic management. Governments regulated the national economy to obtain some mixture of employment, growth, inflation and balance of payments goals.

But, with the collapse of the post-war boom in the early 1970s, it has become widely accepted that the changing structures of the world economy have made successful national economic management impossible.

Jim Tomlinson sets out to examine this belief by firstly analysing the changes which are alleged to have made economic management impossible: the growing dependence on international trade; the internationalisation of financial markets with massive flows of capital in and out of countries; and the growth of multinationals. He finds that while none of these makes economic management any easier, equally none offers an insuperable obstacle to managing the national economy.

He then examines the experiences of three countries as case studies. With Britain in the mid-1970s and France in the early 1980s, he shows that political constraints were at least as important as external pressures in confounding national economic policy. In contrast, Sweden shows how the effects of the structural changes in the world economy can be offset by appropriate policy measures. Sweden's successful export-led growth strategy, begun in 1982, resulted in a fall in unemployment and a rise in industrial profits—because the strategy was based on a political consensus that allowed for control of wages and investment.

A new A-Z of income and wealth— Britain in the 1980s

Thomas Stark

£1.95

ISBN: 0-7163-4014-3

Frank Field MP, former Director of the Child Poverty Action Group, says about this new Fabian booklet:

"It makes available in an accessible form exactly the sort of information the Government is doing its hardest to suppress, and it provides a perfect foil to Government claims that everyone will benefit from current economic policies.

"Publications of this kind are potentially more damaging to the Government than *Spycatcher*."

A new A-Z of income and wealth provides a non-technical summary of income and wealth trends for the first time since the Diamond Commission's *A-Z of income and wealth* (published posthumously in 1980).

The Diamond Commission—the Royal Commission on the Distribution of Income and Wealth—sat between 1974 and 1979. It gave a unique picture of the changing face of Britain. Since its abolition, facts and figures on income and wealth have been buried in various official statistical reports.

A new A-Z of income and wealth is a popular illustrated version of Dr Stark's research paper *Income and wealth in the 1980s*, which was issued by the Fabian Society in September 1987. Copies of this research paper are still available, price £10.00 (£5.00 to members).

A new A-Z of income and wealth is distributed free only to Fabian Society members. Price to non-members: £1.95 including postage. Discounts available on quantities of 10 upwards.

Weekend School, Perth
NORTH & SOUTH—WHAT IS THE **REAL** DIVIDE?
20-21 February
GORDON BROWN MP
KEN LIVINGSTONE MP
Further details from:
John Clifford 031-558-1124

Local Societies

SCOTLAND

Dunfermline: 5 February. "The Way Forward for Labour in Scotland". Speaker: Helen Liddell. Venue: Social Work Department, 3 New Road, Dunfermline. Further details from Bob Eadie, Dalgety Bay 824136.

Edinburgh: 6 pm, Friday 15 January. "The Future of Welfare". Speaker: Robin Cook MP. Venue: Heriot Watt. 7.30 pm, Saturday 23 January. An informal evening with Fabians and friends, at the house of Elisa Trimby and John Clifford, 9 Howard Place, Edinburgh 3. 6 pm, Tuesday 2 February. "Britain's Nuclear Nightmare: What's Wrong With Nuclear Power?" Speaker: Robert Edwards. Venue: Heriot Watt. 6 pm, Tuesday 16 February. "Socialism and the Labour Party: Perception and Reality". Speaker: Hilary Wainwright. Venue: Heriot Watt. Further details from George Jamieson, 031 337 9672.

YORKSHIRE

Sheffield: 4 February. "Inner City Regeneration—What will it do for the Housing Shortage?" Further details from Joan Ward, Sheffield 74684.

York: 8 pm, 29 January. AGM and Hugh Bayley speaking on "How Can Fabians Best Contribute to Labour Victory?" Refreshments provided by members. 8 pm, 26 February. "Working for Racial Harmony in Schools". Speaker: J Unwin. Further details from Hans Breitenbach, 0423 862295.

MIDLANDS

Birmingham: 8 February. "The Poll Tax and Other Wealth Sharing Devices". Speaker: Jack Straw MP. Venue: George Breeze Hall, Fircroft College. Further details from Pamela Davies, 40 Franklin Road, Birmingham B30 2HG.

Black Country: 7.30 pm, 22 January. Meeting with Austin Mitchell MP. Venue: Brooke-Robinson Room, Dudley Town Hall. 7.30 pm, 12 February. Meeting with Bryan Gould MP. Venue as above. Further information from Nick Matthews, 126 Clover Ley, Heath Town, Wolverhampton WV10 0HD.

Grantham: 8 pm, 18 January. "China". Speaker: Nick Butler. Venue: Shirley Croft Hotel, Harrowby Rd. 8 pm, 15 February. "Booms and Slumps—the Weakness of the Capitalist System". Speaker: S Garnett. Venue as above. Further details from Joan Strawson-Guy, 0400 81886.

LONDON

Camden: 12 noon, Sunday 24 January. "Robert Burns Anniversary Party". Buffet and glass of wine. Tickets for £2.50 from Audrey Morris, 5a Turlow Rd, London NW3 5PJ (Tel: 435 3801).

Central London: 7.30 pm, Wednesday 20 January. "Trade Unions and the Law". Speaker: David Bean. Venue: Cole Room, 11 Dartmouth St, SW1. 7.30 pm, Wednesday 17 February. "Amnesty International". Speaker: Marie Staunton. Venue as above. Further details from Giles Wright, 405 4038.

Dulwich: 8 pm, Wednesday 10 February. "Labour and the Media". Speaker: John Lloyd. Venue: 204 Peckham Rye, SE22. 8 pm, Wednesday 9 March. "The Left in the U.S." Speaker: Arthur Lipow. Venue as above. Further details from John Beasley, 693 9412.

Harrow: 8 pm, Thursday 28 January. "The Crisis in the NHS". Speaker: Kathy Attlee. Venue: 53 Sherington Ave, Hatch End. Further details from F Merrison, 866 8035.

Havering: 7.45 pm, 22 January. AGM, followed by Peter Williams who will speak on country parks and open spaces in Havering. Venue: Friends Meeting House, 7 Balgores Crescent, Gidea Park. 8 pm, 17 February. "The Labour Party and the City". Speaker: Lord Williams of Elvel. Venue: Langtons, Billet Lane, Hornchurch. Further details from Basil Newton, 04022 23018.

SOUTHERN

Brighton & Hove: 8 pm, Friday 22 January. "Changes in China". Speaker: Lord (Bert) Oram.Venue: The Cricketers, Black Lion St, Brighton. 8 pm, Friday 12 February. "Health for All". Speaker: Dr Sonia Leff. Venue as above. Further details from George Forbes, Brighton 565191.

North-West Surrey: 3 pm, 17 January. AGM. Guest speaker: Alan Black (UCATT). Venue: 23 Langshott Close, Woodham. Further details from Jean Pickles, Byfleet 45973.

SOUTH WEST

Bournemouth & District: 7.30 pm, Friday 29 January. AGM. Venue: Committee Room 2, Bournemouth Town Hall. Further details from Ian Taylor, 0202 36634.

Gloucester: 4.30 pm, Saturday 16 January. "Tertiary Colleges". Speaker: Gareth Nichols. Venue: Wesley Rooms, St John's Land (opposite Church and Northgate St). 4.30 pm, Saturday 13 February. "The Church and Politics". Speaker: The Very Reverend Kenneth Jennings, the Dean of Gloucester. Venue as above. Further details from F B Wilton, Gloucester 21716.

Plymouth & District: 7.30 pm, 15 January. "The New Education Proposals". Speaker: John Leonard. Venue: Plymouth Arts Centre, Looe St, Plymouth. 7.30 pm, 19 February. "People and Planet—The International Green Movement". Speaker: Christopher Titmuss. Venue as above. Further details from Ms R Goodman, Plymouth 221153.

100 YEARS OF FABIAN PUBLISHING

World Microfilms has recently published in microfiche *100 Years of Fabian Publishing*, compiled by Rashid Kareh, with an introduction by Bernard Crick. This details every book, pamphlet and periodical published by the Society and its subsections from 1883-1987. It costs £60 and is available from World Microfilms, 62 Queen's Grove, London NW8 6ER.

Continued from page 1

**LOCAL GOVERNMENT
CONFERENCE
EDINBURGH**

Saturday 30 January

12.30 pm
George Hotel
George Street, Edinburgh

THE CASE FOR PUBLIC EXPENDITURE

**Gordon Brown MP
John Gunnell**
Chair: Ann Davis

Admission free

VISIT TO THE USA

21 May-3 June 1988

New York ● Washington Boston

Director: Merlyn Rees MP

Organiser: Jenny Jeger

Price: £800 (approx.)

Spending two weeks in the USA in election year, the study visit will include meetings with politicians and trade unionists and perhaps visit a Primary.

Numbers are limited and we would like to send a balanced group. If you would like to be considered for a place, please write for further details to the Fabian Society, 11 Dartmouth Street, London SW1H 9BN. (Members who have already applied will be sent information shortly).

moment, and if our policies fail to match those changing priorities and circumstances we will become no more than an historical curosity.

David Lipsey's important paper to the Labour Party's policy review (attached as a *Briefing* in this mailing), is our first but not our last contribution to the process of rethinking within the Labour Party;

● that without adequate channels of communication and the opportunity for serious debate, ideas are lost or wasted. This was the motivation of the Webbs when they founded the *New Statesman* 75 years ago, and it is why so many Fabians are concerned about the *Statesman's* current problems and its future. I hope that 1988 will give us the opportunity to help to prove that a paper of the left can be well written, serious and attractive and can on that basis be financially viable.

The frustrations of opposition depress us all but defeat gives the Fabians an important role, and a great deal to do.

I hope that 1988 will be remembered not as a year when we nursed our hangovers after a third Conservative victory, but as a lively and creative year, when we rediscovered our self confidence as socialists and sowed the seeds of future victory.

The Fabian Society
needs a

PART-TIME AUDIO TYPIST

Hours can be very flexible to fit in with other commitments.

Write for details to the General Secretary, Fabian Society, 11 Dartmouth Street, London SW1H 9BN

(Tel: 01-222 8877)